Review of Marches and Parades in Scotland

Review of Marches and Parades in Scotland

A Report by Sir John Orr

Published by the Scottish Ministers
Scottish Executive
St Andrew's House
Edinburgh

ISBN: 0 7559 4478 X

© Text: Queen's Printer for Scotland 2005
© Design and Typographical Layout: Astron 2005

All enquiries relating to the copyright in this work should be addressed to:

Office of the Queen's Printer for Scotland
The Licensing Division, St Clements House
2-16 Colegate
Norwich
NR3 1BQ

This report was prepared by Sir John Orr on behalf of the Scottish Ministers.

This publication (excluding the Royal Arms and departmental logos) may be re-used free of charge in any format or medium provided that it is re-used accurately and not used in a misleading context. The material must be acknowledged as the copyright of the Queen's Printer for Scotland and the title of the publication specified.

This publication is also available at www.scotland.gov.uk

Any enquiries regarding this document/publication should be addressed to:

Scottish Executive
Development Department
Equality Unit
Victoria Quay
Edinburgh
EH6 6QQ

Designed and produced on behalf of the Scottish Ministers by Astron B38899

Contents

Foreword vii

Executive summary and summary of recommendations
1. Executive summary — 1
2. Summary of recommendations — 9

Introduction, current processes, information and evidence gathered
3. Introduction: the establishment of the Review, its remit and its conduct — 13
4. Traditions of processions in Scotland — 17
5. The current legislative position: Human Rights Legislation and the Civic Government (Scotland) Act 1982 — 35
6. Current practices in Scotland — 47
7. The number of marches and parades in Scotland — 61
8. A summary of written responses — 73
9. A summary of the telephone survey: 'Review of marches and parades: a survey of views across Scotland' — 109
10. How things are done in England — 117
11. How things are done in Northern Ireland — 127

Recommendations
12. The Period of Notice — 139
13. Informing and involving the community — 147
14. Decision making — 153
15. Numbers and effects on communities — 165
16. Police costs — 181

Appendices

A	Written submissions	191
B	Script for telephone attitude survey	195
C	Meetings	235
D	Extracts from Part V of the Civic Government (Scotland) Act 1982	239
E	Examples of Orders of Exempt organisations made by local authorities	247
F	Examples of codes of conduct of marching organisations	265
G	Examples of band contracts of marching organisations	269
H	Detailed statistics about the number of marches and parades	277
I	Guidance for organisers – elements of a 'How To' guide	299

Index   303

Foreword

I am pleased to present the report and recommendations of the Review of Marches and Parades in Scotland. I believe these recommendations, when taken together, will professionalise and modernise the way that decisions about processions are taken. The package of recommendations should also improve people's experiences of processions, making sure that they are better informed, disruption is minimised and conduct is improved.

I am grateful to all those who have contributed to the Review. Their expertise has been valuable and their suggestions have been helpful. I welcomed the open and constructive dialogue and informed consideration given to the issues raised over the course of the Review. Many organisations provided me with detailed information about statistics and current processes which was not always readily accessible and which took time to collect. Other organisations which arrange marches shared with me their experiences. Without the foundations which that evidence provided, my recommendations could not have been as well informed.

I decided to undertake the Review alone, without a group of specialist advisors. The only person who supported me throughout was Karen Jackson, seconded from the Scottish Executive for the duration of the Review. I am extremely grateful for her energy, wholehearted commitment and significant support with this critical Review.

Not everyone will agree with all aspects of my recommendations. Some may think I have gone too far, others may think I have not gone far enough. However, I hope that they will agree that the process which informed my recommendations was open and robust. I hope also that they recognise that the recommendations strike an essential balance – between the rights of those who want to march and the rights of those who want to go about their daily life undisturbed by such events. During the course of the Review, I continued to be struck by the degree of consensus I have encountered. People of very different perspectives agreed that improvements needed to be made and that my approach represented a fair balance.

I am confident that, when implemented, the arrangements will lead to a fairer and more transparent and inclusive decision making process and one that is appropriate for a multi-cultural Scotland of the 21st century. For the recommendations to deliver the benefits which I believe they can, implementation will require the commitment of many: the Scottish Executive; local authorities; police forces; and march organisers working together in partnership. I look forward to that next stage.

Sir John Orr
December 2004

1 Executive summary

Background to the Review

1.1 The First Minister commissioned me to review the arrangements for marches and parades in Scotland in June 2004. My remit covered five key areas:
- The period of notice organisers give to local authorities, the police and communities;
- The best way to ensure greater community involvement in decisions about marches and parades;
- The basis for determining when to restrict, refuse or reroute marches and parades;
- The number of marches and parades taking place in communities and the effects these have; and
- The policing of marches and parades.

1.2 I was asked to report to the First Minister with recommendations by the end of December 2004.

The Process of the Review

1.3 It was important that my work was informed by the views of those who marched, the communities affected by the marches and the authorities who had responsibility for making decisions about marches and ensuring local safety. I gathered those views in three main ways:
- I wrote to over 1,000 key organisations inviting views relevant to the areas of my remit. I covered a broad range of organisations and encouraged them to circulate it around their networks. The letter was also available on the Scottish Executive website and sent to local media outlets. I was pleased to receive 361 responses to this letter;
- I commissioned an attitude survey to ensure that I received views from the wider community. The survey covered 676 people across Scotland and sought views on a range of issues about marches and parades; and
- I also met with a wide range of people including national and local politicians, the police, faith groups, representatives from business and organisations which arrange marches. To ensure that I gained an insight in respect of approaches outside Scotland, I visited Merseyside, London and Belfast. In collecting information for the Review, I met with around 125 people in 45 separate meetings.

1.4 Chapter 3 describes in more detail the establishment and remit of the Review and the working processes.

Evidence gathered during the Review

Traditions of processions

1.5 My remit covered all marches and parades in Scotland. I thought it important to gather information about the types of processions that took place across the country. There are many reasons for processions: some celebrate community; some commemorate events; and some are a protest against local or national decisions. Many of the processions that receive most media attention are those organised by the Loyalist Institutions (the Orange Order, the Apprentice Boys of Derry and the Provincial Grand Black Chapter of Scotland) or Republican or Catholic groups. I wanted to explore the history and traditions of these organisations to understand better why they organised processions and what they meant to those involved. I also wanted to look at the range of other processions which take place across Scotland. The diversity of these events reflects Scottish traditions, history and culture. Chapter 4 – The Traditions of Processions in Scotland, looks in more detail at the range of processions.

The current legislative position

1.6 It is clear that my recommendations need to sit within the human rights framework. The European Convention for the Protection of Human Rights (ECHR) sets out a range of rights, including the freedom of peaceful assembly. That right protects those who want to march even if their march gives offence to people who are opposed to its purpose. However, that right is also subject to some important qualifications which recognise that people's rights might be in competition. Restrictions on rights must be prescribed in law. The purpose of any restriction of rights must be in line with the purposes stated in the ECHR: *'necessary in a democratic society in the interest of national security or public safety, for the prevention of disorder or crime, for the protection of health or morals or for the protection of rights and freedoms of others'*. The restriction must be proportionate so that any action to restrict a right is appropriate to the seriousness of the threat posed by exercising that right. A restriction should be justified by relevant and sufficient reasons.

1.7 Current arrangements for processions in Scotland are governed by the Civic Government (Scotland) Act 1982. That Act requires organisers to give local authorities seven days notice of their intention to organise a procession. It enables local authorities to prohibit processions or impose restrictions on them after having consulted with the Chief Constable. There have been very few prohibition orders under the Act. The types of restrictions imposed are usually around dates and timing, about routes or about the playing of music. Organisers can appeal to the sheriff against decisions. Local authorities can exempt organisations from the notification requirements and can waive the notification period where appropriate. The number of exempt organisations varied considerably between local authorities, some having as many as 300 others fewer than five.

1.8 Chapter 5 – The Current Legislative Position: Human Rights Legislation and the Civic Government (Scotland) Act 1982 describes the legislative context in more detail.

Current practices

1.9 As part of the Review, I looked in detail at how local authorities currently took decisions about marches and parades. I was grateful for the detailed information many local authorities provided to me about their processes. It quickly became apparent that there were many different approaches.

1.10 In general terms, local authorities require organisers to give written notification, sometimes using a standard application form or otherwise in a letter. While the statutory timetable was seven days, local authorities encourage organisers to give longer and many organisers do so. Once a notification has been received, most local authorities send a copy of it to the local elected member whose ward was affected for comment. They ensure the police received a copy from the organisers. Others circulate it to the roads department within the authority for their views.

1.11 Most local authority officials have delegated powers to take decisions on notifications and they are only considered by councillors at committees if the notification is considered to be controversial. Local authorities take their own decisions on what makes a notification controversial, based on a range of issues, for example: the size of the march; the organiser; or if there are objections from the police or local elected member. While local authorities consider the notification, the police meet with organisers to discuss practical arrangements for the procession. At the end of the consideration, some local authorities write to organisers confirming that they have considered the notification and have no objections. Others simply write if they impose restrictions on the procession.

1.12 Some local authorities have developed a set of standard conditions governing conduct at processions. March organisers also often have their own codes of conduct. Local authorities receive very few formal complaints about processions. The complaints that are received are about noise, disruption, litter, the nature of certain processions, costs and the behaviour usually of onlookers watching processions. A few local authorities have prepared helpful guidance to organisers about how to arrange events, including processions. There was very limited debriefing after processions.

1.13 Chapter 6 – Current Practices in Scotland describes the processes in more detail.

The number of marches and parades in Scotland

1.14 As part of the Review, I collected information about the numbers of marches and parades that took place across Scotland. Local authorities sent me detailed returns about the numbers of processions that were notified to them under the Civic Government (Scotland) Act 1982. These statistics show there were 1,712 notified processions in 2003. Given that some organisations are exempt from the requirements to notify their processions, there will be more processions than this taking place. The past three years has seen a gradual increase of around 8.5% in the number of notified processions taking place. A wide range of organisations arrange processions. Overall in 2003, 50% of all notified processions across Scotland were organised by the Loyalist Institutions (although this rises to 73% in Strathclyde); 1% were organised by Catholic or Republican groups; and 49% were organised by other groups. Marches varied considerably in size from under 50 to over 15,000.

1.15 Chapter 7 – The Number of Marches and Parades in Scotland analyses the statistics surrounding notified processions. Appendix H provides detailed information.

A summary of written responses

1.16 I received 361 responses to my consultation letter, some including very detailed views. In general, a large majority of respondents supported an increase to the notification period, as long as provision was made for certain processions which required shorter notification. On balance, respondents supported greater community involvement in the decision making process and suggested who should be involved and the best ways of involving them. Respondents agreed that, in reaching decisions, local authorities should be able to take into account a wider range of issues. Respondents described their views about the effects marches were having on communities. Views diverged over whether organisers should be required to meet their policing costs.

1.17 Chapter 8 – A Summary of Written Responses records in detail the views expressed. Appendix A lists those who responded.

A summary of the telephone survey of 'Views Across Scotland'

1.18 676 people across Scotland were interviewed as part of the telephone survey of 'Views Across Scotland'. The main topics covered in the survey were: people's experiences of different kinds of processions; the impacts of processions; whether processions were a particular issue and what should be taken into account in reaching decisions; the amount of notice that should be given; who should be involved in decisions; and whether organisers should contribute towards costs.

1.19 The results of the survey show that marches and parades affect a sizeable proportion of the Scottish population. While there can be a number of problems associated with processions, there is also evidence that many people gain positive experiences from them. Respondents consider that procedures for authorising marches needed to strike a balance between minimising the negative impact of marches and maintaining people's freedom to protest, demonstrate and celebrate.

1.20 The survey demonstrated that there is consensus around a number of principles: the need to protect freedom of speech, that marches should be allowed unless there is a risk to public safety and that marches which are likely to inflame racial or religious tensions should not go ahead. These principles are not always compatible and demonstrate the difficulty in balancing one individual's right to march with the authorities' responsibility to ensure public safety and to allow other individuals to go about their daily business.

1.21 The survey showed that the public wanted a wide range of issues taken into consideration when decisions were taken on marches and parades and wanted to make sure that a wider range of organisations and local groups were involved in the decision making process.

Chapter 9 – A Summary of the Telephone Survey 'Review of marches and parades: a survey of views across Scotland' summarises the outcome of the results of the survey. Appendix B provides the full text of the questionnaire used in the survey and the full results of the survey are being published separately *http://www.scotland.gov.uk/marchesandparades*.

How things are done in England

1.22 The legislation in England is different. Under the Public Order Act 1986, the police are responsible for taking decisions on procession notifications. While the legislation is different, in my visits to Merseyside and London, I discovered some good practice in terms of: the planning process which involved organisers in detailed discussions recorded in a 'statement of intent'; expertise built up in specialised planning units; guidance notes to help organisers plan and deliver effective processions; and, by clear and straightforward planning, documents ensuring notifications are handled consistently and key issues are not missed. I also found some valuable examples of providing the community with better information about processions.

1.23 Chapter 10 – How Things Are Done in England describes the processes South of the Border and highlights good practice.

How things are done in Northern Ireland

1.24 Northern Ireland's approach reflects their particular culture and traditions. Decisions on the 3,000 or so processions which take place there annually are taken by an independent body, the Parades Commission. The Parades Commission was established in 1998. It is made up of a Chairman and six members and has an annual budget of £1.2 million. It considers processions under detailed procedural rules against clear guidelines on how those decisions will be reached. It has developed a code of conduct for participants in processions. Although 3,000 or so processions take place a year, most are non-contentious. The Commission issues about 130 determinations about contentious processions which usually set conditions on routes, start and finish times and the playing of music. As well as making determinations on notifications, the Parades Commission has a role in promoting understanding and supporting mediation. The Parades Commission funds a team of 12 authorised officers to assist in mediation. It also uses monitors who are volunteers to observe processions.

1.25 Chapter 11 – How Things are Done in Northern Ireland describes the background to the establishment of the Parades Commission (including the 1997 Independent Review of Parades and Marches, 'The North Review'), its current operation, the review of its operation (Review of the Operation of the Parades Commission, 'The Quigley Review') and the Northern Ireland Affairs Committee (NIAC) inquiry into the Parades Commission and the Public Processions (Northern Ireland) Act 1998.

Recommendations

1.26   I make 38 recommendations to the Scottish Executive. I believe these recommendations, when taken together, will professionalise and modernise the way that decisions about processions are taken. The package of recommendations should also improve people's experiences of processions, making sure they are better informed, disruption is minimised and overall conduct is improved. My recommendations aim to strike a balance between the rights of those who want to march and the rights of communities. My recommendations are grounded in common sense and have been informed by the evidence I have collected and the views I have heard over the period of the Review. It is likely that implementing some of the recommendations will require changes to primary legislation and may take time to effect. Others could be taken forward without legislative changes. Successful implementation is likely to require the commitment of all involved in processions, including the Scottish Executive, local authorities, the police and organisers.

1.27   Chapter 2 – Summary of Recommendations lists all my recommendations. Chapters 12 to 16 deal in more detail with the recommendations associated with each element of my remit.

Recommendations on the period of notice

1.28   My recommendations propose that organisers give 28 days notice of their intention to hold a procession, although this timescale should be waived in certain circumstances, for example where the reason for the procession could not reasonably have been foreseen. No one should be exempt from the requirement to give advance notice of their intention to hold a procession. Local authorities and the police should develop expertise in dealing with notification by putting in place 'single gateways' within their respective organisations to process notifications and to provide a clear source of information for organisers. There should be certain standard steps taken during the extended notice period which will ensure a more consistent approach to decision making and I describe what I consider the key steps might be. As part of the process, local authorities should complete risk assessments and impact analyses on notifications. To ensure that improvements are being made, a monitoring system should be put in place. The development and sharing of good practice should be supported by police and local authority associations and networks.

1.29   Chapter 12 and Recommendations 1 to 8 are about the first element of my remit, the period of notice.

Recommendations on informing and involving the community

1.30   My recommendations will improve the information given to communities by requiring local authorities to prepare and publicise an annual digest of processions and to provide up-to-date information about forthcoming processions. Local authorities should develop an 'opt-in' list of key interests so they are informed about processions. My recommendations also look at how communities can be better involved in the decision making process. Local authorities should develop appropriate mechanisms to ensure that communities have the opportunity to express their views on notifications. Local authorities should consider a wider range of views, including community views, as part of the overall assessment process. Local authorities should also put in place clear procedures for considering community views.

1.31   Chapter 13 and Recommendations 9 to 14 are about the second element of my remit, informing and involving the community.

Recommendations on decision making

1.32   My recommendations aim to improve the current decision making processes. I do not think that creating a new independent body to take decisions on procession notifications is necessary in Scotland and recommend that local authorities should remain responsible for taking decisions. However, in reaching their decisions, local authorities should be able to take into account a wider range of issues and to be able to impose proportionate conditions. Local authorities should respect traditional dates as far as possible and organisers should be prepared to compromise over routes. Organisers should provide written signed notifications. There should be a precursory meeting, facilitated by the local authority and involving at least the police and the organiser, once a notification has been received to discuss the notification resulting in a signed agreement. Local authorities should provide organisers with a 'permit to process' at the end of the notification period outlining what has been agreed and what was expected. Organisers should not be required to pay a fee for a notification. Debriefing meetings should be held after a procession has taken place which provides an opportunity for the local authority, police and the organiser, as well as any other relevant interest, to discuss what happened and to provide evidence that can be taken into account in the future.

1.33   Chapter 14 and Recommendations 15 to 23 are about the third element of my remit, decision making.

Recommendations on numbers and effects on communities

1.34   My recommendations concentrate on three key areas: organisers' responsibility for the numbers of processions; organisers' responsibilities for ensuring processions are properly and professionally planned, supported by detailed 'How To' guidance; and improving overall behaviour associated with processions. While many of my recommendations require action from local authorities and the police, organisers have an important contribution to make in this element of my remit.

1.35   My recommendations encourage organisers to continue to act responsibly in organising processions and consider if events can be combined. Local authorities and the police need to improve their record keeping about numbers and costs. Organisers

1.36 need to think carefully about taking out insurance to cover their processions and might be required to do so in certain situations or provide a behaviour bond. Local authorities should provide guidance to organisers on various aspects of organising processions in the form of a 'How To' guide. Local authorities and the police should also develop a code of conduct for participants in the procession. Organisers need to do what they can to improve the behaviour of onlookers and need to ensure that they have effective stewarding in place for the management of processions. Local authorities and the police may be able to support stewarding with appropriate training. Bands engaged in playing in processions need to take responsibility for their own and their followers' behaviour and identify a named individual to take appropriate responsibility. The police should continue to exercise their enforcement powers appropriately and, in liaison with stewards, ensure that the policing of onlookers is effective. Local authorities without byelaws prohibiting the consumption of alcohol in public places should consider putting them in place.

1.36 Chapter 15 and Recommendations 24 to 35 are about the fourth element of my remit, numbers and effects on communities.

Recommendations on police costs

1.37 My recommendations look at police costs associated with policing processions. Policing processions represents a significant cost to police forces, with annual salary costs alone in the region of £1.5 million. Some 62,000 police hours are used annually in the planning and policing of processions. Three police forces (Strathclyde, Lothian and Borders, and Fife) are responsible for policing over 85% of all processions. I also look at the impact on resources, the level of policing, the numbers of arrests and complaints. Whether organisers should contribute to policing costs promoted an interesting debate and I conclude, on balance, that they should not. It is, however, appropriate for local authorities to consider relevant police costs when reaching decisions about march notifications, although processions should not be prohibited on grounds of cost alone. The police should also improve their liaison with and understanding of organisations arranging marches by ensuring their officers receive appropriate briefing about the reasons for the procession and the background to the organisation.

1.38 Chapter 16 and Recommendations 36 to 38 are about the fifth element of my remit, police costs.

2 Summary of recommendations

First element of remit: period of notice

Recommendation 1
- Organisers should give 28 days notice to local authorities and the police of their intention to hold a procession.

Recommendation 2
- In certain circumstances, where processions are arranged in response to unforeseen events, the 28 days notification period should be waived and organisers should be able to give less notice.

Recommendation 3
- All organisers should notify their intention to march to local authorities and the police.

Recommendation 4
- Local authorities and the police should set up 'single gateways' within their organisations to deal with procession notifications.

Recommendation 5
- Local authorities and the police should take certain key steps to assess notifications during the extended notification period.

Recommendation 6
- Local authorities should complete risk assessments and impact analyses on notifications to provide good quality, factually based information to inform the decision making process.

Recommendation 7
- The Scottish Executive should ensure that there are effective monitoring arrangements in place to demonstrate that local authorities and the police are implementing the new procedures in a way appropriate to their local circumstances with a regular public report produced.

Recommendation 8
- Local authority associations and police associations should ensure good practice is shared more widely.

Second element of remit: informing and involving the community

Recommendation 9
- Local authorities should prepare an annual digest of processions with organisers at the beginning of the calendar year, and update it every quarter and ensure the digest is well publicised and accessible.

Recommendation 10
- Local authorities should provide up-to-date information about forthcoming processions to local communities using the most appropriate means.

Recommendation 11
- Local authorities should maintain an 'opt-in' list for organisations to receive information about processions.

Recommendation 12
- Local authorities should establish mechanisms appropriate to their areas to ensure that communities are able to express views on processions.

Recommendation 13
- Local authorities should take into account wider views, including community views, when taking decisions on procession notifications.

Recommendation 14
- Local authorities should put in place clear procedures for considering community views.

Third element of remit: decision making

Recommendation 15
- Local authorities should remain responsible for taking decisions on procession notifications.

Recommendation 16
- Local authorities should be able to take into account a wider range of issues when reaching decisions on notifications. Their decisions should be evidence based and explained to the organisers.

Recommendation 17
- Local authorities should have discretion to impose conditions proportionate to the notification and to address the issues upon which it based its decision.

Recommendation 18
- Local authorities should respect key traditional dates but organisers should be prepared to compromise over routes where necessary.

Recommendation 19
- Organisers should provide a written, signed notification providing the key information required by the local authority.

Recommendation 20
- There should be a precursory meeting following the submission of a signed notification facilitated by the local authority, involving at least the organiser and the police, resulting in a signed outcome agreement.

Recommendation 21
- Once the notification has been considered by the local authority, the authority should issue organisers with a 'permit to process' outlining what had been agreed and what was expected.

Recommendation 22
- Organisers should not be required to pay a fee for a notification to organise a procession.

Recommendation 23
- Debriefing meetings should be held after processions with the organisers, local authority and the police and other relevant groups resulting in a signed record of what occurred.

Fourth element of remit: numbers and effects on communities

Recommendation 24
- Organisers should continue to act responsibly in ensuring processions are organised for appropriate purposes and consider the scope for combining processions on certain occasions.

Recommendation 25
- Local authorities and the police should ensure that they keep statistics on the numbers of processions taking place and the associated policing costs.

Recommendation 26
- As part of their planning process, organisers should consider whether it is necessary to take out public liability insurance.

Recommendation 27
- Local authorities should produce 'How To' guides for organisers of processions.

Recommendation 28
- Local authorities and the police should develop a code of conduct for organisers and participants and this should be set out in the 'permit to process'.

Recommendation 29
- Organisers should ensure that their existing codes of conduct reinforce the behaviour expected of participants in the 'permit to process'.

Recommendation 30
- In certain circumstances, should the risk assessment demonstrate it is necessary, local authorities should be able to require organisers to take out insurance or provide a behaviour bond.

Recommendation 31
- Organisers should recognise the degree of responsibility they have for the behaviour of onlookers and exercise appropriate influence to improve behaviour where they can.

Recommendation 32
- Organisers should ensure that they have effective stewarding arrangements in place for the management of processions, and local authorities and the police consider whether there is appropriate training that can be offered.

Recommendation 33
- Bands playing at processions should identify a named individual who will be present on the day to be responsible for the conduct of the band and its supporters.

Recommendation 34
- The police should exercise their enforcement powers appropriately and, in liaison with stewards, ensure the policing of onlookers is effective and their actions considered as part of the debriefing process.

Recommendation 35
- Local authorities without byelaws prohibiting the consumption of alcohol in public places should consider putting them in place.

Fifth element of remit: police costs

Recommendation 36
- Organisers of processions should not be required to meet policing costs.

Recommendation 37
- Local authorities should consider relevant police costs when reaching decisions about march notifications.

Recommendation 38
- Police forces should ensure that there is appropriate briefing provided for officers policing processions and that it includes information about the reasons for the procession and the relevant background to the organisation involved.

3 Introduction: the establishment of the Review, its remit and its conduct

Introduction

3.1 Marches and parades have long been a part of life in Scotland. Nearly every town and village across the country has some form of local celebration involving a public procession. Various groups and organisations have particular marching traditions. People have always taken to the streets to celebrate their identity, commemorate a cause or protest against a decision. My work throughout the Review has been informed by those traditions. In our democracy, people have a right to peaceful assembly which must be respected and protected. However, that right is not an absolute one and with that right comes responsibilities. There is a difficult balance to be struck, between what can appear sometimes to be conflicting rights.

3.2 People take part in marches and parades for different reasons. We need to get better at understanding and respecting the reasons and traditions which lie behind processions. In return, those taking part in processions need to get better at understanding the impact they have on the community through which they march.

3.3 My Review has looked at the practical arrangements for making decisions on marches, looked at the impact on communities and how to inform and involve them more effectively and examined the conduct and policing costs associated with marches. My recommendations look at freshening up legislation which has been in place for over 20 years. Clearly things have changed. We have new human rights legislation in place. People expect more of their decision makers. People also expect more involvement in the decision making process.

3.4 I hope that, in future, no one will learn about a procession just a few minutes before it passes by their house. They should have better information and an opportunity to express their views. I hope that local authorities will be able to make more informed decisions, involving organisers at an early stage. I also hope that organisers will take their responsibilities seriously so that processions are better organised and less disruptive.

3.5 It will, of course, be for the Scottish Executive to decide how far it wants to adopt my recommendations. Some will require changes to legislation so will clearly take time. In the meantime, those involved could already go some way to making the improvements I suggest, with better planning, clearer guidance to organisers and a commitment to improving overall conduct at processions.

The establishment of the Review of Marches and Parades

3.6 I was commissioned to carry out a Review of the procedures for authorising marches and parades in Scotland on 28 June 2004. The Review was to last for six months.

3.7 The First Minister had announced his intention to appoint an independent expert to review the procedures for taking decisions on marches and parades to the Scottish Parliament on 17 June. In describing the purpose of the Review, he said it, *'will explore with councils and other interested organisations the frequency, number and routes of marches. It will also consider the rules that govern decisions on marches and parades and how local communities' needs can be considered as part of a reasonable and fair system.'* He went on to say that he believed *'the best decisions will be made locally by local authorities and local police forces through engaging communities… the objective will be to ensure that local rules and regulations that govern decisions about marches and parades – particularly those of a sectarian nature – are designed more effectively to regulate the number and routes of marches and especially to encourage an atmosphere in which voluntary agreements can reduce the number of marches locally without animosity and without increasing community tension.'* In concluding, he made clear that he felt the time was right to do something about the issue of marches and parades which were causing concern in communities *'after many years which most of us have wanted to do something. It is now time to act.'*

3.8 I was pleased to accept the First Minister's invitation to carry out such an important and challenging Review. I made clear from the outset that I was approaching the Review with an entirely open mind and planning to listen to and take account of the range and diversity of views which I expected to be expressed.

The remit of the Review of Marches and Parades

3.9 The remit I was given was to review the procedures for authorising marches and parades in Scotland. The remit covered all marches and parades. In carrying out the Review, I was to:
- Identify the issues surrounding marches and parades from the view of those who wish to march, the communities affected by marches and the authorities who have responsibility for making decisions about marches and ensuring local safety.

There were five key aspects I was asked to look at:
- The period of notice required to be given to local authorities, the police and communities for proposed marches and parades;
- The best way to ensure community input into decisions about marches and parades;
- The basis for determining when to restrict, refuse or reroute marches and parades;
- The number of marches and parades occurring in communities and the effects these have; and
- The costs of policing marches and parades.

I was asked to make recommendations to help local authorities reach decisions that reflect an appropriate range of views and to address the problems being caused by marches and parades. My recommendations were to aim at improving the process for taking decisions on applications for marches and parades, consider how the views of communities could be fed into the decision making process and recommend how best to balance the needs and wishes of communities and the rights of groups and individuals to hold and participate in marches.

The way in which the Review was conducted

3.10 If the Review was to succeed it needed to be evidence based and inclusive. People have strongly held views on marches and parades. I wanted them to be able to express those opinions to me to ensure that the work of the Review was informed by the full spectrum of opinion. I approached gathering that information in three ways:

- **Written submissions** – I began by writing to over 1,000 organisations inviting them to submit views relevant to the key areas of my remit. Given the pivotal nature of the Review, I ensured that my letter went to the widest range of possible interests including: local authorities; the police service; the fire service; the NHS; the enterprise network; tourist boards; community planning partnerships; social inclusion partnerships; housing associations; trade unions; political parties; voluntary organisations; youth groups; sports groups; faith groups; and organisations which arrange marches. I also invited organisations to circulate my letter around their own networks. The breadth of the consultation networks reflected the wide range of possible interests in the Review. To ensure that the work of the Review was brought to the attention of a wide audience, information was also posted on the Scottish Executive web site and circulated to local media across Scotland. I invited comments to be sent to me by 24 September but was prepared to accept submissions after that date. In total, I received 361 written submissions. They came from a wide range of organisations as well as from members of the public. There is a detailed summary of views expressed at Chapter 8 – A Summary of Written Submissions and these were helpful in informing the work of the Review. A list of all who contributed is at Appendix A;

- **A telephone survey** – I wanted to make sure that I explored the views people had on marches and parades in general. TNS Social Research was commissioned to carry out the survey after a selective tendering process. The survey sample was broadly representative of the adult population in terms of age, sex and working status. Results were analysed by police force area. 676 people were interviewed. The survey explored people's views and experiences of marches and parades, the impact marches and parades had on individuals and the community as well as seeking views on the various aspects of my remit, including how the community could be better involved in the decision making process. More details of the survey can be found at

Chapter 9 – A Summary of the Telephone Survey of 'Views Across Scotland'. The full report has been published separately *http://www.scotland.gov.uk/marchesandparades*. The questionnaire used is at Appendix B;

- **Face-to-face meetings** – I supplemented the written material with face-to-face meetings. In gathering evidence for the Review, I met around 125 people at 45 separate meetings. I was able to meet with a wide range of key interest: MPs, MSPs, councillors and council officials, police associations, football clubs, anti-sectarian groups, business interests, representatives from the Roman Catholic Church, representatives from the Church of Scotland as well as organisations which arrange marches (including the Grand Orange Lodge of Scotland, the Apprentice Boys of Derry and Cairde na hÉireann). To understand the approaches and to explore good practice outwith Scotland, I visited Liverpool, London and Belfast. A full list of all those I met is at Appendix C. I found all these meetings extremely helpful and was encouraged that everyone approached them with an open attitude, prepared to share their views and be receptive to rounded and objective discussion. Some interesting points emerged and were valuable in shaping my recommendations.

3.11 I wanted to make sure that the work of the Review was informed by current processes and invited local authorities to provide me with more detailed information about how they implemented the requirements of the Civic Government (Scotland) Act 1982. Local authorities also provided me with statistics about the numbers of notified marches and parades taking place in their areas. Chapter 6 – Current Practices in Scotland looks in more detail at current processes. It was also important that my recommendations were informed by and firmly set in the context of human rights legislation and Chapter 5 – The Current Legislative Position: Human Rights Legislation and the Civic Government (Scotland) Act 1982 looks in more detail at that framework.

Structure of my report

3.12 I have structured my report in three parts. The first provides an Executive Summary and a summary list of my 38 recommendations. The second describes the establishment of the Review, the current legislation, the current processes and the information and evidence I have gathered over the course of the Review. The third sets out my recommendations.

4 Traditions of processions in Scotland

Introduction

4.1 This chapter looks at the very wide variety of marches and parades which take place in Scotland. My remit clearly covered all processions in Scotland and so my recommendations will affect all bodies which organise processions. This has informed me throughout my work and I invited views from a wide range of organisers and also met with representatives of several of them. I welcomed the constructive suggestions and positive approach that all organisations have brought to the Review based on their practical experiences of organising processions.

What is a march or a parade?

4.2 Organisations use different terminology for their processions. Some commonly used words include: cavalcades, commemorations, celebrations, demonstrations, festivals, kirkin', marches, parades, protests, rallies, remembrances, ridings and walks. Organisations also have different reasons for processions, for example: celebration, commemoration, marking traditions and community, or remembrance.

4.3 The administrative arrangements for all these processions are governed by the Civic Government (Scotland) Act 1982 which covers all *'processions in public'*. The definition in the legislation is *'a procession in public'* is a *'procession in a public place'*.

4.4 Dictionaries generally define *'a procession'* as *'a line or a number of people or vehicles moving forward in an orderly or ceremonial manner'*; *'a march'* as *'an organised protest in which a group of people walk somewhere together'*; *'a parade';* as *'ordered march or procession'*; a demonstration as *'a march or public meeting to demonstrate opposition to something or support for something'*; and *'a cavalcade'* as *'a procession of people on horseback or vehicles'*.

4.5 I do not intend to give a prescriptive definition of a procession. I think it is important that the term covers the full range of moving events that occur in public places throughout Scotland. Throughout my report I use the terms 'procession', 'march' and 'parade' almost interchangeably although I have tried to follow the legislation in its use of the term 'procession'.

4.6 My remit concentrated on processions and I have not looked in detail at public assemblies or static protest meetings. They are governed by provisions in the Public Order Act 1986. Under that legislation, organisers are not required to give advance notice. The police can impose conditions on assemblies on the same grounds as they can for processions. Those grounds are to prevent: serious public disorder; serious damage to property; serious disruption to the life of the community: or intimidation to others. A public assembly is defined as an assembly of 20 or more people in a public place wholly or partly open to the air. Public places include roads and places the public has access to, whether free or with payment of an entrance fee.

Marching and parading organisations in Scotland

4.7 A wide range of organisations is responsible for the 1,700 or so processions notified to local authorities every year (for more information on the numbers of processions see Chapter 7). Not all processions are notified as some of the more traditional events are treated as exempt from the requirement of advance notification (for more information on exempt organisations see Chapter 6 – Current Practices in Scotland). It is important to recognise the diversity of processions which take place in communities across Scotland reflecting our own traditions, history and culture. While they are diverse in nature, they also have some common features: they often take place at the same time, at the same place, in the same format each year; they are a celebration of tradition and culture; and they forge community spirit. They can also cause some sort of disruption and have an effect on the wider community. As one respondent put it, processions can be, '*noisy or disruptive or irritating and celebratory, engaging and fun*'. However, they are a part of life in Scotland and my recommendations will affect all organisations which organise processions.

The Loyal Institutions: the Grand Orange Lodge of Scotland, the Apprentice Boys of Derry and the Provincial Grand Black Chapter of Scotland

4.8 The statistics from local authorities detailing the numbers of notified parades taking place in their areas show that, in terms of volume, most are organised by the Loyalist Institutions, which are responsible for organising around 50% of all processions across Scotland (and around three quarters of processions which take place in the Strathclyde Police Force area).

4.9 There are, of course, many documents and academic research on the history of the Loyal Institutions, particularly the Orange Order but I thought it helpful here to highlight some of the key facts about the Loyal Institutions' history and development in Scotland. I have drawn heavily on publicly available information from 'Orangenet' (www.orangenet.org) a website created to provide information about historical, cultural and religious aspects of the Order, from other websites of the Orange Order and from sites created by the Apprentice Boys of Derry. I have also drawn on work by Neil Jarman and Dominic Bryan about the history of the Loyal Institutions, particularly in Northern Ireland, as well as information in Sir Peter North's report, 'Independent Review of Parades and Marches'.

The Loyal Orange Institution – The Orange Order
The history of the Orange Order in Scotland

4.10 The Orange Order has been part of Scottish life for 200 years. The Loyal Orange Institution was formed in Ireland in 1795 after the Battle of the Diamond in County Armagh, when a group of Defenders (Roman Catholics) attacked a cottage owned by Dan Winter (a Protestant). The Loyal Orange Institution built on the traditions of the Protestant Volunteers. Its founding principles were loyalty to the Crown and to the Protestant religion. By 1796, *The Belfast Newsletter* estimated that the Order had 2,500 members and the Grand Orange Lodge was established to give the organisation a sense of coherence, uniformity and strength. The Order held its first parade commemorating the Battle of the Boyne in July 1796, although similar parades had been organised by other groups previously.

4.11 The Order in Scotland had a military foundation and was brought to Scotland by Scottish regiments which had fought in the Irish Rebellion of 1798. Some soldiers served in Ireland alongside members of the newly formed Orange Order. The regiments brought back lodge warrants with them. The first warrants were granted to the Breadalbane Fencibles and the Argyll Fencibles between March and May 1798. Around 12 other fencible regiments took out Orange warrants to hold Orange Lodges in their Regiments over the next few years, including the Ayr, Tay, Dumfries, North Lowland and Caithness Fencibles. Fencible Regiments were defence forces, raised during hostilities for the duration of the war only and were designed to liberate the regular army from the United Kingdom for service abroad, limited to home service unless members voted to go overseas.

4.12 It appears that the first civilian lodge was established in Maybole in 1808. By the late 1820s, there were 40 lodges established in Scotland mainly in Ayrshire, Glasgow and Galloway but as far north as Dundee, to the east at Dalkeith and Musselburgh as well as in Edinburgh. By the 1830s full Districts had been established at Airdrie, Dumfries, Edinburgh, Glasgow, Kilmarnock, Maybole, Paisley and Stranraer.

4.13 All these lodges came under the control of the Grand Lodge of England, formed in Manchester in 1808 and moved to London in 1828 when the Duke of Cumberland was its Grand Master. The Order became known as the Loyal Orange Institution of Great Britain. When the London Grand Lodge sent an officer in 1833 to visit Airdrie, his open carriage dressed in Orange ribbon was met outside the town and paraded through its streets. He was treated in the same manner when he visited Stranraer. Due to the Order's political activities to oppose Catholic Emancipation and the Reform of Parliament, a Select Committee of the House of Commons was appointed to carry out an enquiry into the Order's activities. The findings of the Committee were difficult for the Duke of Cumberland and he officially disbanded the Order in 1836.

4.14 This caused unrest and confusion. Lodges were divided, some joining the Grand Protestant Confederation formed to replace Orangeism. Others remained outwith any constituted authority, later enrolling with the Grand Lodge of Ulster. Other Lodges united immediately and formed the Grand Orange Association of Scotland in 1836. The headquarters of the new Lodge was the King William Tavern in the Gallowgate in Glasgow. The fragmentation continued until 1850 when Orangemen in Scotland appeared to have sought unity and all the Lodges in Scotland enrolled with the Grand Protestant Association of Loyal Orangemen of Great Britain which had emerged from the Grand Protestant Confederation. With a larger membership, the Grand Protestant Association organised a system of Provincial Grand Lodges and, in 1853, the Provincial Grand Lodge of Scotland was raised to the full status of a Grand Lodge. Following the establishment of the Grand Orange Lodge of Scotland, the Order grew and developed an increasing political awareness as it sought to defend Protestant beliefs at the polls.

4.15   The Order suffered a set back in 1859, when it split apart over the right to march. Its processions had attracted opposition and skirmishes. Coatbridge Orangemen had been seriously assaulted in 1857, a procession planned for Inchinnan in 1858 had to be called off when it was prohibited by the Sheriff and a local demonstration at Linwood in 1859 ended with a loss of life. The Sheriffs of Ayr, Lanark and Renfrew ordered a ten year ban which was accepted by the Grand Lodge. Some Scottish lodges left to join the Liverpool based 'Institution of Great Britain'.

4.16   Despite a period of a disunified structure, both branches of the Order continued to grow, in part due to the migration of Ulstermen into Scotland and in part due to a reaction by Scottish Protestants to a feeling that Catholics were being granted concessions by the Liberal Government. Membership of the Order peaked in the years between 1874 and 1878. The Order in Scotland was reunited during this time, in 1876 and the Loyal Orange Institution was constituted. The Order forged links with the Conservative party at the end of the nineteenth century.

4.17   The early twentieth century, in 1910, saw the Order under new and clear leadership with a new Grand Master, David Ness. He encouraged the Ladies Section of the Order, created in 1909, and gave fresh impetus to the juvenile movement. The First World War took its toll on the Order as some of its members lost their lives. Membership of the Order increased during the 1920s and 1930s, partially in response to the 1918 Education Act and to the revival of the Home Rule question for Ireland. The Order's first Annual Divine Service was staged in Glasgow Cathedral in 1933. Various MPs and Peers were members of the Order. At this time the Order broke off its formal ties with the Unionist Party and temporarily established its own party, with an MP being returned for Motherwell in 1923. The Order continued steadily throughout the mid years of the century with a recovery in the 1970s when the Grand Order was reorganised and several new District Lodges established. Current issues of interest for the Order, as it passes its 200 years in Scotland, remain linked to continuing to protect the Protestant faith and concern about issues in Northern Ireland. The Order no longer has political ties to any party and members come from all political persuasions.

Structure of the Orange Order in Scotland

4.18 The present day structure of the Orange Order reflects its historical development. The lodge remains the basic unit of the Order and lodges are created where and when members want to set them up. There are an estimated 911 lodges across Scotland. Each lodge elects a number of officers annually, headed by the Master and sends representatives to one of 62 District Lodges. In turn the District Lodges send representatives to one of the four County Grand Lodges, covering Glasgow, Central Scotland, the East and Ayrshire, and Renfrewshire and Argyll. The Grand Orange Lodge of Scotland is made up of representation from the County Grand Lodges and each District Lodge in Scotland. The Grand Lodge has around 300 members at each meeting and meets formally four times a year, in March, June, September, and has its Annual General Meeting in December. It works through a number of committees. The Orange Order has an estimated 50,000 members across Scotland. Almost a third of the adult membership is female and there is an active junior section.

The beliefs of the Orange Order

4.19 The Orange Order emphasises its religious foundation and, to underline the importance of its religious basis, an open Bible is displayed when a lodge is in session. Each lodge has a chaplain who will open and close proceedings in prayer and read a portion of the bible. The Order describes its belief system is as 'Christian, Protestant, patriotic and fraternal' and summarises its purpose as:

- To maintain intact the Protestant Constitution and Christian heritage of the United Kingdom;
- To cultivate Christian character, promote brotherly love and fellowship; and
- To expose and resist by all lawful means every system opposed to the mental, political and spiritual freedom of the individual.

4.20 Its principles are set out formally in the Qualifications of an Orangeman which state that an Orangeman should:

'have a sincere love and veneration for his Heavenly Father; a humble and steadfast faith in Jesus Christ, the Saviour of mankind, believing in Him as the only Mediator between God and man. He should cultivate truth and justice, brotherly kindness and charity, devotion and piety, concord and unity and obedience to the laws; his deportment should be gentle and compassionate, kind and courteous; he should seek the society of the virtuous and avoid that of the evil.

He should honour and diligently study the Holy Scriptures, and make them the rule of his faith and practice. He should uphold and defend the protestant religion and sincerely desire and endeavour to propagate its doctrines and precepts. He should strenuously oppose the fatal errors and doctrines of the Church of Rome, and scrupulously avoid countenancing (by his presence or otherwise) any act or ceremony of Popish Worship. He should by all lawful means resist the ascendancy of that Church, its encroachments and the extension of its power, ever abstaining from all uncharitable words, actions or sentiments towards Roman Catholics.

> *He should remember to keep holy the Sabbath day, and attend the public worship of God, and diligently train up his offspring and all under his control, in the fear of God, and in the Protestant faith. He should never take the name of God in vain, but abstain from all cursing and profane language, and use every opportunity of discouraging those, and all other sinful practices in others. His conduct should be guided by wisdom and prudence, and marked by honesty, temperance and sobriety. The glory of God and the welfare of man, the honour of his Sovereign, and the good of his country should be the motives of his actions.'*

4.21 The Orange Order takes its name from King William III, Prince of Orange, celebrating his role in bringing constitutional monarchy to Britain with the Bill of Rights. They consider William III brought religious toleration, freedom of speech and of the press, liberty of the subject, independence of judges to interpret the law and the development, both at home and overseas, of parliamentary democracy and constitutional monarchy.

The parading traditions of the Orange Order

4.22 Parades are a very important part of the Orange tradition and heritage and are often the most visible part of the Order's activities to the public, although it is important to the Order that parades are not viewed as the only part of their activities which encompass wider fraternal, social and charitable pursuits. However, to many members of the Order, the annual parade is often regarded as the highlight of the lodge year. The Order's formal submission to me explained the intrinsic importance of parades:

> *'And we flatter ourselves that we are good at it. Sunday best dress, the bright lodge sashes, the expensive oil painted banners and the bands produce a street theatre of noise and colour that is unmatched by any other organisation in Scotland. A strict code of public behaviour is only rarely breached by members and is then subject to lodge discipline and lodge processions are well stewarded by our own marshals. The police are not required to expend any time or effort in stewarding and are able to concentrate on their traffic and public order duties.'*

4.23 The Orange Order believe that parades represent a medium to witness for their faith and to celebrate their cultural heritage. The Order see their tradition of parades as building on the existing traditions of the Protestant community. Parades commemorate various events from the remembrance of the fallen at the Somme to the 12th of July commemorating William III's victory over James II at the Battle of the Boyne. There are also local church parades and Divine Services. Parades are a way of marking a sense of tradition and family and the maintenance of freedoms.

4.24 Parades usually involve a number of lodges parading together within the District. The parade is led by a colour party carrying the national flag, followed by a parading band, followed by the lodge banner and the members of the lodge. Banners depict biblical scenes, famous people or events in history. Members wear collarettes or sashes and the bands wear uniforms.

4.25　Orange processions in Scotland have had a long history. July processions were common in Ayrshire, Wigtown and Dundee in the 1840s and 1850s. The Grand Orange Lodge of Scotland organised its first 12th of July parade at Moodiesburn in 1857, although the first recorded Scottish 12th of July celebration was thought to have taken place in Glasgow in 1821. However, the parades did not always pass off peacefully and there were assaults in 1857, followed by a prohibition of the march the following year and more violence in 1859. Processions were then banned by the Sheriffs of Ayr, Lanark and Renfrewshire for ten years. It has been alleged that Father Jeremiah Coakley had to leave East Lothian in 1861 because he had compelled the authorities to put a stop to an Orange march in Bo'ness placing his life in danger from enraged local Orangemen.

4.26　Marches appear to have grown in size in Glasgow over the middle nineteenth century. In 1868 records show that 600 took part in 12th of July procession but 10,000 were taking part in the 1870s. In 1878 there were an estimated 100 lodges in Glasgow with a membership of 14,000 – 15,000. Marches were taking place across Scotland. One of the earliest parades in West Lothian was in 1892 in Armadale. Broxburn saw a major parade in 1922 with 5,000 participants. *The West Lothian Chronicle* records the parade set out with '*bands playing and banners flying… A force of 43 policemen was distributed along the route some of whom were mounted, fortunately though little call was made on their services.*' The Order's first Annual Divine Service was held in Glasgow Cathedral in 1933 where the Order later returned to celebrate its 200 years in Scotland in 1998.

The main parades of the Orange Order

4.27　The Orange Order's main parades take place around 12th of July commemorating William III's victory over James II at the Battle of the Boyne. There are sometimes 'feeder parades' on the same day as the commemorative parades held by a lodge from their hall to their point of departure. A lodge may walk through a part of local town or village before leaving for the main parade. Sometimes they parade from their hall to collect their Grand Master from his house. Following their participation in the main event, the lodge may parade back to their Orange hall. As well as the main parades, the Orange Order organises parades to and from church services. At these parades, the bands will play only religious music. There are also local parades celebrating more localised events such as the founding of the lodge or the unfurling of a new banner.

The Royal Black Institution – the Provincial Grand Black Chapter of Scotland

Background and beliefs of the Royal Black Institution

4.28　The Royal Black Institution was formed in Ireland in September 1797 and sees itself as a predominantly religious organisation. The aims and objectives of the organisation are based on Christian teaching as found in the Holy Scriptures and on the principles of the Reformation. Its members are encouraged to study the scriptures, increase the knowledge of the reformed faith, engage in Christian and charitable outreach and continue and further develop social and responsible citizenship. Membership is confined to men who must first be members of the Orange Order.

The Provincial Grand Black Chapter of Scotland

4.29　The Royal Black Institution has a tiered structure, with the local preceptory the base, rising to district and county levels and the Imperial Grand Black Chapter of the British Commonwealth, the governing body, which has representatives from the various provincial chapters. The Royal Black Institution has representation in Scotland through the Provincial Grant Black Chapter of Scotland which has a total of 60 Preceptories spread over 11 District Chapters. These are to be found in and around the Greater Glasgow area, Ayrshire and in the Lothians.

Main commemorative parades of the Royal Black Institution

4.30　In Northern Ireland, the first major Royal Black Institution parades take place on 13 July in County Down. The second half of August is the key time for Royal Black Parades with local parades held before the main six County parades on the 'Last Saturday' of August. In Scotland, the Royal Black Institution has one main parading day on the second Saturday in August. Preceptories around Scotland organise parades at this time, for example in 2003 there were 11 parades in Glasgow and 15 parades in North Lanarkshire organised in August. Like the Orange Order there will be 'feeder parades' to the main parade. Royal Black parades are a public manifestation of the member's Christian faith and others are linked to 'Divine Services'. The Royal Black Institution has internal stewarding appointed for the purpose of ensuring that those who take part adhere to their code of conduct.

The Apprentice Boys of Derry

History and development of the Apprentice Boys of Derry

4.31　The Apprentice Boys of Derry was formed to commemorate the Siege of Derry which took place in 1689. It commemorates the actions of 13 apprentice boys who seized the keys to the gates of Londonderry and closed them in the face of the advancing army of James II. James II's army laid siege to the city in April 1689 for 105 days before William III's forces were able to relieve the city at the end of July.

4.32 The first Apprentice Boys club was formed in 1714. The present day organisation of the Apprentice Boys dates from 100 years later when the Apprentice Boys of Derry Clubs were founded. At the heart of the organisation are the eight Parent Clubs which are based in the Memorial Hall in Londonderry. Six of these are named after leaders of the siege: Baker, Browning, Campsie, Mitchelburne, Murray and Walker, the other two being the Apprentice Boys of Derry Club and the No Surrender Club. The Baker Club was formed in 1927, the Campsie Club as recently as 1950, while the other five clubs were founded in the nineteenth century.

4.33 Besides the Parent Clubs, the organisation consists of around 200 Branch Clubs across Northern Ireland, in Scotland, England, the Republic of Ireland and three in Canada. Each Branch Club is established through, and affiliated to, a Parent Club. Branch Clubs in each area are also linked together by Amalgamated Committees which function as sub-committees of the main organisation. There are eight Amalgamated Committees in Northern Ireland, one in Scotland and one in England. Overall organisation and management of the Apprentice Boys is controlled through the General Committee.

4.34 There are an estimated 1,500 members in Scotland. The Clubs were first established in Scotland in 1903. The Apprentice Boys do not have a junior organisation and have no female members. The organisation is independent from the other loyal orders, although many Boys are also members of the Orange Institution.

Main parades of the Apprentice Boys of Derry

4.35 The first celebrations of the Relief of Londonderry took place on the walls on 28 July 1689 and the first organised service on 8 August that year. The Apprentice Boys now hold parades to commemorate the two main events of the Siege of Derry: the closing of the city gates by the apprentice boys in December 1688, and the relief of the siege with the arrival of the Mountjoy in August 1689. These two events have been commemorated in the city in some form since the late 17th century. The first parades in Scotland appear to have taken place in 1959. In Scotland, the Apprentice Boys have two main parades a year. The 'Relief of the City Parade' takes place on the third Saturday in May each year with each branch club taking turns to host the parade, under the control of the Scottish Amalgamated Committee. 'The Closing of the Gates Parade' and service is held on the second Saturday in December each year and is held in Glasgow, again under the control of the Scottish Amalgamated Committee.

Catholic marching organisations: Ancient Order of Hibernians

4.36 The Ancient Order of Hibernians is no longer very active in Scotland. It is difficult to know exactly when the Ancient Order was formed. It would probably trace its own routes back to 1565 but only gained its present title in 1838. It grew out of the Ribbon Society which was prevalent in Ireland in the eighteenth and nineteenth centuries. The aim of the organisation is to protect the interests of Roman Catholics and to defend and foster their religion. In Northern Ireland, its parades take place on St. Patrick's Day and Lady's Day (15 August) with bands, banners and members wearing green coloured sashes. The organisation is now seen as a religious, cultural and social grouping.

4.37 The organisation was strongest at the turn of the century. It took on the role as a friendly society as well as providing political support for Irish Nationalism. In 1905 there was a constitution agreed and a new President and Vice President who allied the organisation with the campaign for Home Rule. However, its membership has declined throughout the twentieth century.

4.38 There are very few parades now organised by the Ancient Order. These generally take place in the Strathclyde Police Force area, mainly around Inverclyde and Port Glasgow and also in North Lanarkshire.

Republican marching organisations: Cairde na hÉireann

4.39 Cairde na hÉireann is a relatively newly established national network of groups and individuals campaigning for a new Ireland, built on the principles of justice and equality. It has a political purpose rather than a religious affiliation. It coordinates the activities of groups, bands and individuals which support its aims as laid out in its constitution:
- to campaign for a united Ireland;
- to support sister organisations in Ireland;
- to promote a new Ireland based on the principles of justice and equality;
- to support initiatives aimed at improving the material conditions of the Irish community in Scotland; and
- to campaign against racism and sectarianism.

4.40 Cairde na hÉireann's main work includes campaigning, providing an information service, taking forward political education and organising marches and bands. The Republican bands within Cairde na hÉireann have an agreed code of conduct. The group estimates it represents around 2,000 people, including 300 from the James Connolly society and a number of flute bands with between 55 and 70 members each. 3,000 people had attended their recent marches in Coatbridge. Cairde na hÉireann has worked to improve the conduct of marches and highlight the now trouble-free nature of the James Connolly march in recent years as an example of the success they and organisations affiliated to it have had.

4.41 In the written submission they made to me, Cairde na hÉireann describes the purpose of its marches:

> '*Republicans march in support of various campaigns. Recently these have included anti-collusion marches. We also commemorate significant people and dates in our calendar, for example the annual James Connolly commemoration in Edinburgh. Our marches are followed by political rallies which have been addressed by representatives of Sinn Fein, the Labour Party, the Scottish National Party, anti-racist campaigners and many other campaigns. These events may not be universally popular. People may profoundly disagree with our political analysis. However, these events are not sectarian.*'

Band Parades

4.42 There is an increasing number of Band Parades taking place representing both Protestant and Republican Traditions. Band Parades have been traditional in Northern Ireland but less so in Scotland. Some bands have links to the Loyalist Institutions, many do not and those Loyal Institutions are not responsible for organising their processions nor for controlling behaviour of bands at those processions. For a band to take part in a Loyalist Parade, they must be a member of one of the band associations across Scotland, such as: the Prize Flute Association and the Scottish Accordion Band Association and the four regional divisions of the Scottish First Flute Band Association. The associations aim to improve the standard of dress, playing and decorum within member members. The Grand Orange Lodge of Scotland operates an approved list of bands. Some of the larger band parades celebrating the Loyalist traditions take place in Whitburn, Broxburn, and Stoneyburn.

4.43 Republican bands are part of the Cairde na hÉireann structure. This includes bands which were formerly part of the West of Scotland Bands Alliance. Some of the West of Scotland Bands Alliance parades organised in recent times in Wishaw received considerable media attention. There are also a few marching bands aligned to the Ancient Order of Hibernians.

Other marches and parades in Scotland

4.44 It would be wrong to think that marches and parades are just a feature of and organised by the Loyalist Institutions or Republican or Catholic groups. Public processions are part of the traditions of communities across Scotland and are important to a very wide range of people. These events include the traditional community celebrations that take place throughout Scotland from the crowning of summer queens, gala days and common ridings in the Borders to celebrations which represent new traditions. These events very often take place at the same time every year, in the same place and take the same format. Some processions are organised to celebrate or commemorate certain times of the year. There is also a history of political protest and demonstration. Such events are part of the civic and political life of Scotland.

Traditional Community Events

Crowning of Summer Queens

4.45 Since the early 16th century, Queens of May have been recorded in Scotland. The practice of crowning a summer Queen is still widespread and basically the proceedings followed are similar with the ceremonious arrival of the Queen and her attendants, crowning on a decorated dais, a procession, sports and games. Many of the Summer Queens have distinctive names. For example the summer queen in Largs is known as the Brisbane Queen. In Lanark, the Lanimar Queen is crowned on Lanimar Day, one of the highlights of Lanimar Week, in early June. Some people date it back to 1140 while others suggest 1488, when there is the first recording of the event which arose from the marking of the Burgh's boundaries.

Gala days

4.46 Many towns and villages across Scotland have annual gala days, bringing these areas together in a celebration of history and culture as well as community life. These events are often organised by voluntary committees. Historically, galas days took place in mining communities and there were often two gala days, one in May to celebrate the miners' one-day holiday and the other in June. Gala days were a chance to dress up. Bands turned out to play music for a procession of children, which ended in a park where the rest of the day's events took place.

4.47 Gala days still take place across Scotland with pipe and flute bands playing at events like the Strathaven Gala Day, the Lilias Day Parade in Kilbarchan and the Springside Gala Day in Ayrshire. Kilwinning holds its Segdoune Gala Day in June, choosing the Segdoune Queen from each of its primary schools in rotation. There are over 30 gala days in West Lothian including galas in Bathgate, Armadale and the Deans Gala in Livingston. Many gala days remain aimed at children such as the children's gala in Linlithgow & Linlithgow Bridge. Sometimes gala days are linked to particular aspects of communities' past histories, like the festival week in June organised by the Stewarton Bonnet Guild. This can trace its history back to 1933 and was established to lift the spirits of children during the days of the depression. Some local authorities offer particular assistance to gala day committees, reflecting the particular traditions in their area.

Highland games

4.48 Highland games take place from May to September throughout the summer in towns and villages in the Highlands (and sometimes also in the Lowlands). They developed as a celebration of legends and stories of strong men with athletic ability and were associated with the arts of war but have since grown into organised gatherings. Today they involve athletics, tugs of war, heavy events, highland dancing as well as massed pipe band processions and road and hill races. Sometimes they celebrate the agricultural traditions of the area. Highland games often have a long history. For example, the Braemar Gathering which takes place on the first Saturday in September can trace its routes back 900 years, although has only been organised in its current form by the Braemar Royal Highland Society for the last 188 years.

Scottish Borders – common ridings and festivals

4.49 I am grateful to the Scottish Borders Tourist Board for information about the traditions of commons ridings and festivals in the Borders. In general, the annual commons ridings and festivals held in each town are a survival of the old practice of riding the town's boundaries to preserve the burgh rights and to prevent encroachment by neighbouring landlords. Long after they ceased to be essential they continued in commemoration of local legend, history and tradition. Today they are distinctive and colourful expressions of civic pride and tradition and often involve large numbers of people on horseback following the Burgh Standard as it is carried on its traditional route by a young man chosen each year from among the town's bachelors. Ribbons are tied to the Standard by the principal lass, recalling the days when a knight's lady attached her ribbon to his lance before battle. Each town in the Borders celebrates its history once a year during June and July.

4.50   There are common ridings across the Borders towns: Hawick, Selkirk, Galashiels, Jedburgh, Kelso, Lauder, Coldstream, Peebles, Duns, and Melrose. Examples include:

- The Coldstream Civic Week – inaugurated in 1952 which begins on a Sunday with the investiture of the Coldstreamer, the principal figure in the celebrations, and the bussing of the Burgh Flag. A week's activities follow with rideouts, gymkhana, sports and parades. The highlight of the week on the Thursday is the ride to the Flodden Memorial to commemorate the dead of 1513. Wreaths are laid, a short service held and an oration delivered by a guest speaker. Friday evening sees a torchlight procession and firework display. The Civic Week ends on the Saturday with horse racing, fancy dress parade, the return of the Burgh flag and Beating Retreat.
- The Galashiels Braw Lads Gathering – established in 1930 to celebrate the town's history. Preliminary events precede the main ceremonies on the Saturday which begin with the Braw Lad receiving the Burgh Flag and leading his mounted supporters to the Raid Stane. Here in 1337 Gala lads killed English raiders in a field of wild plums. The stream ran red with blood and 'soor plooms' became the Burgh emblem. The ride continues with a crossing of the Tweed to Abbotsford and a return to the Old Town cross where the creation of Galashiels as a Burgh of Barony in 1599 is recalled. The ceremony of sod and stone (sasine) is enacted and red and white roses mingled on a base of thistles to commemorate the marriage of James IV of Scotland and Margaret Tudor, descendant of the Royal Houses of York and Lancaster. The rideout concludes with an Act of Homage at the War Memorial. Sports and gymkhana bring the week's festivities to a close, with the final act being the laying of flowers at the War Memorial by the Braw Lass.
- The Hawick Common Riding – links the traditional riding of the town's lands with a commemoration of the callants, young Hawick lads who in 1514 routed English plunderers, capturing their flag. Records of the Common Riding principals go back to 1703. A young man is chosen as Cornet and in the weeks before the main ceremonies he leads his mounted supporters on a series of rideouts. Those who complete the long rough ride to Mosspaul and back are made members of the Ancient Order of Mosstroopers. Official proceedings begin on Thursday evening, when in a ceremony of speech and song, the Burgh Flag is bussed and entrusted to the Cornet. The next day bands, civic dignitaries and the mounted cavalcade process around the town. The Cornet with 'the banner blue' leads his followers in the chase,

a ride at full gallop in memory of the victorious youth of 1514. The traditional refreshment of curds and cream is taken. The riding of the marches, horse racing and the dipping of the flag in the River Teviot follow. Saturday events include laying the wreaths at the War Memorial, horse racing and professional games. The Common Riding concludes with the Cornet returning the flag to the Provost.

- Peebles Beltane Week – with Queen Victoria's Diamond Jubilee in 1897 the burgh revived the old ceremony of riding the marches, linking it with the Beltane Fair, which traced its origins to a charter granted by James VI in 1621. Beltane signifies the fire of Bell or Baal and originated from the pagan Celtic festival in honour of the power which in early summer gave light, warmth and growth. Fires were lit and games held. Following an inaugural service on the Sunday a week of events takes place with children's sports, disco, Beltane concert and a fancy dress parade just some of the highlights. Wednesday evening sees the installation of the Cornet followed by the Riding of the Marches and a ceremony at Neidpath Castle where the Cornet is given a welcome by the Warden of Neidpath. The mounted procession leaves for the River Tweed and following a series of horse races the evening ends with the dancing of the Cornet's Reel in the High Street. Festival Day on the Saturday, after an early morning rideout, begins with the proclamation of the historic Beltane Fair and the crowning of the Beltane Queen, followed by a grand procession around the town. Sports and Highland dancing are held in the afternoon and the festival ends with Beating of Retreat.

- Selkirk Common Riding is at least 400 years old and stems back to the time of the 'Burleymen', Burgh Law men who had the task of ensuring no one was encroaching on the town's common lands. In 1513, 80 men from Selkirk followed James IV into battle at Flodden. Only one, Fletcher, survived to return, weary and wounded. but bearing a captured English flag which he raised aloft and then cast to the ground. The Flodden legend came to be associated with the Common Riding, with the Royal Standard Bearer as the central figure and the casting of the colours the main ceremony. Proceedings begin on the Thursday with 'crying the burley' as riders are summoned to attend. The bussing of the flags follow. Various trades and corporations are represented, each with their own standard bearer, who join the Royal Burgh Standard Bearer the next day. The town rises early to follow the band and witness the bussing of the Burgh Flag. The Riding of the Marches, which involves fording the River Ettrick, lasts about four and a half hours and the riders return to the Market Place for the solemn casting of the colours. The Burgh Flag is returned to the Provost and celebrations continue onto the next day with horse racing, gymkhana, Highland dancing and professional games.

4.51 As well as common ridings, there are other festivals in the Borders, many of which involve at least one procession, such as the Eyemouth Herring Queen Festival where the Queen (chosen from High School pupils) arrives in the Harbour on a traditional voyage by sea from St Abbs. The procession tours the town halting at the War Memorial and Memorial to the 129 Eyemouth men lost in the 1881 fishing disaster.

Other community celebrations

4.52 Many other communities organise processions to celebrate their community identity or traditions.

Lesbian, Gay, Bisexual and Transgender Community – The Pride March

4.53 The first Pride March took place in the summer of 1995 in Scotland and has grown and developed since. In 2004, Pride Scotia (Glasgow) was responsible for organising Scotland's national Lesbian, Gay, Bisexual and Transgender (LGBT) Pride event. It involves a traditional march and rally where politicians, community activities, celebrities and individuals turn out to march through the city centre celebrating personal identity and diversity. Pride marches often have a theme and in 2004 this was 'Pride Scotia – celebrating 10 years of Diversity in Scotland'. The march is usually followed by a festival event. Participants come from around the country to take place. Planning begins early. 3,000 to 5,000 people are estimated to attend. For many participants it is the first opportunity they have to make a safe public statement of their pride in their sexual orientation or gender identity. It is also the only opportunity many non LGBT people have to see that this community exists in Scotland. Pride makes a key contribution to national and local aims of equality, diversity, social inclusion and cohesion.

The Hindu Community – the Ram Lila Parade, Edinburgh

4.54 The Ram Lila Parade is organised by the Scottish Indian Arts Forum as a culmination of the celebrations for the Hindu Dusherra festival in mid-October. It is attended by local and national Hindu communities, as well as the general public. Organisers estimate up to 10,000 people took part in 2003. A parade of floats and bands starts from Lothian Road and makes its way up to Calton Hill, where a bonfire is lit and effigies of Hindu demons are burnt.

The South Asian Community – Edinburgh and Glasgow Melas

4.55 Edinburgh and Glasgow Melas were founded by members of the Pakistani, Indian and Bangladeshi communities. Their key objectives have been to reflect and celebrate Scotland's cultural diversity, while retaining its roots in the South Asian communities. In July in Glasgow and in August or September in Edinburgh, they bring together people from a diverse range of cultures and backgrounds to celebrate international and local talent in music, dance, and art. Crafts bazaars, food stalls, children's activities and sports are organised too. This year's Melas were held in Pilrig and Kelvingrove Parks respectively. Organisers estimate around 40,000 people attended last year's festival over two days in Edinburgh. Edinburgh's Mela has a marching band, Ronak Baja, made up of two bagpipers, two trombonists and a dhol player.

The Sikh Community – the founding of the Khalsa

4.56 The Sikh community in Glasgow organise a procession every year in April to commemorate the founding of the Khalsa, the community of baptised Sikhs in 1699. The procession visits all Gurdwaras (Sikh place of worship) in Glasgow. The aim of the procession is to unite all human beings and enhance their spirituality and faith in God. The procession is led by the holy Sikh scriptures, the Guru Granth Sahib, with the congregation following and singing the praises of God. All are welcome to participate in the procession and partake in a community meal at the end.

Youth groups

4.57 Many youth groups organise processions from the traditional annual parades of the Scouts Association, the Boys Brigade and the Girls Brigade to youth festivals such as the International Youth Festival which took place in Aberdeen involving 700 young performers in a street carnival.

Other processions

Sporting events

4.58 There are more and more charity walks, fun runs, road races, half and full marathons taking place across Scotland. While perhaps not everyone's idea of a procession, they need to be carefully arranged, have many of the same effects as more traditional processions, and organisers will be covered by many of my recommendations. There are also processions arranged to mark sporting events, particularly victories, or to protest about decisions such as moving football grounds.

Processions which mark particular dates

4.59 There are some key dates in the calendar which are associated with processions. Remembrance Sunday is such a date with many different organisations arranging processions to war memorials to commemorate and remember those who have died in conflicts over the years. Churches also sometimes organise parades around important days in their calendars, for example Palm Sunday. There are processions arranged to celebrate national days, for example the Norwegian constitution day in May. There are also processions around art festivals, for example Edinburgh hosts the festival cavalcade in August.

4.60 Scotland also has a particular culture of celebrating the passing of the old year with many events organised around Hogmanay. Some of the most interesting include:
- the Ancient Fireballs Ceremony which takes place in Stonehaven, north of Aberdeen. At midnight the high street is lit up as local fireball swingers make their way swinging their fireballs above their heads. The ceremony dates back from a fisherman's festival in the nineteenth century;

- the torchlight Up-Helly-Aa procession in Lerwick which takes place on the last Tuesday in January. Up to 1,000 costumed people bearing torches drag a Viking galley through the streets of Lerwick to a designated burning spot;
- Orkney also has a unique burning ceremony on 11 January (to mark the old Hogmanay) where a 'clavier', a burning half barrel filled with wood shavings and tar, is carried around the streets of Burghead stopping at the houses of eminent citizens to present a smouldering piece of wood for good luck before being taken to a fort on a nearby hill;
- the biggest Hogmanay festival is now organised in Edinburgh where a torchlight procession takes place on 29 December involving anything up to 12,000 people. The torch carriers are accompanied by pipes and drums of both traditional and contemporary groups.

Council organised events

4.61 Councils also organise processions. Many councils have an annual 'Kirkin' of the Council' when councillors parade from the town house to a local kirk for a dedication and service with the parade led by a local pipe band. In June, Glasgow Council organises the Lord Provost's Procession with floats representing community groups, charities, businesses and other organisations, with a wide range of participants from piping bands to African drummers. It marks the beginning of Glasgow's Summer in the City Festival.

Protest marches

4.62 The final category of processions is protest marches that take place in a democracy enabling people to make their views heard in a public way. While there are many other ways of demonstrating, collective action in the streets is still a popular way of making feelings heard.

Political and Trade Union marches

4.63 The Scottish Trades Union Council represents some 630,000 trade union members in Scotland from 40 affiliated organisations. The STUC and its affiliates have been organisers of or involved in some of the major marches and demonstrations in Scotland's communities and workplaces on a range of issues over more than a century as well as annual May Day marches. Recent protests have involved supporting nursery nurses in their dispute over pay levels. The STUC is responsible for organising an annual Scotland wide demonstration, the St Andrew's Day March against Racism and Fascism. The march takes place on the Saturday nearest to St Andrew's Day and attracts trade unionists, politicians, media, public, voluntary and private sector organisations, as well as individuals.

4.64   Scottish CND has organised a series of protests in various parts of the country against nuclear weapons as well as organising anti-war marches and rallies on behalf of the Scottish Coalition for Justice not War. These events provide an organised framework for people to express their concern about political issues. Their marches mainly take place at Faslane and in Edinburgh and Glasgow.

Protest groups

4.65   Many other groups arrange processions to publicise their view or their cause. These can be to support or protest about local decisions such as the closure of a hospital or a sewage works to national decisions such marches against the war in Iraq or against anti-hunting legislation or simply to bring attention to an issue such as Epilepsy Scotland. There have been marches against events occurring in other countries, such as China and Russia.

5 The current legislative position: Human Rights Legislation and the Civic Government (Scotland) Act 1982

Introduction

5.1 This chapter of my report sets out the legislative framework within which decisions about marches and parades are currently taken. There is other legislation which will apply to some marches and parades and I consider this in more detail in Chapter 15 (recommendation 27 on 'How To' guides for organisers).

Human rights legislation

5.2 I consider the freedom to peaceful assembly and to freedom of expression to be fundamental rights in a democratic society. These rights are protected by international and domestic legislation. This is clearly a very complex area of legislation, the subject of considerable academic research and case law, and I do not pretend to be an expert. Many others have studied this area in more depth than I and, in preparing this chapter, I have drawn on Sir George Quigley's analysis of the human rights legislation in that chapter of his Review of the Parades Commission as well as submissions sent to me by a number of local authority lawyers.

5.3 I think it is important to give a flavour of the human rights legislation which set the work of Review in its statutory context and illustrate the framework into which my recommendations must fit. I have looked at Article 11 of the European Convention for the Protection of Human Rights which provides for the freedom of peaceful assembly and at some important opinions about the extent of the rights given by those Articles.

Human rights legislation – European Convention on Human Rights (ECHR) and the Human Rights Act 1998

General

5.4 The European Convention for the Protection of Human Rights and Freedoms sets out a range of rights from the right to life and personal liberty to the protection of privacy and family life, freedom of thought, conscience and religion, freedom of expression and freedom of assembly and association. It is a treaty of the Council of Europe and has now been ratified by 45 countries. The Convention is enforced by the European Commission on Human Rights and the European Court of Human Rights. The Human Rights Act 1998 incorporated the European Convention on Human Rights into UK law, enabling people to enforce their Convention rights in UK courts. Since October 2000, all UK public bodies have a statutory duty to undertake all their functions in conformity with the Convention.

The European Convention as it applies to marches and parades

5.5 In the context of marches and parades, Article 11 concerning the freedom of peaceful assembly is key. The text of Article 11 provides that:

'Everyone has the right to freedom of peaceful assembly and to freedom of association with others, including the right to form and to join trade unions for the protection of his interests;

No restrictions shall be placed on the exercise of these rights other than such as are prescribed by law and are necessary in a democratic society in the interest of national security or public safety, for the prevention of disorder or crime, for the protection of health or morals or for the protection of the rights and freedoms of others. This Article shall not prevent the imposition of lawful restrictions on the exercise of these rights by members of the armed forces, of the police or of the administration by the State.'

5.6 Many aspects of the provisions of Article 11 of the Convention have, of course, been considered in detail in cases brought to the European Commission of Human Rights. Key opinions have set out the Commission's and the Court's views:

- that it is appropriate to have an authorisation procedure to consider processions;
- that rights under Article 11 cover public processions and apply both to individuals and corporate bodies;
- that, as long as the organisers' intention is for peaceful assembly, the possibility of violent counter-demonstrations is not reason alone for prohibiting processions;
- that the rights under Article 11 cover processions which may annoy or give offence to people opposed to the ideas or claims that it is seeking to promote.
- that states should protect those involved in processions and take reasonable and appropriate measures to enable lawful demonstrations can proceed peacefully; and
- that rights under Article 11 do not cover processions if organisers and participants have violent intentions which result in public disorder.

Key Opinions

5.7 The Commission held in **Rassemblement Jurassien and Unite Jurassienne v Switzerland (1979) (17 DR 93, 119, ECommHR)** that the subjection of meeting in public thoroughfare:

'to an authorisation procedure does not normally encroach upon the essence of the right. Such a procedure is in keeping with the requirements of Article 11(1) if only in order that the authorities may be in a position to ensure that the peaceful nature of a meeting and accordingly does not as such constitute interference with the exercise of the rights.'

5.8 In **Christians Against Racism and Fascism v UK (1980) (21 DR 138)**, the Commission stated that:

'freedom of peaceful assembly covers not only static meetings but also public processions. It is, moreover, a freedom capable of being exercised not only by the individual participants of such a demonstration but also by those organising it including a corporate body such as the applicant body. Under Article 11(1) of the Convention, the right to freedom of peaceful assembly is secured to everyone who has the intention of organising a peaceful demonstration. In the Commission's opinion the possibility of violent counter demonstrations, or the possibility of extremists with violent intentions, not members of the organising association, joining the demonstration cannot as such take away that right. Even if there is a real risk of a public procession resulting in disorder by developments outside the control of those organising it, such a procession does not for this reason alone fall outside the scope of Article 11(1) of the Convention, but any restriction placed on such an assembly must be in conformity with the terms of paragraph 2 of that provision.'

5.9 In **Plattform 'Artze fur das Leben' v Austria (1988) (13 EHRR 204)**, the European Court of Human Rights stated that:

'a demonstration may annoy or give offence to persons opposed to the ideas or claims that it is seeking to promote. The participants must be able to hold the demonstration without having to fear that they will be subjected to physical violence by their opponents; such a fear would be liable to deter associations or other groups supporting common ideas or interests from openly expressing their obligations on highly controversial issues affecting the community. In a democracy the right to counter demonstrate cannot extend to inhibiting the exercise of the right to demonstrate.

Genuine effective freedom of peaceful assembly cannot, therefore, be reduced to a mere duty on the part of the state not to interfere; a purely negative conception would not be compatible with the object and purpose of Article 11. Article 11 sometimes requires positive measures to be taken even in the sphere of relations between individuals if need be.

While it is the duty of contracting states to take reasonable and appropriate measures to enable lawful demonstrations to proceed peacefully, they cannot guarantee this absolutely and have a wide discretion in the choice of the means to be used. In this area the obligation they enter into under Article 11 of the Convention is an obligation as to measures to be taken and not as to results to be achieved.'

5.10   **G v Federal Republic of Germany (1989) (60 DR 256, ECommHR)** made clear that Article 11 does not apply to a:

'demonstration where the organisers and participants have violent intentions which result in public disorder.'

Limitations of rights

5.11   Various rights under the European Convention on Human Rights are not without qualifications. This is an important principle as it recognises that people's rights might be in competition with each other and with public interests and there may be a need to impose restrictions. Article 11 states that restrictions are those *'prescribed by law and are necessary in a democratic society in the interest of national security or public safety, for the prevention of disorder or crime, for the protection of health or morals or for the protection of rights and freedoms of others.'*

5.12   The grounds for restricting rights must be relevant and sufficient. The limitation must be legal and must be *'necessary in a democratic society'* which case law has clarified is a society characterised by *'pluralism, tolerance and broadmindedness'* where the rights of minorities are protected. The purpose of any restriction of rights must be in line with those stated in the Convention: protecting national security or public safety, preventing disorder or crime, protecting health or morals and protecting the rights and freedoms of others. The implementation of any restriction must be proportionate to the purpose of the restriction. This ensures that any action taken to restrict a right is appropriate to the seriousness of the threat posed by exercising that right. Authorities have a measure of discretion open to them, *'the margin of appreciation'*, to judge the necessity of a restriction given that they are best placed to judge their national circumstances. However, that discretion is closely monitored by the Court.

5.13   The European Commission of Human Rights has given a number of opinions on the appropriateness of actions taken to limit Article 11 rights:

The Austrian authorities banned a demonstration because of the noise expected at the demonstration and the Commission held that it can: *'be regarded as 'necessary in a democratic society'' to prevent excessive noise of a demonstration and it was not disproportionate in the present case to do so by the prohibition of the demonstration rather than by its subsequent dissolution. Having regard to the previous experience, it was in no way unreasonable or arbitrary to assume that the proposed demonstration would also lead to unnecessary noise.'* **(Application 13812/88 by S v Austria);**

The UK authorities banned a rally in Trafalgar Square as part of a general ban on demonstrations relating to Northern Ireland and the Commission held that *'Having regard to the fact that a refusal of permission [on grounds of public order] did not amount to a blanket prohibition on the holding of the applicants' rally but only prevented the use of a high profile location (other venues being available in central London)… the restriction in this present case may be regarded as proportionate and justified in a democratic society.* **(Application 25522/94 by Rai et al);**

The UK authorities had prohibited all assemblies within a radius of four miles from the junction of roads adjoining Stonehenge Monument for four days in view of past incidents and disorder caused by Druid followers. The Commission referred to previous disorder at Stonehenge and said: *'The Commission notes that the ban did not affect groups of less than 20 people and that it was open to the applicant to practise his religion or belief in a smaller group within the four mile exclusion zone. Bearing all the factors in mind, the Commission considers that the interference with the applicant's right of freedom of assembly can be regarded as 'necessary in a democratic society... for the prevention of disorder'.* **(Application 31416/96 by Pendragon).**

Sheriff Judgements about processions in Scotland

5.14 Sheriff courts in Scotland have also considered appeals against authorities' decisions to restrict Article 11 rights and prohibit processions.

5.15 In **Aberdeen Bon-Accord Loyal Orange Lodge 701 v Aberdeen City Council (September 2001)** the court was of the opinion that the council's reasons for its decision were not made out and an outright ban was disproportionate. The Sheriff stated that: *'This right [under Article 11] is not restricted to those whose views accord with the majority. It is the essence of a civilised democratic society that many points of view may be expressed in public.'* The Sheriff went on to indicate that the right to public assembly may be restricted in certain circumstances but that it was for the public authority to show that it was necessary to curtail that basic right before any such restriction would be upheld. The action proposed needed to be proportionate to the risks which might arise and provide a reasonable response to the perceived risk. The Sheriff considered that *'a complete prohibition requires much more than a 'concern that the procession might promote religious intolerance and might interfere with the rights of other citizens to go about their business freely and lawfully'... It is the right of individuals and groups in a civilised society to express their views as long as neither their words nor their actions contravene the law. Tolerance is what is required in a democratic society and that includes toleration of views or sentiments which may not coincide with one's own.'*

5.16 In the case of the **County Grand Lodge of Ayrshire, Renfrewshire and Argyll v Argyll and Bute Council** it was noted that while Strathclyde police had commented that the procession may well arouse latent emotional tendencies resulting in disorder, the Sheriff stated that *'it seems quite clear that... there is a right for individuals and groups to express their views as long as neither their words nor their actions contravene the law and a mere concern that a procession might promote religious intolerance and might interfere with the rights of other citizens to go about their business freely and lawfully is not sufficient to justify a prohibition'.*

5.17 Another recent case of relevance was the **Wishart Arch Defenders Loyal Orange Lodge 404 v Angus Council (April 2001)** where the Sheriff found that the authority's statement of reasons did not justify a restriction of Article 11 rights. The Sheriff did not consider that the Council's case had foundation in fact. He was concerned by the lack of specificity about how the proposed procession would interfere with the rights and freedoms of others and how those rights might suffer as a result of the procession.

The Sheriff warned against making decisions based on *'emotion or personal feeling'*. He accepted that it was appropriate to take into account local knowledge of a local area but noted that it was necessary to explain the basis of decisions taken based on that local knowledge and that the Council needed to demonstrate the foundation of their decisions including their understanding of public perception.

Statutory framework for holding public processions in Scotland: The Civic Government (Scotland) Act 1982

Background

5.18 Part V (Public Processions) of the Civic Government (Scotland) Act 1982 (referred to in the following paragraphs of this Chapter as the Act) sets out the statutory framework for the arrangements for holding public processions in Scotland. It rationalised previous provisions about powers to prohibit and impose conditions on processions. This chapter looks at the provisions of the Act in some detail. The relevant extracts from the Act are at Appendix D. I have also gathered information about the current operation of the Act which I discuss in more detail in Chapter 6. Information about the Act, its operation and people's experience of it have informed my recommendations as to the improvements that can be made in the arrangements for dealing with marches and parades in Scotland (in Chapters 12 to 16).

5.19 In general terms, the Act requires organisers to notify the local authority and the police of their intention to hold a procession seven days before that procession takes place. It sets out the information the organiser is required to provide. It sets out the processes the local authority should follow in handling the notification, including their order making powers allowing them to prohibit or set conditions on the procession after consultation with the chief constable. The Act also sets out the process for appeal against local authority decisions and the offences and enforcement powers.

Discussion of the Civic Government (Scotland) Act 1982

5.20 I have received mixed views about what the Act requires of local authorities and what degree of conditions they can impose which I explore in more detail in Chapter 6. However, the principle is clear in that in submitting a notification, organisers are **not** seeking local authorities' permission to process. Organisers are not therefore applying for permission or for any type of 'licence'. Rather they are informing the local authority of their intention to hold a procession. Recommendation 21 in Chapter 14 deals with this aspect of the Act.

5.21 The Act gives local authorities power to prohibit or impose conditions on the march. These powers can only be exercised after consultation with the chief constable. Local authorities have interpreted this as meaning that the initiative for a ban must come from the chief constable. Like previous local legislation governing processions (for example local legislation like section 385 of the Burgh Police (Scotland) Act 1892 and the Edinburgh Corporation Order Confirmation Act 1967) the Act is, in fact, silent on when the powers to prohibit or set conditions can be exercised. This is very different from the provisions in the Public Order Act 1936 giving the chief constable powers to issue directions to regulate or ban processions only when he considers that serious public disorder may be occasioned. The Public Order Act 1986 widens the circumstances in which the chief constable can make directions to prevent serious damage to property, serious disruption to the life of the community and intimidation to others. Those are police powers and can only be exercised in Scotland when the procession assembles or is underway. The Civic Government (Scotland) Act 1982 empowers the local authority to set conditions in advance of the procession.

5.22 Provisions in the Act must be applied within the framework of the rights set out in the European Convention of Human Rights. It is clearly established that the existence of an authorisation process does not in itself constitute an interference with those rights. Article 11 is a qualified right and recognises that the right to peaceful assembly is not an absolute right and other factors in the interest of national security or public safety, for the prevention of disorder or crime, for the protection of health or morals or for the protection of rights and freedoms of others can be considered.

Detailed provisions of the Civic Government (Scotland) Act 1982

5.23 This section looks in detail at the provisions in Part V of the Act.

Detailed provisions: Section 62 – Notifications of Public Processions

Requirements on organisers to give notice of their intentions to hold a parade

5.24 Under sections 62(1), (2) and (3) of the Act a person proposing to hold a procession is required to give advance written notice of the proposal both to the local authority where the procession is to be held and to the chief constable. If the procession is to be held to any extent in a National Park, the organiser must also notify the National Park authority. The notice must be given no later than seven days before the date of the proposed procession. The notice should specify:

- the date and time when the procession is to be held;
- its route;
- the number of people likely to take part;
- the arrangements for the control of the procession that the person holding the procession is making; and
- the name and address of the person who is holding the procession.

Changes to the notification period

5.25 Section 62(4) gives the local authority discretion to make an order to dispense with the seven days notice period. This recognises the immediacy of some processions. While the timescale may be changed, under section 62(5) the same information should be provided. Section 62(9) requires the local authority must consult the chief constable before exercising these order-making powers.

Exempt groups

5.26 Section 62(6) gives the local authority power to make an order exempting people from the requirement to give notice of their intention to hold a procession. They may do this as the result of an application or at their own discretion. Section 62(8) gives the local authority discretion to set conditions on exempted parades (eg such as size), an ability to classify processions according to any factor or factors whatsoever and to vary or revoke any orders made. Section 62(9) requires the local authority to consult the chief constable before exercising these order-making powers.

Customary processions

5.27 While section 62 does not apply in relation to processions commonly or customarily held, a local authority can make an order under section 62(7) to apply section 62 to customary processions. Section 62(8) gives the local authority discretion to set conditions on customary processions, an ability to classify processions according to any factor or factors whatsoever and to vary or revoke any orders made. Section 62(9) requires the local authority to consult the chief constable before exercising these order-making powers.

Publicising Orders made under the Act

5.28 If a local authority makes, varies or revokes an order about exempt groups or customary processions, section 62(11) requires them to give public notice of that fact through a newspaper or newspapers circulating in their area.

Definitions

5.29 Section 62(12) provides definitions. 'Procession in public' is simply defined as *'a procession in a public place'*. This is the same definition used in the Public Order Act 1986 (section 16). I understand that those drafting the legislation at the time did not consider it *'practicable to define the term procession'* itself. 'Chief constable' is defined as being *'the chief constable of the police force for the area which comprises of or includes the area of the local authority'*. 'Public place' is also defined as having the same meaning as in Part II of the Public Order Act 1986 which includes *'a road and any place to which the public or any section of the public has access, on payment or otherwise, as of right or by virtue of express or implied'*.

Detailed provisions: Section 63 – Functions of Local Authorities in Relation to Processions

Local authority order-making powers in response to notifications

5.30   Section 63 of the Act sets out the process for handling notifications. Under section 63(1), the local authority may, after consulting the chief constable, make an order prohibiting the holding of the procession or imposing conditions on the holding of it. There is no requirement on the local authority to make an order. Once an order is made, section 63(1A) provides that a local authority, after consulting the chief constable, may vary or revoke the order or make a new order. If the procession is to be held in a National Park, they should consult the National Park authority as well.

5.31   Section 63(2) sets out the conditions that the local authority may impose on the holding of the procession. These may include conditions:

- on the date, time and duration of the procession;
- on its route; and/or
- prohibiting its entry into any public place specified in the order.

5.32   Section 63(3) provides that a local authority must deliver at least two days before the proposed date of a procession, to the person who gave the notice:

- where they have made an order, a copy of it and a written statement of the reasons for it (section 63(3)(a)(i));
- where they decide not to make an order or to revoke an order already made, notification of that fact (section 63(3)(a)(ii));
- where they have varied an order, a copy of the order as varied and a written statement of the reasons for the change (section 63(3)(a)(iii)).

5.33   Section 63(3)(b) provides that where a local authority makes an order prohibiting a procession or imposing conditions on it they must make arrangements to ensure that the people who might take or are taking part in the procession are made aware of the fact that an order has been made (and if the order has been varied, that it has been varied) and of its effect. Section 63(4) requires the local authority to comply with subsection (3) as early as is practicable rather than, for example, waiting two days if they had been given more notice.

Detailed provisions: Section 64 – Appeals against orders under Section 63

5.34   Section 64 makes provision for appeals to the sheriff against an order made by a local authority prohibiting or imposing conditions on the holding of a procession, or against a variation of such an order.

Who can appeal?

5.35   Section 64(1) provides that the person who has or falls to be treated as having given notice of a proposal to hold a procession in public can appeal against the local authority order or any variation of it.

Process of appeal

5.36 Section 64(2) provides that an appeal under section 64 shall be made by way of summary application and shall be lodged with the sheriff clerk within 14 days from the date on which the copy of the order and statement of reasons for it were received by the appellant. Section 64(3) provides that the sheriff can hear an appeal after the expiry of the 14 day period if good cause is shown.

Grounds of appeal

5.37 Section 64(4) provides the grounds of appeal upon which the sheriff may uphold the appeal. The grounds are that the local authority erred in law; based their decision on any incorrect material fact; exercised their discretion in an unreasonable manner or otherwise acted beyond their powers. Section 64(5) empowers the sheriff in considering an appeal to hear evidence by or on behalf of any party to the appeal.

Upholding or dismissing an appeal

5.38 Under section 64(6) the sheriff may uphold the appeal and either remit the case to the local authority to reconsider their decision or, if there is insufficient time, he can vary the local authority's order or make a different order. The sheriff may specify a date by which the local authority must reconsider their decision and to modify any procedural steps which would otherwise be required to be taken so that reconsideration can take place more quickly, for example to vary the local authority's standing orders. The sheriff may also dismiss the appeal under section 64(6). Before exercising any of his powers in relation to the appeal, under section 64(7), the sheriff must make sure that all reasonable steps have been take to secure that the local authority which made the order has been given notice of the appeal and an opportunity of being heard. Under section 64(8) the sheriff may include in his decision provision about expenses.

Appeals against the sheriff's judgement

5.39 Section 64(9) provides that the parties to an appeal to the sheriff may appeal to the Court of Session against the sheriff's decision but only on a point of law. The appeal must be made within 28 days of the date of the decision.

Detailed provisions: Section 65 – Offences and Enforcement

5.40 Section 65 specifies offences in relation to both the *holding* of a procession in public and *participating* in certain such procession and specifies the penalties for such offences. It also makes provision for a power of arrest in relation to these offences.

5.41 Section 65(1) creates four offences for the holding of a procession:
- holding a procession without having given at least seven days notice (or giving notice if the local authority has dispensed with the time limits for giving notice) and without there being an exempting order in force;

- holding a procession in contravention of an order made by the local authority or the sheriff prohibiting the holding of the procession;
- holding a procession otherwise than in accordance with a condition imposed by an order made by the local authority or the sheriff in relation to the procession; and
- holding a procession otherwise than in accordance with the particulars of its date, time and route specified in the notice given or application for an order made under section 62.

5.42 The penalties for those guilty of an offence under section 65(1) are, on summary conviction, a fine not exceeding level 4 on the standard scale (currently £2,500) or imprisonment for up to three months or both.

5.43 Section 65(2) sets out similar offences for people participating in those processions which fall under section 65(1). However, the offence is not simply of participating but of participating and refusing to desist when required to do so by a constable. The penalty for those guilty of an offence under section 65(2) is, on summary conviction, a fine not exceeding level 3 on the standard scale (currently £1,000).

5.44 Section 65(4) gives a constable a power to arrest without warrant a person whom he reasonably suspects of committing or having committed an offence under section 65.

Detailed provisions: Section 66 – Relationship of Sections 62 to 65 with the Public Order Act 1986

5.45 Arrangements for processions in England and Wales are governed by the Public Order Act 1986. That Act requires organisers to give notice to the police six clear days before the date of the procession. The police have powers to impose conditions on a procession and the local authority does not have the same formal role as in Scotland. However, Section 12 of the Public Order Act 1986 gives powers to the police to give directions imposing conditions on those organising or taking part in the procession conditions to prevent serious public disorder, serious damage to property or serious disruption to the life of the community or intimidation of others. Section 12 extends to Scotland and therefore gives the police the same powers to impose directions on processions in Scotland. Section 66 of the Civic Government (Scotland) Act 1982 generally provides that sections 62 to 65 of the 1982 Act are subject to the Public Order Act 1986. It further provides that any order made under those sections shall be subject to any directions given under section 12 of the 1986 Act insofar as they relate to the same matters. Anything done in conformity with any such directions or omitted, in conformity therewith, to be done shall not be an offence under section 65 of the 1982 Act.

Other legislation which might apply to marches and parades

5.46 There is other legislation which might apply to marches and parades depending on the particular facts and circumstances of each march/parade. I consider this legislation in more detail in Chapter 15 (recommendation 27 on 'How To' guides for organisers). In summary, the following legislation may be relevant:

- Common law – organisers have a common law duty of care to take reasonable care not to cause foreseeable death, injury, illness or damage etc. Failure to take reasonable care could result in civil action and claims for damages from third parties against the organisers for injury or loss to person;
- Health and Safety at Work etc Act 1974 and its associated Regulations apply particularly where people are employed to work at the event. Under the Management of Health and Safety at Work Regulations 1999, organisers have a duty to carry out risk assessments which should determine any control measures necessary to avoid risk or to reduce it to acceptable levels. This legislation may also apply to major events and place a responsibility on local authorities to ensure as far as is reasonable and practicable, the safety of its employees and members of the public. There is also a legal requirement to carry employer's liability insurance;
- Food Safety Act 1990 applies where food is provided or sold;
- Occupiers Liability Scotland Act 1960 – duty of care – may impose liabilities on the landlord or tenant of the venue;
- Licences, permits, certifications – depending on the nature of a march or parade some will require licences, permits or certifications, for example: a public entertainment licence; a liquor licence; a theatre licence; a street trader's licence; a lottery permit; or a market operator's licence. If the event involves the use of a regulated spectator stand (over 500 spectator capacity) or requires the erection of a temporary stand or raised platform with public access, a Special Safety Certificate is required;
- Traffic Legislation – such as the Road Traffic Regulation Act 1984 as amended by the Road Traffic (Temporary Restrictions) Act 1991 and the Road Traffic Regulation (Special Events) Act 1994. If there is a requirement for restrictions such as road closures, diversions, signs or cones then a Temporary Traffic Regulations Order (TTRO) may be needed;
- Control of Pollution Act 1974 – provisions about use of loud speakers;
- Public Order Act 1936 – prohibition of the wearing of uniforms etc signifying association with any proscribed organisation;
- Public Order Act 1986 – already discussed in this Chapter; and
- Terrorism Act 2000 – provisions relating to membership and support of and fundraising for a proscribed organisation must also be observed.

6 Current practices in Scotland

Introduction

6.1 This chapter of my report describes the current processes for taking decisions about notifications of marches and complaints. I have been grateful to local authorities and police forces for the useful and detailed information they have provided about how they handle notifications submitted under Part V of the Civic Government (Scotland) Act 1982.

6.2 During the Review, I have reflected carefully on this information and on people's views of how things are currently done to see if there are areas where improvements can be made and good practice shared. Overall, I have come to the conclusion that processes are very varied across Scotland, and, while I recognise absolutely the importance of ensuring processes are appropriate to local circumstances, I think a greater degree of consistency is important. Clearly, processes have evolved over the 22 years that the legislation has been in existence. During that time, there has, of course, been major changes to local government in Scotland through reorganisation and to central government in Scotland through devolution. I think it is time to look afresh at the ways things are done, to freshen up, modernise and professionalise the process. My recommendations for change are contained in Chapters 12 to 16. They have been informed by what I have found currently happens.

Current processes
How notification is given

6.3 Many local authorities have a standard form for organisers to complete to give notice of their intention to hold a march or parade. The form sets out clearly the information required from the organiser and is based on the requirements of the Civic Government (Scotland) Act 1982. Forms vary across local authority areas but the required information includes:
- the name and contact details (address and telephone number) of the organiser;
- the organisation he/she represents;
- the date and time of the procession;
- the proposed route;
- the estimated number of participants;

- the estimated number of vehicles; and
- details of stewarding and arrangements for control.

6.4 Some local authorities ask for more information to help them come to a decision on the notification including:
- the reason for the procession;
- the nature of the event;
- a check that the organiser has notified the police;
- whether it is a sponsored event;
- whether it is an annual event;
- will there be a street collection;
- the estimated number of coaches bringing participants;
- the time and point of assembly;
- the dispersal time;
- the names of any accompanying bands; and
- details of any return processions.

6.5 In all cases the form must be signed by the organiser. The forms are often accompanied by simple instructions about their completion. Forms also give the contact detail of the local authority department to which notifications should be submitted. Some forms also include a summary of the standard conditions relating to the conduct of marches and parades, ensuring that these are clear to the organiser at the outset.

6.6 Those authorities which do not have standard forms require notice to be submitted in writing. They feel it is difficult to cover all the information in a standard form because of the variety of processions being notified. However, they require very similar information of the organiser.

How much notice is given

6.7 The legislation only requires organisers to give seven days notice. However, many organisers given considerably more notice. Organisers I have spoken to stress that they always give as much notice as they can, many giving at least 28 days if not more. Local authorities feel that the current system only works because organisers act responsibly and give them more notice. Local authorities stress to organisers the need to give them longer than seven days and emphasise this in their application forms and guidance. Some local authorities specifically ask for 28 days notice to be given whenever possible, others ask for two months.

6.8 Some areas are looking at how to improve advance planning and, in one local authority area, the police wrote, at the beginning of 2004, to all organisers of events which took place in 2003 enclosing the notification form and asking them to complete the application form for any events they were planning in 2004 and 2005. This was to ensure that the police could make effective arrangements for policing events well in advance to minimise disruption to police officers.

6.9   Chapter 12 considers the period of notice and recommendations 1 and 2 propose changes.

How notifications of marches and parades are currently handled: general processes

6.10   While there is no one model of how local authorities and police forces deal with notifications of marches and parades submitted to them under the Civic Government (Scotland) Act 1982, there are some broadly similar themes in the way in which notifications are processed.

Local authorities

6.11   On receipt, the notification is circulated to the elected members for the wards through which the procession will go, inviting their views. A copy is also sent to various departments within the local authority for comment (in most cases the roads department for traffic disruption and in some cases environmental services for cleansing, transportation services, land services, legal services, parking enforcement). Some local authorities also send a copy to the local police station and, sometimes, the relevant police central events planning office specifically inviting a report on the notification (although the organisers are themselves responsible for ensuring that a copy of the notification goes to the police). Other local authorities have a wider range of interests they consult, particularly for larger processions, including where appropriate the management company for trunk roads, British Transport Police, the fire service and the ambulance service. Clearly, the amount of time given to respond depends on the amount of notice given by the organiser. Many local authorities feel that the current system only works because organisers are responsible and give more than the seven days notice.

6.12   Some local authorities send out an acknowledgement letter to the organiser, explaining the process and that they will be in touch once they have considered the notification.

6.13   In most local authorities, officials have delegated powers to take decisions on non-controversial notifications. The definition of what is non-controversial varies. However, it is generally based on whether:

- objections or concerns have been expressed about the notification;
- the purpose of the procession and its organiser. Some local authorities require the appropriate committee to consider notifications for marches from various organisations (the British National Party, the National Front, Combat 18, the James Connolly Society and independent Loyal Orange Lodges);
- the predicted size of the event. Some local authorities require the appropriate committee to consider all adult 'sectarian' parades with 500 or more participants, but officials are able to make decisions on smaller parades or juvenile parades; and
- whether it requires major road closures. Some local authorities require the appropriate committee to consider notifications which would require a major road closure, but

officials are able to make decisions on notifications which would only require a temporary traffic restriction.

6.14 If no objections to the notification are received, the notification does not fall into a controversial category and the police confirm they are content, then officials take the decision under their delegated powers. However, in a few local authorities, all notifications go before a committee.

6.15 For most local authorities, notifications are only considered by a committee if objections or concerns are raised about the notification. The Committee which considers notifications depends on the structure of the local authority. Generally, notifications are considered by the Licensing Committee, or a sub-Committee of the Licensing Committee. In other local authorities it is the General Purposes Committee or the Planning and Regulatory Committee which consider notifications. The committee considers all the comments in front of it and, based on its assessment following consultation with the chief constable, can make an order prohibiting the procession, an order imposing conditions on it or to agree to the procession going ahead. In considering the notification, most committees have a representative of the chief constable in attendance and some committees invite the organisers to their meeting. Clearly, the notification timetable makes it difficult to convene committees and the current system appears to work only because most notifications are non-contentious and most organisers give more than the statutory seven days notice.

6.16 At the end of the process, most local authorities send a letter to the organisers confirming that they may proceed with the procession and drawing their attention to the general conditions which they have in place governing the conduct of processions and whether the police have imposed any additional conditions. Some local authorities take the opportunity to indemnify the authority from claims for injury. Other local authorities only send a letter to the organiser if there are specific conditions to be imposed.

Police forces

6.17 In parallel, the police have their own processes to follow. In many areas, the police hold meetings with organisers of processions to discuss the practical issues surrounding the timing and routes of their event, the extent of any disruption and any concerns that the police may have. These meetings are held with the local officer, normally of sergeant or inspector rank, over the practicalities of the event. They often discuss marshalling and stewarding. They sometimes discuss the standard conditions about how processions should be conducted which various police forces have developed. Some police forces explain these conditions and the responsibilities of the organiser and require the organiser to sign a declaration. These are generally informal meetings and are rarely formally recorded. However, they are usually productive in ensuring arrangements for marches and parades are successful and go well on the day. I understand that organisers, in the main, approach these meetings in a constructive way and are receptive to these discussions and are prepared to reach compromises over the practicalities.

6.18   Local authorities are rarely involved in these practical discussions, although some areas have joint working parties or planning groups to deal with larger processions involving the local authority and sometimes a wider group of relevant interests. Sometimes the police will give the local authority a summary of meetings and the conditions that they discussed both at the meeting with the organiser, supplemented by the views of a more senior officer. If there are any concerns that have not been resolved with the organiser these are highlighted in the report. If there are adverse concerns expressed in the report, the local authority Committee will consider them in reaching their decisions about notifications.

Related recommendations

6.19   Chapter 12 (specifically recommendations 4, 5 and 6), Chapter 13 (specifically recommendations 12, 13, and 14), Chapter 14 (specifically recommendations 15, 15, 17, 20, 21, 22, and 23) consider the way notifications are handled and the decision making processes.

Exempt organisations: organisations which do not require to notify their intention to hold a march or parade

Exempt organisations

6.20   Under Section 62(6) the Civic Government (Scotland) Act 1982, local authorities can make orders exempting organisations from the need to notify their intention to hold a march or parade. The intention behind this provision seems to have been to allow local discretion to local authorities to exempt community groups, for example gala day parades, from the notification process. Orders under this section vary considerably across the country and local authorities appear to have interpreted it very differently. Some local authorities require all organisations to notify their intention to organise a procession, although make an exception for the Salvation Army and the Scouts and Guides Association under the provisions relating to processions 'customarily or commonly held'. Other local authorities have long lists of groups that are exempt, a number with around 70 organisations. A couple of local authorities have adopted the full list of organisations that were exempt under the former Strathclyde Regional Council, which runs to over 300 organisations (although some are now defunct). These exempt organisations are required only to advise the police of their intention to hold a procession. Very often the police still meet with the exempt organisation to discuss the events to ensure that they can plan effective policing for the procession. Many organisations also notify the local authority and are in contact with departments within the local authority.

6.21   Groups that are listed as exempt include: community councils, community associations, gala day committees, highland games committees, committees organising common ridings, groups organising community festivals, servicemen and veterans groups, various religious groups and some unions. The exemption order only covers the local authority area in which it was made. A fuller list illustrating the organisations which are exempt can be found at Appendix E. Chapter 12, recommendation 3, considers the position of exempt organisations.

Processions that are 'commonly or customarily held'

6.22 Under Section 62(7) of the Civic Government (Scotland) Act 1982, processions that are 'commonly or customarily held' are not subject to the notification requirements. The intention behind this provision was to have a general provision exempting organisations such as the Salvation Army and the Scouts and Guide Associations from the notification requirements of the Act. Some local authorities have, however, included those organisations in their list of exempt organisations to clarify their position.

Exceptions to the exemption procedures

6.23 Under Section 62(8) of the Civic Government (Scotland) Act 1982, local authorities can set conditions on an exempting order or on processions that would otherwise be regarded as being 'commonly or customarily held'. This might reflect the organiser of the procession or the time of the procession. It enables a local authority to take account of a change in circumstance or of experience gained of the procession in the previous year or of similar processions. Very few authorities have used this power and would argue if a group was not specifically on the exempt list, or the Salvation Army or Scout or Guides Association, then the requirements to notify a procession otherwise applies.

6.24 Those authorities which have made orders under this section variously list some of the following organisations requiring them to notify their intention to hold a procession:
- Allan McLean Memorial Flute Band
- Ancient Order of Hibernians
- Apprentice Boys of Derry
- Bridgeton Republican Flute Band
- Clydeside Troops Out Movement
- Coatbridge Harp Flute Band
- Glasgow Irish Freedom Action Committee
- Loyal Orange Order
- Provincial Grand Black Chapter
- Thornliebank Flute Band
- West of Scotland Bands Alliance

6.25 In areas, where section 62(8) orders are not made, organisations are required to notify their intention to process unless they are specifically listed as exempt.

Conditions set on the conduct of marches

6.26 Over time, many local authorities together with the police have developed a set of standard conditions that march organisers and participants should follow. These cover very practical issues and generally set out the expected conduct for organisers and participants. In effect, they form the basis of a code of conduct for processions. However, these are not consistent across Scotland and not every list of conditions include all these provisions. Generally, in those local authorities areas which set out conditions they have between 10 and 16 standard conditions which apply to all processions. The sorts of issues covered include:

- *Conditions to ensure that the details in notification are followed* – These conditions make clear that all processions should assemble and commence at the time stated in the notification. They also make clear that all processions should keep to the route stated in the notice. Some authorities make clear that the procession must only promote the reason or the organisation described in the notification;

- *Conditions about where to march* – These conditions explain that the police will give instructions about the width of the carriageway which may be used by the participants depending on the type of carriageway and these instructions should be obeyed. They explain that where there are no footpaths, participants should keep to the right hand side of the road. They also make provision about the width of the march, generally stating that the march should be between four and six abreast and keep to the near or left hand side of the street, except one way streets where they will keep to the right hand side. There is often a general condition requiring that no obstruction should be caused;

- *Conditions to minimise disruption to traffic and pedestrians* – These conditions make clear that the procession should be split into sections in order to avoid serious dislocation of traffic. They require organisers to assist the police in ensuring that passage is allowed for traffic and pedestrians, ensuring provision is made for regular and sufficient pedestrian passage across the parade. Parades will continue moving and no part will stop unless for emergency purpose on direction of or with agreement of the police, or where specifically authorised to do so in advance or at the parade route end;

- *Conditions about stewarding* – These conditions make provision for a minimum of marshals who must be clearly identified and must wear high visibility jackets or tabards with the word 'Steward'. Some ensure that the colour worn must not clash with on duty police officers. Sufficient stewards and marshals shall be present to ensure that participants comply with directions. Some local authorities recommend the level of stewarding they feel to be appropriate, which varies from a minimum of four marshals for each procession or, where the number of participants is over 160, the ratio of marshals to participants should be no less than 1 to 40, another suggests a 1:10 ratio;

- *Conditions requiring marchers to obey police instructions* – these conditions require organisers and participants to comply at all times with the directions or instructions given to them by the police. General conditions are set to ensure that no cause for complaint should be given;

- *Conditions relating to organisers' responsibilities* – These conditions set out clearly the responsibility of organisers before and during the march. Some require an identified official be appointed to liaise with the police before the march. Most require the organiser to identify himself to the police officer in charge of the procession before the procession starts. These conditions make clear that the organiser is responsible for ensuring that conditions about the march are brought to the notice of people, bodies and bands participating. Other authorities emphasise that the responsibility for conduct and safety of participants lies with organisers and recommend that they take separate advice on the question of liability for anyone who might be involved in an accident and suggest short term insurance cover;
- *Conditions about the playing of music* – Generally, these conditions make clear that there should be no music played when approaching or passing places of worship while services are in progress. Some allow for only a side drum to be played when passing places of worship when a ceremony or service is taking place for 50 yards before or after that location to retain the beat. Other conditions go further and require bands to cease playing when approaching and passing places of worship. Other conditions require music only to be played during the procession and not when the procession is assembling;
- *Conditions about when music can be played* – The majority of conditions allow music to be played between 7.30am and 9.00pm. However, that is not consistent and some authorities make provision that music can only be played later, after 8.00am or after 9.00am. Some require music not to be played after 8.00pm;
- *Conditions about loudhailers* – These conditions explain some of the other legislation which applies to the conduct of processions and make clear that the conditions of section 62 of the Control of Pollution Act 1974 in relation to the use of loudspeakers need to be observed. That provides that no loudhailers will be used other than for parade control or participant address;
- *Conditions about what can be carried during a procession* – these conditions prohibit the carrying of halberds and weapons of any description shall be carried. They also prevent the display of banners, placards, flags and posters bearing inflammatory images or words; and
- *Conditions about what can be worn during a procession* – These conditions explain some of the other legislation which applies to the conduct of procession. They make clear that the terms of the Public Order Act 1936, in relation to the prohibition of the wearing of uniforms signifying association with political organisations, must be observed. They also provide that no paramilitaristic uniforms will be worn and that the terms of the Terrorism Act 2000, relating to membership and support of and fundraising for a proscribed organisation, must also be observed.

6.27 As well as these general conditions, some authorities have other more specific conditions requiring:
- first aid facilities to be available;
- children to be carefully supervised; and
- provision to be made by the organiser to clear litter from the assembly and dispersal points.

6.28 Chapter 15 considers issues relating to organisers' responsibilities, including a code of conduct (recommendations 28 and 29), stewarding (recommendation 32) and responsibility for onlookers (recommendation 31) and the behaviour of bands (recommendation 33).

Making changes to notifications – changes through discussion, orders and prohibitions

Changes through informal discussion

6.29 Informal discussions with the police sometimes result in changes to timing and routes of notifications. This often reflects the positive nature of informal discussions and organisers' willingness to reach sensible accommodation. The sorts of issues which are taken into account are practical ones about traffic disruption, avoiding clashes with other events and rerouting because of street closures.

Changes through orders

6.30 Most notifications are accepted and do not require changes to be made. One authority estimated it only set conditions on a couple of processions a year. However, local authorities do make orders to impose conditions on processions. These orders are made for the same practical reasons that are also covered in informal discussion.

6.31 Local authorities have made orders to avoid clashes of dates, times and routes with other processions, to enable proper arrangements to be made for police supervision, for better traffic management and to allow road closures and rerouting of bus services. They can reflect amendments to routes following police and transport service concerns. Health and safety considerations also have been taken into account. Examples of restrictions imposed include, a change to the time of a Trades Council parade, a change to a route of a Church of Scotland parade due to traffic congestion, a change to the time and assembly point of a march organised by a political party, a change made to the start time of a band parade to minimise disruption and ensure effective policing. Some have made provision about where music can be played, preventing it being played outside a sheltered housing complex. There was one example of an order being made to allow the carrying of weapons at an army volunteers parade.

6.32 Occasionally organisers appeal the conditions set out in orders. For example a change to a route was successfully appealed. This is rare and most organisers accept the reasons for the conditions set in the order on the notification.

Prohibition orders

6.33 Occasionally, it has been necessary for local authorities to make an order prohibiting a procession from going ahead. This has been done extremely rarely in Scotland. Under the previous legislation governing the holding of processions in Scotland, there were a few examples of prohibitions. In March 1980, Strathclyde Regional Council banned marches by the National Front for a month following their proposal to organise a 'Smash the IRA' march. In April 1981, the Council imposed a three month ban on processions concerned with or connected to directly or indirectly with Northern Irish affairs or organised by persons associated with those affairs. This was prompted by a series of demonstrations and counter-demonstrations related to prisoners and conditions in prisons in Northern Ireland by various Irish groups. There was a further one month ban in September 1981. The terms of the banning order needed to be carefully drawn up and were, in fact, amended to ensure that other processions like gala days and political protest marches could go ahead.

6.34 Under the Civic Government (Scotland) Act 1982, there continue to be very few prohibition orders. Orders are made extremely rarely and indeed most local authorities record that they have never needed to make a prohibition order. Those local authorities which have made prohibition orders have done so for various reasons (broadly based on concerns about public order). Their decisions are the subject of considerable interest which reflects how rarely processions are banned in Scotland. Experience has shown that they are often appealed by the organisers and in a number of cases the appeal has been upheld and the order overturned. I have discussed various Sheriff judgements in more detail in Chapter 5 looking at the legislative context. It might be helpful to briefly reprise them:

> In **Aberdeen Bon-Accord Loyal Orange Lodge 701 v Aberdeen City Council (September 2001)**, the Sheriff summed up Aberdeen Council's reasons for prohibiting the procession as a general *'concern that the procession might promote religious intolerance and might interfere with the rights of other citizens to go about their business freely and lawfully'* and the court was of the opinion that the council's reasons for its decision were not made out and an outright ban was disproportionate;
>
> In **The County Grand Lodge of Ayrshire, Renfrewshire and Argyll v Argyll and Bute Council**, the Sheriff was not convinced of Argyll and Bute's reasons for a ban based on a general feeling that the procession may well arouse latent emotional tendencies resulting in disorder and *'a concern that a procession might promote religious intolerance and might interfere with the rights of other citizens to go about their business freely and lawfully is not sufficient to justify a prohibition.'*
>
> In **Wishart Arch Defenders Loyal Orange Lodge 404 v Angus Council (April 2001)**, the Sheriff did not consider that the Council's case had foundation in fact and was concerned by the lack of specificity about how the proposed procession would interfere with the rights and freedoms of others and how those rights might suffer as a result of the procession.

Dundee Council also made a prohibition order preventing an Orange Order march but this too was overruled by the Sheriff and permitted following the appeal.

6.35 North Lanarkshire Council has made two banning Orders in January 2003 and 2004 banning a proposed procession by the West of Scotland Band Alliance. The General Purposes (Processions Sub-Committee) made the Orders. This followed information from the police that there was reliable information that there would be a significant threat of serious disorder, violence and damage to property with an attendant threat to public safety. A previous march involving one of the bands had lead to disruption to the town centre and counter demonstrations resulting in a number of arrests. The orders were made on the basis of the need to protect public order and public safety and the risk that the procession posed. The 2004 order also took account of the extent of the disruption to the town centre and the need to protect the right of members of the public to have access to the centre. The Committee concluded that protection of public order and public safety and the right of access could not be achieved by less stringent means.

6.36 One of the most recent, high profile prohibition orders has been Aberdeen Council's decision to make an order banning a National Front march. The Licensing Committee took this decision after advice from the police that the march represented a potential threat to public order and safety. The police had specific information that local soccer thugs, reinforced by football hooligans from other parts of Britain who were sympathetic to the National Front, were threatening to cause disorder on the day of the march. The police also warned that counter-demonstrations opposing the National Front presented a situation where the risk to public safety would increase to an extent which was *'difficult to quantify'*. The Council also banned a counter-demonstration being planned by Aberdeen Trades Council on the identical grounds that its march, also planned for 28 November, posed a risk to the safety of Christmas shoppers in the city centre. Following the decision, the organisers decided not to appeal.

Organisers' codes of conduct

6.37 Many march organisers also have codes of conduct which apply to their members taking part in parades. These deal with the behaviour of marchers. They cover uniforms, what can be carried, the music that can be played, and alcohol. They are strictly enforced by the organisers. March organisers which also employ bands ensure that they have contracts with those bands. Examples of current codes of conduct are at Appendix F and of band contracts at Appendix G.

6.38 March organisers are also looking at improving the training of their stewards. The Apprentice Boys of Derry is developing a pilot scheme for parade marshals. They have senior certified marshals who were trained by the Chief Steward at Leeds United Football Club. They hold meetings before their main parades to go over the details and arrangements and make sure that they have a full knowledge of the route of the procession and possible trouble areas. The Loyal Orange Order also provide some training to their stewards. Other organisers also provide some training for their stewards. The STUC for example provide instructions to those stewarding about the nature of their duties and their role accompanied with guidance for those involved in the march. Cairde na hÉireann, an umbrella group representing Irish organisations supporting a united Ireland, hand out leaflets to their stewards.

Advice to organisers

6.39 A number of local authorities have developed very straightforward guidance for those organising processions. This is helpful in bringing together all the various issues which organisers need to address in arranging a successful procession. They cover issues such as the legal requirements, the insurance requirements, requirements for other licenses and permits, how to go about the planning process, how to complete a risk assessment, information about stewarding, accidents and welfare arrangements and first aid requirements. I have had sight of helpful guidance from Edinburgh Council, Fife Council and Scottish Borders Council. While the guidance is aimed at those planning events, there are parts of it which I consider to be applicable to those organising processions. Some authorities have events teams which help those planning events. I return to both these aspects later in Chapter 12 (recommendation 4) and Chapter 15 (27 recommendation).

Complaints about processions

6.40 Local authorities have advised me that they receive very few formal complaints about parades. Those that do receive complaints say that they are generally in single figures and have been about:
- *Noise* – being disturbed early in the morning by flute bands assembling before an early morning parade, the general noise from bands, that the music starts too early in the morning;
- *Disruption* – closure to taxi ranks, general frustration about the disruption to traffic and bus services, road closures, not being able to park due to parking suspensions;
- *Litter*;
- *Nature of processions* – people feel some marches are sectarian in nature, some processions promote bigotry;
- *Costs* – to police and local authority; and
- *Behaviour of onlookers and some band members* – bad language, urinating in public or drunkenness.

6.41 In evidence to me, individuals and organisations have also expressed their concerns about some marches and parades. This is recorded in more detail in Chapter 8 which summarises the views expressed in response to my consultation. While I recognise that a lot of this is anecdotal material, there is a sufficient spread of information to demonstrate that some people are frustrated by the disruption they face to their daily lives and do feel intimidated by certain processions.

After the procession – arrangements for debriefing

6.42　From the evidence, there seems to be very little debriefing that currently takes place after processions. One local authority recorded that it would happen only where an unforeseen difficulty or incident has occurred and so it happens very rarely because there are very few incidents. Another authority holds debriefing meetings after large events and brings together a wide range of interested parties who had been involved in the event (including the local authority, the police, other emergency services, including those providing first aid, as well as the organiser).

6.43　Some police forces do carry out internal debriefing. The officer in charge of the policing of the procession submits a debrief report after the event. The report contains information about the numbers involved in the procession, the number of stewards the organiser provided, the number of people arrested or reported, the number of police involved and any other general comments about the conduct of procession including for example, levels of drunkenness, disorder and the standard of stewarding. The reports are collated to Operation Planning Units and any particular issues are sometimes discussed by officers from the local police area with the organiser. The reports are kept and referred to if the organisation were to submit a future notification.

6.44　I believe that debriefing should form an important part of the processes for handling notifications. This is an issue I return to in Chapter 14 (recommendation 23).

Work by local authorities to develop a policy on marches and parades

6.45　While I was carrying out the national Review, Glasgow City Council was also carrying out work to develop a policy on public processions and demonstrations, appropriate for circumstances in Glasgow. This reflected the concern that had been expressed at the conduct of some processions, and the potential disruption to local residents and to city life more generally, caused by the volume of processions taking place in Glasgow. It is clear from the statistics that more notified processions take place in Glasgow than in any other local authority area. The Council wanted to gauge public opinion on processions through a wide-ranging consultation. I was pleased to see that Glasgow decided to undertake a focused programme of work on an issue that was important to people in Glasgow.

6.46　The Council carried out a specific consultation on a draft policy and guidance on public processions. The draft policy acknowledged that processions were important to participants but emphasised that organising and participating in a procession brings responsibilities in terms of ensuring that the rights of others are not infringed. The draft policy tried to describe, for organisers and the public, some general guidelines on processions setting out the sorts of issues that the council took into account in reaching decisions about notifications. It also provided some general guidelines to organisers and participants about the appropriate conduct of processions.

6.47 I understand that Glasgow are considering the results of the consultation and will consider how best to take forward some of the issues it raised in light of the recommendations of the my national Review. I hope that they will be at the forefront of taking forward some of the recommendations in my report.

7 The number of marches and parades in Scotland

Introduction

7.1 This chapter provides statistics on the numbers of processions taking place across Scotland. Before I look in detail at the statistics, it is important that I explain a little about the way I have categorised marches and what these statistics actually demonstrate.

A note on my categories

7.2 For ease of recording and then analysing statistics about processions, I needed to group the processions into categories. I decided to use three categories and my shorthand descriptions for the categories were: 'Orange', 'Catholic' and 'Other'. It might be helpful to explain what lies behind those categories.

7.3 I decided that these were readily understandable categories and already used by the general public in identifying the different processions taking part in their communities. However, they do not distinguish between the various groups within those overarching categories. I recognise that a variety of different sorts of marches take place in each category.

7.4 I included all the Loyal Institutions under the 'Orange' category and so it covers parades organised by the Orange Order (at all levels – Grand Lodge, County Grand Lodges, District Lodges and Private Lodges) the Apprentice Boys of Derry and the Provincial Grand Black Chapter of Scotland. The 'Catholic' category includes processions organised by Catholic groups including the Ancient Order of Hibernians. It also includes groups which would describe themselves as Republican and political rather than religious, such as the James Connolly Society and the West of Scotland Bands Alliance. It also includes marches organised by a new group, Cairde na hÉireann which has been established as a coordinating group of Republican organisations. The 'Other' category was, of course, the widest ranging from political protest through to gala day processions, with a considerable variety between. Chapter 4 on The Traditions of Processions gives a flavour of that variety.

A note on interpreting the statistics

7.5 As part of the Review, I asked local authorities to provide me with statistics on the numbers of processions notified to them under the Civic Government (Scotland) Act 1982. However, as they record only those which need to be notified, these statistics will not show the total number of processions taking place across Scotland. As discussed in Chapter 6 on Current Practices, some local authorities have made orders exempting various groups from the need to give notice and other local authorities regard some processions as 'commonly or customarily' held under section 62(7) of the Civic Government (Scotland) Act 1982. For example, Scottish Borders Council treat the common riding processions as exempt, for the purposes of the Act, and there is often more than one procession in most of the ten towns which have annual Common ridings. They also treat as exempt other community festivals which take place across their area. Other local authorities have upwards of 300 exempt organisations. Given local authorities have different numbers of exempt organisations, the comparison between the numbers of processions taking place in each local authority area will not always be comparing like with like.

7.6 Record keeping within local authorities also varies. Some authorities keep detailed records showing a month by month analysis of the numbers and types of processions being notified. Others do not have the same historical data and I have had to use estimates for some of the earlier years to give a more complete picture.

7.7 Some processions involve both an outward and a return procession. Most local authorities require only one notification and the statistics record a single procession, although in reality two will have taken place. For example, of the 42 Orange walks which were notified to take place in South Lanarkshire in July 2003, 20 involved both an outward and return procession. During the Review, people drew attention to these outward and return processions as being of some concern to communities. There was a commonly held perception that these led to disruption throughout the day, with the outward procession taking place early in the morning and the return procession not coming back until the early evening.

What the statistics show

7.8 Detailed tables showing the statistics about the number of marches and parades I collected as part of the Review are at Appendix H. In this chapter, I look at statistics on:
- the numbers of notified processions (figure 7.1);
- the number of notified processions in each category (figure 7.2);
- the proportion of notified processions in each category (figure 7.3);
- the spread of processions across Scotland (by police force area and local authority area) (figures 7.4, 7.5 and 7.6);

- the regional spread of the proportion of notified processions in each category (by police force area and by local authority area) (figure 7.7);
- the spread of processions throughout the year (figure 7.8); and
- the size of marches.

Numbers of notified processions

7.9 During the Review, I was aware of the strongly held belief that many people felt the numbers of processions across Scotland was increasing. The statistics show that this has, in fact, been the case and there has been a gradual increase of around 8.5% between 2001 and 2003:

- in 2001 there were 1,577 notified processions;
- in 2002 there were 1,600 notified processions;
- in 2003 (the year which has the most accurate records) there were 1,712 notified processions; and
- in the first nine months of 2004 there were 1,428 notified processions.

7.10 The following table shows the number of notified processions taking place annually across Scotland from 2001 to September 2004.

Total number of all notified processions 2001-2004 (Figure 7.1.)

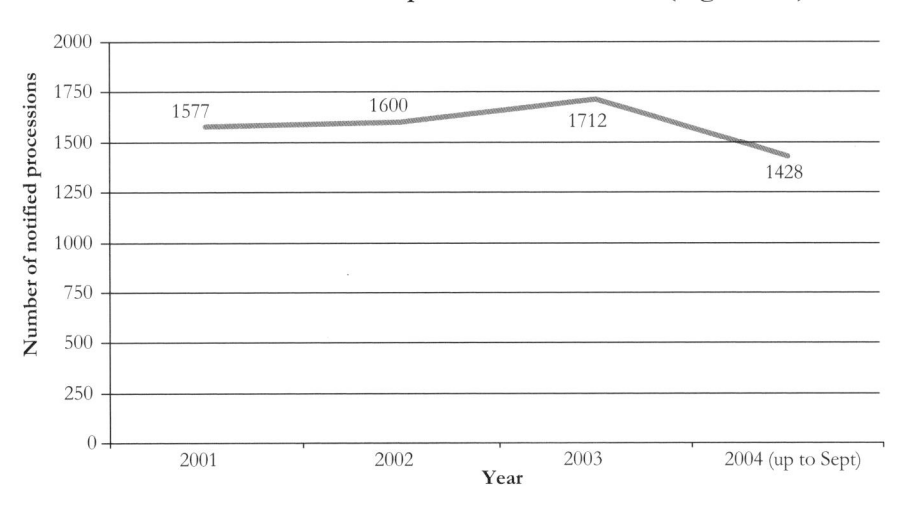

Numbers of notified processions by category

7.11   It is interesting to look at the differences in increases between categories. The 'Orange' category has seen the steadiest growth from 800 in 2001, 832 in 2002 and 853 in 2003; the 'Catholic' category has remained more or less static and the 'Other' category has varied with 756 in 2001, a decrease to 751 in 2002, and an increase to 839 in 2003.

7.12   The following table shows the number of notified processions by category taking place annually across Scotland from 2001 to September 2004.

Number of notified processions by category 2001-2004 (Figure 7.2)

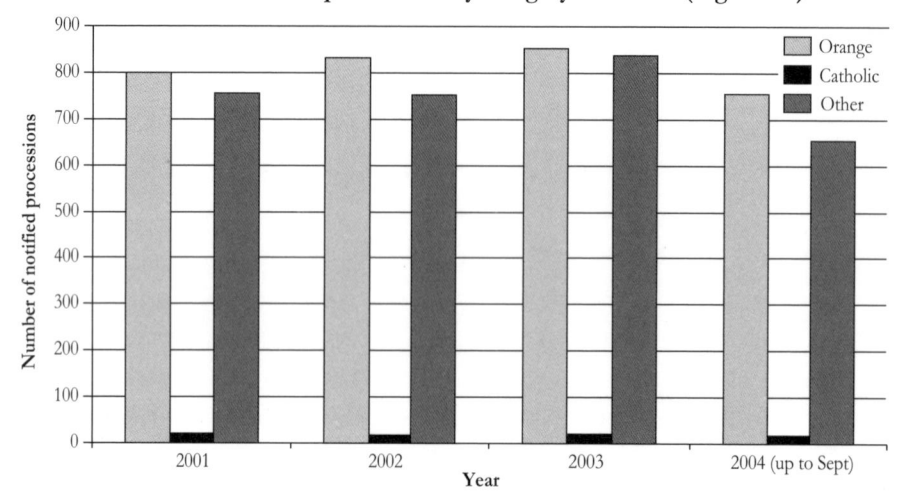

Proportion of notified processions in each category

7.13   The statistics show the proportion of processions being arranged by different organisers. Overall in 2003, half of all notified processions (50%) were in the 'Orange' category, 1% in the 'Catholic' category and 49% in the 'Other' category. These proportions need to be treated with a little caution as there are other processions organised by exempt groups, in addition to those that need to be notified, and by their nature these would fall into the 'Other' category. Generally the proportion in each category remained similar.

Proportion of notified processions by category 2001-2004 (Figure 7.3)

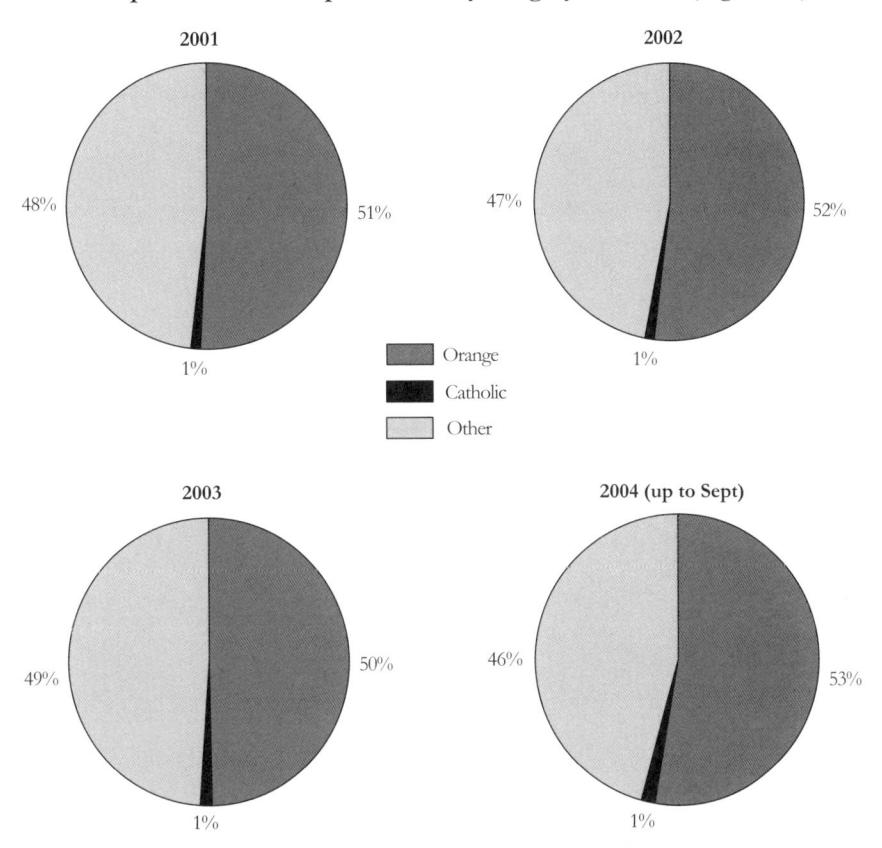

2001: Orange 51%, Catholic 1%, Other 48%

2002: Orange 52%, Catholic 1%, Other 47%

2003: Orange 50%, Catholic 1%, Other 49%

2004 (up to Sept): Orange 53%, Catholic 1%, Other 46%

Spread of notified processions across Scotland

7.14 The statistics show that there is not an even spread of processions across Scotland and the following tables show the numbers of notified processions which took place across Scottish Police Force Areas in 2003.

Numbers of notified processions across police force areas in 2003 (Figure 7.4)

Police Force Area	Orange	Catholic	Other	Total
Strathclyde	713	16	250	979
Lothian and Borders	86	2	210	298
Fife	13	1	161	175
Tayside	7	1	93	101
Central Scotland	31	0	56	87
Grampian	0	0	54	54
Northern	0	0	15	15
Dumfries and Galloway	3	0	0	3
Total	853	20	839	1,712

Number of notified processions by police force area 2003 (Figure 7.5)

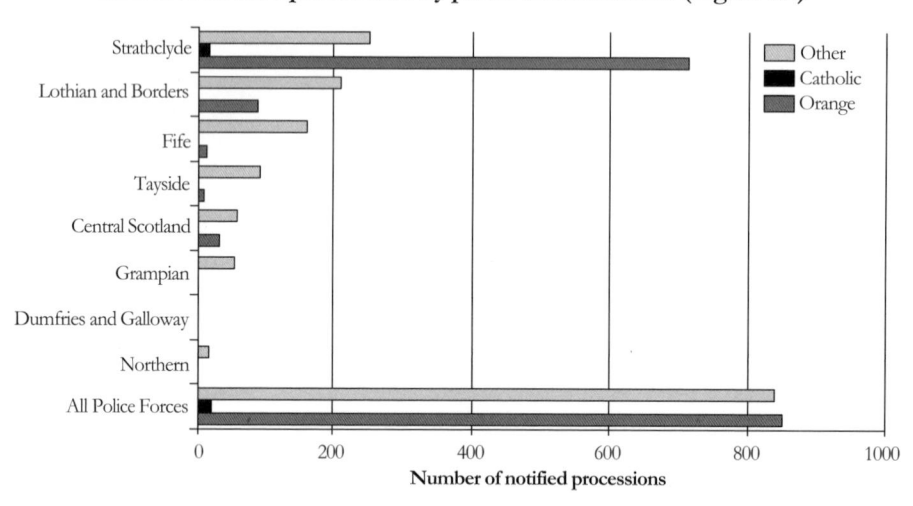

7.15 Some local authorities have a disproportionate number of processions in proportion to their population size, as can be seen in the following table:

Numbers of notified processions in 2003 (Figure 7.6)

Ranking no of marches		Total	Orange	Catholic	Other	Population size (2003)	Ranking – population size
1	Glasgow	338	287	11	40	577,090	1
2	Fife	175	13	1	161	352,040	3
3	South Lanarkshire	162	111	0	51	303,010	5
4	North Lanarkshire	160	157	3	0	321,820	4
5	West Lothian	109	75	0	34	161,020	10
6	North Ayrshire	93	63	0	30	136,030	14
7	East Lothian	83	7	0	76	91,090	23
8	Edinburgh	72	1	2	69	448,370	2
9	Perth and Kinross	58	3	0	55	135,990	15
10	Renfrewshire	57	31	1	25	170,980	9
11	Falkirk	43	20	0	23	145,920	12
12	Argyll and Bute	42	0	0	42	91,300	22
13	East Ayrshire	40	26	0	14	119,530	16
14	South Ayrshire	31	9	0	22	111,580	17
15	Stirling	29	8	0	21	86,370	26
16	Midlothian	28	3	0	25	79,710	28
17	Angus	23	1	1	21	107,520	19
18=	Aberdeenshire	20	0	0	20	229,330	6
18=	Dundee	20	3	0	17	143,090	13
18=	Moray	20	0	0	20	87,460	25
21	East Dunbartonshire	18	10	0	8	106,970	20
22=	Clackmannanshire	15	3	0	12	47,680	29
22=	East Renfrewshire	15	9	0	6	89,680	24
24=	Aberdeen City	14	0	0	14	206,600	8
24=	Highland	14	0	0	14	209,080	7
26	Inverclyde	12	9	1	2	83,050	27
27	West Dunbartonshire	11	1	0	10	92,320	21
28	Scottish Borders	6	0	0	6	108,280	18
29	Dumfries and Galloway	3	3	0	0	147,210	11
30	Orkney	1	0	0	1	19,310	32
31=	Eilean Siar	0	0	0	0	26,100	30
31=	Shetland Islands	0	0	0	0	21,870	31

The regional spread of the proportion of notified processions

7.16 There are considerable differences in the regional spread of organisers. In 2003, in the Strathclyde Police region, 73% of all notified processions were in the 'Orange' category, 2% in the 'Catholic' category and 26% in the 'Other' category, whereas in Lothian and Borders Police Force region, 29% were in the 'Orange' category, less than 1% in the 'Catholic' category and 70% in the 'Other' category. Almost 36% of notified processions in the Central Police Force area fell into the 'Orange' category and 64% in the 'Other' category.

7.17 The following table shows the spread for local authority area. Percentages have been rounded.

Proportion of processions organised in each category in 2003 (Figure 7.7)

Ranking no of marches	Council Area	% 'Orange'	% 'Catholic'	% 'Other'
1	Glasgow	85	3	12
2	Fife	7	1	92
3	South Lanarkshire	69	0	31
4	North Lanarkshire	98	2	0
5	West Lothian	69	0	31
6	North Ayrshire	68	0	32
7	East Lothian	8	0	92
8	Edinburgh	1	3	96
9	Perth and Kinross	5	0	95
10	Renfrewshire	54	2	44
11	Falkirk	47	0	53
12	Argyll and Bute	0	0	100
13	East Ayrshire	65	0	35
14	South Ayrshire	29	0	71
15	Stirling	28	0	72
16	Midlothian	11	0	89
17	Angus	4	4	91
18=	Aberdeenshire	0	0	100
18=	Dundee	15	0	85
18=	Moray	0	0	100
21	East Dunbartonshire	56	0	44
22=	Clackmannanshire	20	0	80
22=	East Renfrewshire	60	0	40
24=	Aberdeen City	0	0	100
24=	Highland	0	0	100
26	Inverclyde	75	8	17
27	West Dunbartonshire	9	0	91
28	Scottish Borders	0	0	100
29	Dumfries and Galloway	100	0	0
30	Orkney	0	0	100
31=	Eilean Siar	0	0	0
31=	Shetland Islands	0	0	0

Spread of notified processions throughout the year

7.18 The statistics I collected do not, unfortunately, give a full spread of processions across the year as some local authorities do not collate statistics on that basis. However, the statistics I did receive show that in 2003 the peak month for all processions was June (with 392), with many taking place in July (259), May (174) and August (157) followed by November (142). The peak months for marches in the 'Orange' category were June (250) and July (202) with May the next most popular (108). Processions in the 'Catholic' category took place in May and June (five each month) with others in March and August (three each month). The peak month for 'Other' marches was June (137) with November (110) and August (82) seeing a fair number too.

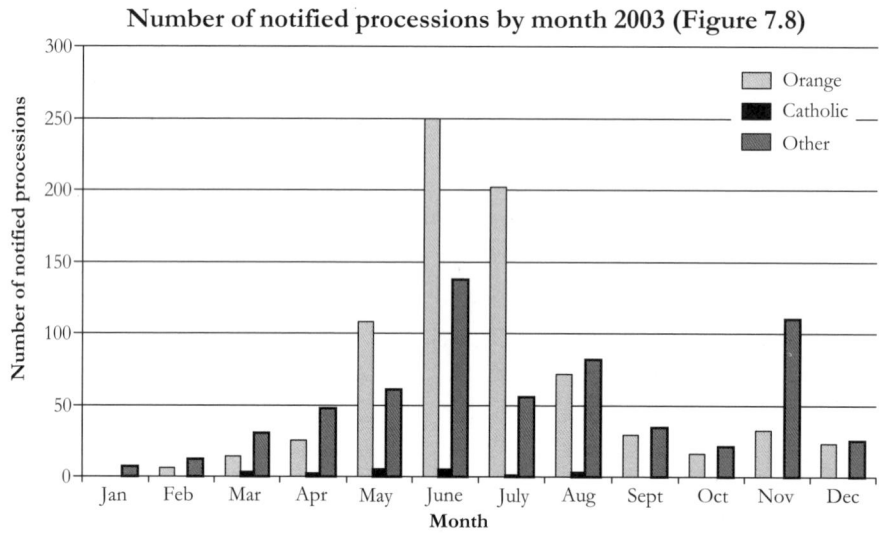

Number of notified processions by month 2003 (Figure 7.8)

Note: The above figures are incomplete as some local authorities do not keep figures showing a monthly breakdown.

7.19 What these figures don't show, of course, is the number of processions occurring on the same day. Most processions take place in the summer months of May, June, July and August with November providing another peak. Weekends are naturally popular for a lot of organisations and many organisations have important traditional dates which the various parts of their organisations want to celebrate annually. Looking in more detail at some of the notifications for 2003 can show how many processions take place on the same day, leaving to one side the other unnotified processions which might also be taking place at the same time. A few examples illustrate the spread:

- There were over 50 processions notified to North Lanarkshire Council on 5 July 2003 involving a wide range of Private and District lodges, ladies lodges, as well as the Grand Orange Lodge and Flute Bands. The numbers at the various processions varied considerably. Most were under 100 although nine had over 200 participants (including three over 500);

- The Provincial Grand Black Chapter of Scotland notified 12 processions to North Lanarkshire on 9 August. Most of the processions involved under 100 participants, although two predicted more than 400 participants;
- There were five Orange Order processions on 26 June 2003 in East Lothian around Prestonpans starting at 7.30am;
- There were nine different events in various parts of Edinburgh on 14 June 2003 ranging from gala days to a motorcycle action group run;
- In Renfrewshire on 3 July 2004 there were ten processions, nine organised by various Loyal Orange Lodges and one by Renfrewshire Arts (half of the processions took place in parts of Paisley).

Size of marches

7.20 It is clear from the statistics that the numbers participating in notified processions varies considerably from tens to thousands. I was not able to collect overall figures showing how many people participate, however the telephone survey I commissioned demonstrated that 28% of those asked had participated in a gala day parade, 15% in a protest or demonstration and 3% in an Orange walk or Republican parade.

7.21 Some local authorities provided information about the scale of events in their areas. For example, the average number of participants in Dundee was around 40, although several hundred had taken part in the marches against the war in Iraq. In East Renfrewshire, Orange walks similarly varied in size, from 20 to 400 with other processions ranging from 50 to 500. South Lanarkshire recorded 15,200 people taking part in Orange walks in 2000 reducing to 14,241 in 2003. At the national Orange Order walk at Blantyre on 10 July 2004, 12,000 people attended. Processions in Edinburgh also varied considerably in size with organisers estimating that: 800 participated in the annual May Day Rally, 1,000 in the James Connolly march; 3,000 in Pride Scotia; and 4,200 in the Provincial Grand Black Chapter Parade. Fewer people attended smaller issue based processions: 100 at an excluded parents demonstration and 100 at a sewage works protest march.

7.22 The disruption caused and policing requirements will vary considerably according to the predicted size of the processions. People commented that the larger processions in small villages can effectively cut villages off.

8 A summary of written responses

Introduction

8.1 I wrote to over 1,000 organisations inviting their views on the areas covered by my remit:
- The period of notice required to be given to local authorities, the police and communities for proposed marches and parades (currently seven days);
- The best way to ensure community input into decisions about marches and parades;
- The basis for determining when to restrict, refuse or reroute marches and parades;
- The number of marches and parades occurring in communities and the effects these have; and
- The costs of policing marches and parades.

8.2 Given the pivotal nature of the Review, I ensured that my letter went to the widest range of possible interests including: local authorities; the police service; the fire service; the NHS; the enterprise network; tourist boards; community planning partnerships; social inclusion partnerships; housing associations; trade unions; political parties; voluntary organisations; youth groups; sports groups; faith groups; and organisations which arrange marches. I also invited organisations to circulate my letter around their own networks. The breadth of the consultation networks reflected the wide range of possible interests in the Review. To ensure that the work of the Review was brought to the attention of a wide audience, information was also posted on the Scottish Executive web site and circulated to local media across Scotland. I invited comments to be sent to me by 24 September 2004 but was prepared to accept submissions after that date.

Responses

8.3 In total, I received 361 written submissions. They came from a wide range of organisations as well as from members of the public. A list of all who contributed is at Appendix A. I would like to thank everyone who responded. The submissions I received have helped to inform my recommendations. They were valuable in supplementing the other views I have heard from the face-to-face meetings I held and survey information I collected. They ensured I heard the views of a wide range of people with an interest in my work.

8.4 This chapter of my report summarises in some detail the main points that emerged from the submissions. I have grouped the views according to the categories of respondents and in line with the five areas of my remit:
- submissions from local authorities and local authority associations (32);
- submissions from police associations (3);
- submissions from other parts of the public sector (4);
- submissions from community councils (14);
- submissions from business organisations (6);
- submissions from transport organisations (6);
- submissions from the voluntary sector (5);
- submissions from religious organisations (12);
- submissions from MSPs (1);
- submissions from organisations which arrange marches (12);
- submission from individuals (30);
- standard submissions from individuals (216); and
- views forwarded from the Scottish Executive (20).

A summary of the general issues emerging from the response

Period of notice

8.5 Over 95% of those who commented on the period of notice agreed that the current seven day period was too short to allow meaningful consideration of notifications by local authorities and the police. It allowed no time for any wider consultation, including with the community. Suggestions for lengthening the period ranged through 14 days, 21 days, 28 days, one month, two months, six weeks, three months to six months for certain sorts of processions. Over 80% thought 28 days represented a more appropriate notification period. Around 5% drew attention to the need for a shorter notification for exceptional circumstances, for processions organised in response to unforeseen local, national or international events. Respondents recognised that organisers were already acting responsibly in giving more than seven days notice. Those who thought seven days was long enough were in areas where there were limited numbers of processions taking place.

Community input

8.6 On balance, respondents generally supported the idea of greater community involvement. Respondents considered who should be involved and suggested in addition to community councils, local authority interests and the police, the following groups could be included; community groups; groups that could demonstrate that they were representative of the community; residents groups; businesses (direct or through chambers of commerce); professional or trade bodies; public transport operators; churches, places of worship and faith groups; and youth groups.

8.7 Some respondents expressed caution about community input into the decision making process, feeling it risked a vocal minority with strongly held views dominating the process. The role and responsibility of councillors in representing their community views needed to be recognised and continue. The purpose of consultation and what community could influence needed to be clear. The time and resource implications of community consultation also needed to be borne in mind. There was a need to think about who would have a right to comment or object, and the process for considering those comments and objections as part of the decision making process. Some people felt the current legislation needed to be changed to ensure that community views could be taken into account.

8.8 Respondents made practical suggestions as to how consultation with the community could be achieved. Generally there was support for advertising notifications about processions in the local media. Organisers could be required to advertise their parade and to demonstrate that they had done this. Organisers could be required to distribute flyers to local residents and particular groups such as churches. Notifications could be posted in libraries and other public or local authority buildings. Notifications needed to make clear the timescale for objections and where those views should be sent. Local authorities could make use of existing mechanisms for gauging views, such as local community planning structures or their local area committees. A few respondents suggested a general poll or referendum to establish communities' views.

Decision making

8.9 Respondents agreed that there was a careful balance to be struck between the rights of marchers and the rights of communities to go about their daily lives without unnecessary disruption.

8.10 A majority of respondents agreed that local authorities should continue to take decisions about notifications. In reaching those decisions, local authorities should be able to take into account a wider range of issues. Respondents suggested that those wider issues could include:
- protection of public safety;
- protection of public order;
- the level of disruption to traffic;
- the level of disruption to public transport;
- the level of disruption to pedestrians;
- the level of disruption to the life of the community;
- the likelihood of public nuisance;
- minimising noise;
- the views of the communities;
- whether organisers were 'fit and proper' to organise a march;
- the background of the organisation, no history of illegality or confrontation;
- experience and behaviour associated with previous marches;

- the object and purpose of the march;
- the possibility of intimidation;
- whether the march was deliberately provocative;
- whether the march was likely to provoke considerable counter demonstration;
- the atmosphere created by the march and the impact on community relations;
- if the march caused offence to the majority of the community;
- the previous behaviour and experience of marches – for example were previous conditions properly observed;
- the implications for police time and resources;
- whether there were other events on at the same time;
- numbers and frequency of marches taking place;
- general health and safety issues; and
- the scale of police resources necessary to police a march.

8.11 Respondents thought local authorities should have flexibility to impose appropriate restrictions including those on the route, time, date and duration. Routes were an important area where there could be compromise. Respondents suggested a variety of approaches including that: marches should only be permitted in residential areas if a minimum level of intrusion can be guaranteed; marches should be restricted to main arterial routes where possible; marches should avoid small narrow streets in residential areas; marches should avoid shopping centres; if the march was considered to be religious or sectarian in nature it should avoid areas of a predominantly different religion than those of the marchers or not walk past a place of worship if a service is in progress; generally marches should not be held in town centres but in parks or other locations, to minimise disruption. It might be possible to agree specific routes for marches to take.

8.12 A minority of respondents suggested confrontational processions which demonstrate a religious or racial bias or promoted sectarian behaviour should be banned.

8.13 Local authorities and some others thought that detailed guidance would be helpful in ensuring that there was a more consistent approach to decision making across Scotland. Decisions had to be explained to organisers and the process needed to be properly informed and transparent.

Numbers and effects on communities

8.14 While local authorities and the police received few formal complaints about marches, it was clear from other respondents that some marches, particularly those described as 'sectarian' were causing issues for communities. Some respondents recorded the disturbance and intimidation they experienced at these marches. They felt that such marches had a detrimental effect on Scotland's image. Such marches were particularly disruptive to people's ability to go about their daily lives, ranging from small irritations such as not being able to cross roads until the march had passed to requiring changes to be made to previously planned church services, weddings and funerals. Some of the large annual marches effectively shut off small villages.

8.15 Generally the specificity of the examples which respondents highlighted related to the numbers of processions taking place and the frequency of disruption, the behaviour of onlookers, including drunkenness, and general anti-social behaviour. Marches were felt to have a negative effect on business turnover. They disrupted public transport and also disrupted people's daily arrangements.

8.16 Many respondents identified the contribution that organisers had in mitigating the effects on communities and reducing the amount of disruption caused. Some supported a code of conduct for marches. Some organisers already had these in place and a code would need to build on these. The behaviour of participants was important in how the community was affected by the march. Others suggested organisers needed to look at the numbers of marches being arranged by their organisations and ensure that marches were being arranged for appropriate and substantive reasons.

8.17 Some respondents suggested that guidance for organisers would be helpful. It should set out rights, obligations and responsibilities. It could cover health and safety issues. Organisers needed to ensure that they had effective stewarding and marshalling in place. Organisers were receptive to this, describing initiatives they had underway and recognising the need for more training. The guidance could look at the stewarding arrangements and local authorities, or the police, should be prepared to look at training for stewards.

Policing costs

8.18 The policing costs of parades were considered to be significant. Views on police costs diverged, with respondents divided as to whether organisers should be required to contribute to costs or not. Those opposed to the suggestion that organisers be required to pay for policing costs, felt it prejudiced political freedoms, the freedom of speech and people's right to peaceful assembly. As most marchers were taxpayers, some respondents felt that they had already contributed to police costs. On balance most respondents were opposed to the suggestion. Those that supported the suggestion that organisers pay for policing costs, felt it was right marchers should pay rather than expecting the community to meet their costs. Some suggested that organisers should at least pay a proportion of their costs and others suggested that a charge could be discretionary with the police able to charge when they though appropriate, for example if the march required a higher level of policing than usual. Given police resources were finite, costs should be able to be taken into account when considering notifications. A number of respondents were concerned about the effects on normal policing levels. Rather than charging for police, some suggested organisers be required to take out insurance or a bond against damage.

A summary of submissions received from local authorities

8.19 I received responses from 30 local authorities as well as two local authority associations, COSLA and SOLACE. All 32 local authorities also provided statistics on the number of marches which had been notified to them and some provided some very detailed and helpful information on their current processes. I have drawn on this material elsewhere in the report, in Chapters 6 and 7 on current processes and statistics. The responses broadly welcomed the review as an opportunity to look at the arrangements for marches and parades, given the legislation governing the processes had been in place for over 20 years, allowing those arrangements to be considered in the changing human rights context.

Local authorities' views on the period of notice

8.20 Without exception, local authorities considered the seven days notification period inadequate and two commented that it definitely should not be shortened. Local authorities felt that seven days did not allow them sufficient time to consider notifications properly, liaise with other services, inform the public, nor did it allow any discussion with organisers to take place. Local authorities stressed that although they met current timetables, the current system worked only because most notifications were non-controversial and organisers of marches and parades acted responsibly and gave considerably more notice than seven days required in statute. Seven days would not allow councils to arrange committee meetings. Many authorities in their guidance for march notifications, highlighted the importance of giving as much notice as possible, most encouraging organisers to give one or two months. To improve advance planning, the local police in one local authority area had written to organisers of events in 2003 to ask them to complete notifications outlining their intentions for 2004 and 2005 events.

8.21 There were mixed views on what an appropriate notification would be and suggestions made varied from 15 days, 21 days, six weeks, one month, two months through to three months. Over 45% (15) of respondents agreed that a month (28 or 30 days) was a more appropriate time period. Others suggested a longer timetable for large marches which would require more bodies to be involved in making arrangements.

8.22 20% (6) said that it was important to have an exceptional provision allowing local authorities to dispense with the full period of notice if it were appropriate, for example in circumstances which could not have been foreseen.

Local authorities' views on community input

8.23 Under current processes, local authorities rely on elected members to represent their community views about march notifications. Three local authorities commented specifically that this system worked particularly effectively, given the existing statutory framework, as elected members had a high awareness of the feelings and concerns of their communities. Under present arrangements, some local authorities considered the views of their roads department and of the police and felt that the priority should continue to be afforded to their views.

8.24 A majority of the local authorities, commenting generally, supported wider community input in the decision making process. However, this support was qualified by some important caveats:

- **Scope of current legislation** – Several local authorities commented that they felt that the current legislation did not allow them to take into account public opinion. They were of the opinion that the law needed to be amended to allow them to do so. They felt that court decisions had demonstrated, that under the current legislation, public opinion was not sufficient grounds to ban a parade. There was no provision in the current legislation for communities to comment and so felt that the community had no formal role in feeding into the decision making process;

- **Purpose of consultation** – Some respondents highlighted that there was a fine balance to be drawn between people's right to march and the community's right to conduct their normal daily lives. Any wider consultation needed to be carefully framed as, while it was clear that members of the public found certain parades distasteful, peaceful protest was a fundamental right. There was a risk of raising and then frustrating expectations of the public if they felt that their views were being ignored. There needed to be clarity about what the public could influence and how their views would be taken into account;

- **Implications for time and resources** – Local authority respondents felt that any wider consultation would be time consuming and resource intensive. It would therefore be important to ensure that local authorities had the discretion to decide how best to gauge community views in their own area which fit best their own circumstances. There was scope to use existing consultation methods: people's panels, local community planning, area committee structures and community councils. Arrangements for consultation needed to be practical and workable; and

- **Who had a right to comment** – A number of authorities commented that it would be difficult to define who had a right to comment (for example, was it the whole of the local authority area or people living on the route) and to make sure that views being expressed were genuinely representative and not simply the views of a vociferous few.

8.25 Some authorities made practical suggestions as to how community views could be invited including:

- inviting views on larger parades through a newspaper advert;
- requiring organisers to advertise their parade for 14 days and for objections to be submitted to the local authority to consider in reaching their decision;
- requiring organisers to advertise their parade through flyers to local residents and businesses and to make direct contact with local churches and to put a notice in the press;

extending a list of people who required to be consulted under statute to include local community groups, community councils and particular groups affected, for example, churches. At least four authorities raised the role that community councils should have.

8.26 Four respondents thought that there was merit in considering the processes for licence applications under the Civic Government (Scotland) Act 1982 where there was an established process for direct community involvement.

8.27 Respondents also commented on how objections from the community should be considered. Organisers of marches needed to be made aware of them to allow them to be considered and should have the chance to be able to put forward their views. Local authorities thought it would be appropriate to consider community views as part of their overall consideration and, if objections had been raised, this should be at a meeting of the appropriate council committee.

Local authorities' views on the basis for decision making

8.28 The key issue for local authorities in reaching decisions about marches was to find an appropriate way to balance the rights of freedom of expression and of peaceful expression with the rights of others. The most appropriate way of striking that balance was looking carefully at routes and that is where they felt that there was most scope for compromise and discussion. Local authorities recognised the inherent difficulties in reconciling sometimes conflicting views.

8.29 Local authorities commented that decisions on notifications should remain with them. Most local authorities thought that the current decision making framework was too narrow and restricted their ability to make decisions about marches in their area. The framework for making decisions needed to be objective and fair. The current scope that local authorities had for making decisions was limited and not well understood by the public.

8.30 Local authorities agreed that public safety and public order issues should be the principal criteria in informing decisions. Police views would continue to be very important. However, they felt that it would be helpful to broaden the sorts of issues which could be taken into account. Suggestions of the issues which could be taken into account included:
- the level of disruption to traffic;
- the level of disruption to public transport;
- the level of disruption to pedestrians;
- the level of disruption to the life of the community;
- the likelihood of public nuisance;
- the views of the communities;
- whether organisers were 'fit and proper' to organise a march;
- the background of the organisation, no history of illegality or confrontation;
- the object and purpose of the march;

- the possibility of intimidation;
- whether the march was deliberately provocative;
- whether the march was likely to provoke considerable counter demonstration;
- the previous behaviour and experience of marches – for example, whether previous conditions were properly observed;
- the implications for police time and resources;
- whether there were other events on at the same time; and
- general health and safety issues.

8.31 Local authorities also made suggestions about the appropriateness of certain routes for marches and suggested some general principles for reaching agreements over routes including:
- marches should only be permitted in residential areas if a minimum level of intrusion can be guaranteed;
- marches should be restricted to main arterial routes where possible;
- that marches should avoid small narrow streets in residential areas;
- marches should avoid shopping centres;
- if the march was considered to be religious or sectarian in nature it should avoid areas of a predominantly different religion than those of the marchers;
- if the march has a religious or sectarian nature it should not march past a place of worship when a service is in progress; and
- marches should, in general, not go through town centres or pass places of worship.

8.32 Some local authorities highlighted the need for some clear and national statutory guidance. This should set out the reasons that could properly be taken into account in reaching decisions. It would help when decisions were challenged in court, ensure consistency, fairness and openness in reaching decisions and remove political pressure to ban marches arranged by lawful organisations which were generally disapproved of. The ideology of a march should not, by itself, be a factor for a ban. The guidance should cover the formal procedures for the consideration of objections at a hearing. Guidance should be developed by the Executive in consultation with local authorities and the police.

8.33 Some authorities thought it would be helpful to share good practice, for example in looking at ways of facilitating mediation. Some local authorities suggested it would be helpful to hold debriefing meetings after marches to learn from experience. The meetings should involve local authority departments, the police and the organisers. Another suggested that local authorities should get a report from the police after the march.

Local authorities' views on numbers and effects on communities

8.34 Local authority responses made clear the variety in the numbers of marches happening across Scotland. Those with few marches felt that the numbers and the effects on communities were manageable. However, there was more disruption and detrimental effects in those local authorities with a greater number. In general, local authorities received few formal complaints about marches.

8.35 There were mixed views about whether quotas should be set for the numbers of marches that took place in any one community. Some authorities thought this would undermine the freedom of peaceful assembly. Others thought that looking at the amount of disruption experienced by a community was appropriate and local authorities ought to be able to take into account the frequency of marches as well as the routes to minimise disruption and the impact on community relations. They thought that measures to encourage the consolidation of marches would be helpful and achieve reduced disruption and costs.

8.36 Some local authorities thought a statutory code of conduct for marches, drawing on the conditions already set by many local authorities for marches as well as organisers' codes of behaviour, would be helpful. The code would govern the conduct of a march and cover topics such as: organisers' responsibilities for the conduct of a march, levels of stewarding, the width of a march, what could be carried and displayed at a march, the playing of music, sanctions for future marches if things went wrong and other possible penalties. Such a code would only work with the co-operation of marching organisations.

Local authorities' views on policing costs

8.37 There were mixed views on the merits of charging for police time and for local authority time. Those that opposed the suggestion felt that there was a risk that it could prejudice political freedom. They accepted that the costs should be found from general resources, although thought that allocations from central government funding should take account of these costs. Some authorities recovered costs associated with traffic management measures, others did not or exempted certain community groups from the requirement.

8.38 However, there was some support for requiring organisers to make a partial contribution to policing and administrative costs, as long as it was not too excessive to make it impossible to organise events. They drew attention to the parallel with football clubs which had to meet policing costs within their stadia. One authority thought that local authorities should have the discretion to recover costs as and when appropriate. Another thought that the chief constable ought to have the discretion to charge when the march required a higher level of policing than would normally be required. There was support for requiring organisers to take out insurance or a bond against damage which would ensure that local communities did not have to meet all the costs of marches in their area.

8.39 A few councils looked at the possibility of charging an administrative fee for various events, for example for marches not recurring annually, and whether it would be appropriate to charge a fee for notifications. Most concluded that it would not. Other local authorities thought that organisers should meet the costs of administrative work associated with notifications, and the cost of any adverts, if a notification required to be advertised.

A summary of submissions from police associations

8.40 The eight police forces commented through the three police associations. Their responses were set against the general presumption of people's right to march and the need to achieve a balance between that right and the rights of others not to be disturbed and disrupted.

Police associations' views on the period of notice

8.41 All three associations felt that the seven days notice period was too short. It did not give sufficient time to the police to consider notifications or prepare for marches nor did it allow communities to be consulted. 28 days would allow time for consultation and public notification to be given to communities, giving them a set amount of time to comment. Decisions should only be taken once those views had been considered.

8.42 The police associations recognised that some organisations already gave more than seven days notification but it would be helpful to set this on a statutory footing. Larger marches needed a considerable amount of police planning. It was recognised that there was a need to have an exceptional circumstances clause. There needed to be some consistency with other timetables – for example, formal road closures required around eight weeks.

Police associations' views on community input

8.43 The police associations supported wider community input into the decision making process. Currently the community could really only comment through their local councillor. Consulting the community would ensure that local authorities were better informed of the range of issues associated with a march. Communities would be well placed to comment on the scale of disruption. Local authorities could receive information that would allow them to consider the march's impact on the: restriction of movement including access for emergency vehicles and public transport; restriction of normal community activity; restriction of access to public amenities such as hospitals; and restriction of access to places of worship. The community might express views on costs; intrusion; tensions and fear and the impact on shops and other businesses.

8.44 They made the point that proper consultation required time to complete. The police associations suggested that march notifications could be published in the local media and posted in public buildings. The notification would advise people who wanted to express a view of the timescale and an address for comments. Communities should be allowed a reasonable amount of time to express their views – one association suggested at least two weeks. Consultation should also include community groups.

Police associations' views on the basis for decision making

8.45 Generally the police associations thought it right that local authorities remained responsible for taking decisions on march notifications. They felt that there was some confusion about the role of the police and it could appear that decisions were based on the police's views. One association suggested that it might also be appropriate to consider the establishment of a Commission, covering the whole of Scotland, as the appropriate place to take decisions, with that Commission being obliged to publish decisions, although they felt that current arrangements were working.

8.46 The police associations thought that it was important that local authorities were able to take a wider range of issues into account when reaching decisions on notifications. Currently, decisions were generally taken after formal consultation only with the police. The police based their comments on public safety. They were in a difficult situation if required to admit that there could be situations with which they could not cope. Local authorities should be able to weigh up wider views, including community comments, to allow them to take a view on the relative benefits of a march and costs in terms of disruption and policing. It was important that local authorities could consider wider inconvenience and disruption to community life, such as traffic disruption and the changing nature of roads which could be busy and dangerous. This was appropriate under the terms of the human rights legislation, as the right to peaceful assembly was a qualified one.

8.47 Local authorities should also be able to take into account previous behaviour as evidence of the likelihood of future disorder, including the behaviour of non-participants and onlookers which would prevent public disorder or crime. The police association which suggested this felt that would be appropriate in human rights terms, under an authority's right to use the margin of appreciation in interpreting ECHR decisions, to allow them to take account of their knowledge of national circumstances.

8.48 It was suggested that it would be helpful for local authorities to give a written determination, setting out clearly which of the qualifications under Article 11 of the ECHR were being applied in a decision. This would help to ensure organisations understood the decision making processes which, in one police association's view, needed to be transparent and the reasons for decisions properly explained to organisers.

8.49 The police associations thought that there should be scope for councils and organisers to negotiate on the number of processions and for restrictions to be set on the number. Organisers needed to act responsibly and co-operatively to restrict the number of minor unnecessary parades which occupy police time and cause disruption. Organisers could self police their notifications and perhaps prioritise their parade notifications. The frequency, in some areas, was felt to lead to a concentration of attention, tension and disruption.

8.50 Local authorities should be able to impose restrictions on route, time, date and duration and be required to notify organisers of the restriction. There may be other restrictions appropriate for local authorities to impose and they should have powers to do so. For example, there might be merit in holding parades away from public highways, in parks. While participants might consider this to be overly restrictive it would limit disruption to communities who might support such a proposal. It was important organisers continued to have a right of appeal.

8.51 Generally the police associations thought there needed to be more clarity around the legislation and whether local authorities were, in fact, giving permission for marches. Currently the legislation gave them the power to restrict or prohibit processions. If local authorities did neither it could reasonably be argued that they were *de facto* approving the procession. There was support for a formal approval given, underlining the local authority's responsibility and making accountability clear. A pre-parade document would help to define responsibility and accountability mechanisms.

8.52 One police association raised the issue of spontaneous events with no advance warning which could cause operational difficulties for the police. The legislation governing these events, the Public Order Act 1986, was not easy to enforce as it was often difficult to identify the person in charge and difficult to prove if an offence had been committed.

Police associations' views on numbers and effects on communities

8.53 The police associations thought it important to recognise the diversity of marches taking place across Scotland and that most processions were relatively peaceful events which did not cause risks to public safety. However, it was also important to recognise that most processions were organised by groups often described as 'sectarian'. The sectarian nature of some parades was a particular feature of one aspect of Scotland's history and culture. The Irish influence was clear and opposing elements collided at parades, with implications for the way those parades were regulated. Such processions, and the events that happened around them, caused significant concern, disturbance and intimidation to some residents, business people, religious congregations and visitors. These processions often posed the biggest challenge for the police and to community harmony. The behaviour of onlookers at these parades caused particular concern. One association thought that Republican and Loyalist organisations appeared to be increasing their profile through organising a greater number of marches and extending the traditional marching season along new and sometimes controversial routes.

8.54 The police highlighted the difference in resources needed from one or two officers to large numbers of staff. Some marches along busy roads required a higher number of officers to ensure public safety and to divert transport which could cause disruption. Officers could be unable to deal with every offence that takes place on a march day which could appear, to observers, that the police were ignoring offences or allowing them to occur. Observers were not aware of all the facts an officer had to consider in policing a parade. The frequency of minor parades was occupying police time and causing disruption.

8.55 The police associations felt it would be helpful to have detailed guidance for organisers. There was currently guidance available for organisers of general and of sporting events. That guidance could set out rights, obligations and responsibilities. It was also important that the guidance covered responsibilities about marshals and stewards. The police associations thought that there was scope for professionalising stewarding. It might be that members of the organisation who are closely connected to those participating in the parade, and are unwilling or unable to regulate behaviour, were not the most effective stewards. The numbers of stewards required needed to be determined in agreement with police and the relevant local authority, following a risk assessment.

Police associations' views on policing costs

8.56   The police associations accepted that policing marches was a legitimate police duty but all felt that the cost of policing parades represented a significant call on police resources which should be examined. Resources were finite and the policing of marches that required a sizeable police presence reduced resources available for overtime patrols. Some parades required a disproportionately high call on resources. While there were no circumstances which presented an unmanageable problem, there could be circumstances which presented such a threat to public order that the police presence required would be an unacceptable burden to the police budget. Such a heavy police presence would have negative connotations for the police service in terms of public reassurance and overall community engagement strategies.

8.57   The police associations explained that the competing demands on police resources, with a significant number of officers deployed whether through frequency of parades or in response to a threat to public order, could have detrimental effects on normal policing levels in communities. It should be appropriate for local authorities to factor competing demands into setting restrictions. Ensuring that there was an integrated policy framework to resolve possible disputes over contentious parades would be valuable to the police.

A summary of submissions from other parts of the public sector

8.58   I had four responses from the wider public sector. Three responses from parts of the National Health Service and one from Historic Scotland.

8.59   The NHS responses highlighted that it would be useful to ensure that they were consulted, as a matter of course, when march notifications were being considered to ensure that the health and welfare of those taking part could be taken into account. It would also allow hospitals to plan for a possible increase in referrals. If there was trouble at a march, then that could put a strain on health service resources. There was concern about the effects of the misuse of alcohol. One response also suggested that marches could have a detrimental effect on people's health if they perceived a threatening atmosphere and felt intimidated.

8.60   In commenting, the Scottish Ambulance Service drew attention to the variable effects of marches for its services. It was important that they received information about the duration, route and diversions, and numbers and purpose. That allowed the service to complete a risk assessment of its services and resource cover. In areas where there were more marches, that had an implication for resources and response times, due to disruption.

8.61 Historic Scotland described the impact of marches for them as minimal, although some of their properties were involved as assembly areas, for example for local 'riding of the marches' and for other local groups. Edinburgh Castle was also affected but the police ensured that they had good information in advance.

A summary of submissions from community councils

8.62 I received 13 submissions from community councils and one from the Association of Scottish Community Councils.

Community councils' views on the period of notice

8.63 Most community councils had a view on the period of notice. Three thought seven days was an appropriate timescale – any longer would appear 'big brotherish' – which currently worked but during that period there was a need to give information to the community. The majority, however, thought the period should be lengthened. There was a range of views about the appropriate time period: 14 days, 21 days, six weeks, 28 days or three months. The favoured response was 28 days.

Community councils' views on community input

8.64 Eleven respondents commented on community input. A couple felt that community views were best represented through the elected member and wider consultation might not be beneficial if there were particularly partisan views within the community. However, the majority welcomed wider community consultation.

8.65 Six thought that community councils should have a formal role in the process, as they did for other notifications and licence applications, and made suggestions as to the role. Two suggested that communities could feed their views through community councils to coordinate and forward to the local authority which could be seen to fall under their duty in the Local Government (Scotland) Act 1973 to *'ascertain, coordinate and express to local authorities'* the views of local people.

8.66 As well as community councils, seven respondents suggested other organisations that should be consulted. These included a broad range of local organisations and mentioned specifically residents groups, trade associations and youth organisations. They should be fully consulted about the time and route of a proposed march and be able to make objections about marches taking place in their immediate area. Local authorities would be required to consider any objections raised.

8.67 Four respondents made suggestions as to how the community could be informed. Most favoured information being given through an advert in the local press, others suggested the local authority website, posters in local authority offices and flyers distributed asking for opinions.

Community councils' views on the basis of decision making

8.68 Community councils mentioned the need to balance the rights of marchers with the public's rights to go about their business without disruption. However, it was important that there was a balance and the right to march had to be seen as 'a public right which has to be exercised with due regard for the rights of other members of the public'. One community council felt that the rights of marchers appeared to take priority over the rights of residents. It was important to respect private and family life.

8.69 There were mixed views on who should be responsible for making decisions. Some community councils thought that the police should be responsible for making decisions rather than local authorities whereas others thought that it should remain with local authorities. The types of issues that community councils thought should be taken into account when decisions were reached about marches, included:
- considerations about public order;
- considerations about public safety;
- considerations about health and safety;
- disruption to traffic;
- disruption to local businesses;
- disruption to the community;
- ways of minimising noise;
- whether the purpose of the march was likely to lead to violence;
- whether the march was deliberately provocative;
- whether there was likely to be trouble;
- behaviour at previous marches;
- the community's views about the march and the outcome of any general feedback;
- whether the community felt there were too many marches;
- whether the march causes offence to the majority of the community;
- whether the police are able to police the march effectively; and
- the scale of resources required to police a march.

8.70 In reaching decisions about routes, the following were suggested as issues to consider. Routes should:
- be developed that cause the minimum impact on residents;
- avoid town centres;
- avoid possible flashpoints for trouble;
- avoid disrupting emergency services; and
- generally avoid housing estates.

Community councils' views on banning processions

8.71 In their responses, community councils recognised that there was a need to respect people's human rights. However, some thought that certain marches should be banned, such as *'confrontational marches which demonstrate religious, racial or sexual bias'* or *'religious or sectarian marches'* should be banned, or at least limited, or *'all religious marches should be banned as they cause trouble and disruption and reinforce the image of bigotry in the West of Scotland'*.

Community councils' views on numbers and effects on communities

8.72   Community councils had mixed views on the numbers and effects. Some community councils noted their concern about the numbers of marches taking place. Others felt that the numbers were not causing a particular problem. Noise and general disruption were raised as issues of concern. The behaviour of onlookers was also causing problems in some areas, detracting from the quality of life and 'giving a bad impression to visitors and tourists'. Others felt that marches were positive in bringing visitors to towns.

8.73   Responses also drew attention to problems caused through alcohol consumption and wanted to see the police being more proactive in tackling drunkenness. Some community councils wanted to see quotas set for marches, or only marches which involved 75% of the local population going ahead.

Community councils' views on Policing costs

8.74   Eleven respondents commented on the issue of police costs, and opinions were mixed. Two felt that costs should be met, as currently, through council and police budgets. Four suggested that organisers should be required to pay or, at the very least make a significant contribution to, the policing costs of their march. Others felt that whether payment was required should depend on the purpose of the march. For example, marches that were of benefit to the population, or were community marches or were by youth groups should not be required to meet costs whereas others, for example those with limited or no connection to the local population, should pay.

8.75   One respondent felt that the community which pays the council tax should have a chance to comment on whether they feel it an appropriate use of resources, given that most marches are a minority activity and of little relevance to most people. Another respondent, commented on their perception that there was increased policing associated with some Orange Order marches and it was important that the scale of policing was proportionate.

A summary of submissions from business organisations

8.76   I received six submissions from businesses and organisations representing businesses.

Business organisations' views on the period of notice

8.77   Three respondents offered views on the period of notice. All felt that seven days was inadequate. Twenty-eight days seemed a reasonable period to allow *'a systematic system of checks and assessments to be undertaken'*. During this period, they felt that businesses should also be given notice of forthcoming marches.

Business organisations' views on community input

8.78 Three respondents thought it important to ensure that business views were considered as they were an important part of the community. There were existing mechanisms for gathering business views, through chambers of commerce, community councils or local area committees. They should have access to information and an opportunity to register their concerns. Businesses make plans about staffing, distribution and stocks well in advance and needed to be given sufficient notice to change their plans if necessary.

Business organisations' views on the basis for decision making

8.79 Business respondents were clear that it was important to respect people's rights to peaceful assembly although that needed to be balanced with the rights of others to go about their normal activities. They thought that organisers should take their responsibilities seriously and recognise that their march caused an often negative economic impact. Two respondents commented that in a democracy there were many other more effective ways to draw attention to a cause, which should be encouraged.

8.80 Business respondents thought that there should be restrictions on the routes and timing for marches and, wherever possible, marches should not go through the city centres and should not take place at peak trading periods. One respondent suggested that there should be a limited number of marches permitted within a specific timetable and organisers should bid for slots. There was also a suggestion that particular routes should be developed for marches, avoiding the city centre, possible bottlenecks and key routes through cities. There needed to be authorised alternative routes for public transport operators. The police should be able to move marches to less sensitive areas. Respondents felt there was some confusion in the current system about who had the authority to make decisions. Businesses looked at the reasons for marches, commenting that there needed to be a serious reason for marching. Some marches were not and created a negative image. There was some agreement that marches which were offensive, for example in promoting sectarian or racist views, should not be permitted.

Business organisations' views on numbers and effects on communities

8.81 Business respondents described the economic impact of marches. They were in no doubt that marches affected business saying that if marches resulted in street closures *'tills stop ringing'* and retailers lost *'the serious shopper and serious money'*. The majority of marches appeared to have *'a negative impact on businesses, particularly retail business'*. They felt people avoided city centres, preferring to shop at out of town shopping centres. The disruption was not restricted to the duration of the march and lost turnover was never regained. Businesses recognised that there were positive aspects to some marches which were a demonstration and celebration of different facets of a multi-cultural society and enjoyable for residents and visitors alike. However, they were clear that was not always the case and there were instances where *'marches cause severe and lengthy disruption to civic and business life and are viewed with bemusement by tourists'*.

Business organisations' views on policing costs

8.82 Four respondents commented on the question of policing costs. Most were sympathetic towards requiring organisations to meet at least some of the costs associated with their marches, which were often significant, although this should not impact negatively on smaller organisations without financial resources. One respondent thought that, in recognition of the capital city status, Edinburgh should be given additional funding to cover the costs of policing marches. Two respondents thought that organisations should pay the full social costs of marches, including compensation to businesses which lose turnover due to the march.

A summary of submissions from transport organisations

8.83 I received six submissions from transport organisations, managing trunk roads or providing public transport.

Transport organisations' views on the period of notice

8.84 Four organisations commented on the period of notice, agreeing that seven days was not long enough. Bus operators wanted a longer period from 14 days to six weeks to ensure that they were able to plan and deliver altered routes and to tell their customers of the changes. One organisation said that it would be important to ensure that the notification period allowed sufficient time to take into account the possible need to close roads and to ensure those procedures could be properly followed.

Transport organisations' views on community input

8.85 One organisation commented that transport operators ought to be better and more consistently informed about marches. It was felt that the current system of advance notice was a little erratic.

Transport organisations' views on the basis for decision making

8.86 All six respondents commented. The bus operators felt it was important that decisions on march routes take into account the need to maintain access and freedom of movement for those not involved on the march. Respondents recognised the right of people to march but they felt that the routes should not cause severe disruption to normal life. Decision making should take into account the disruption to bus services and the approved routes should minimise that disruption.

8.87 Other respondents suggested that priority routes be protected and bus routes be taken into account in considering what was a priority route. Developing standard diversion routes would be helpful so that people became familiar with those diversion routes which were the same each time. A more consistent better planned approach could limit the scale of the disruption to the overall network. One respondent thought that disruption could be minimised if the times when marches could take place were

8.88 restricted, avoiding peak periods and Saturdays in city centres. More careful consideration should also be given where two or more events were taking place in the same day requiring the same road to be closed at different times. Sporting events and road works should also be considered alongside the notification to allow an overall assessment of disruption.

8.88 Current legislation did not require local authorities to consult with roads authorities and one operator thought that ought to be standard procedure to ensure that the effects on traffic was taken into account. Another respondent felt that marches should generally be discouraged from trunk roads as they were not suitable due to vehicle speed and volume of heavy goods traffic on those roads. Should a march take place on a trunk road, there needed to be a formal road closure in place.

Transport organisations' views on numbers and effects on communities

8.89 Five organisations commented on the numbers and effects of marches. Most respondents commented on the disruptive effect that marches had on public transport, particularly bus transport. The disruption undermined the efficiency of the system. Passengers could not rely on bus services when disrupted by march routes. One operator had experienced 31 road closures in the first six months of 2004. The effects of road closures were felt throughout the day, not just when the march was taking place or just in the vicinity of the march, but more widely through the network. The lack of advance planning meant that it was difficult for bus operators to offer services to those participating in the march. The disruption had a direct financial cost on bus operators.

8.90 One organisation was concerned by the *ad-hoc* nature of current traffic management procedures. They wanted to see procedures properly regularised in the interest of all road users.

Transport organisations' views on policing costs

8.91 Respondents did not specifically comment on policing costs.

A summary of submissions from the voluntary sector

8.92 I received five submissions from organisations in the voluntary sector, covering residents' groups, a council for the voluntary sector and a group tackling sectarian behaviour.

Voluntary sector views on the period of notice

8.93 Four organisations commented. Two respondents agreed that given the number and nature of processions in their area, the current arrangements worked well. 2 organisations felt that seven days was inadequate to allow notifications to be properly considered by local authorities. A longer period would allow them to consult more widely with organisers, the police and the local community and would allow the police more time to plan their deployment of resources. One felt 28 days would be appropriate, another suggested that for annually recurring marches, six months could be given. One organisation highlighted the need to allow exemptions to a longer notification period.

Voluntary sector views on community input

8.94 Two organisations commented. One thought that the community council and other representative bodies should be able to comment on marches that were considered to be controversial. Another respondent thought it important that while the final decision on marches should continue to lie with local authorities, local communities should have a chance to make their views known, particularly around frequency, timing, routes and the previous behaviour of the participants. Local authorities could seek views through advertisements in the local media and in prominent places, and views should be given to the local councillor or direct to the local authority.

Voluntary sector views on the basis for decision making

8.95 Four organisations made comments related to the decision making process. Two respondents agreed that given the number and nature of processions in their area, the current arrangements worked well. The police were involved in advising on routes and timing and the small number of marches passed without incident.

8.96 Two organisations felt that there should be changes to the process. One residents' group felt that all marches which *'intimidate, deliberately or otherwise'* should be restricted as local communities should have a right not to feel threatened, intimidated or needlessly inconvenienced. They felt there was a need to ban all marches which appeared sectarian. To minimise disruption there should be scope for marches to take place outwith the city centre, in industrial estates. One respondent felt it was right that local authorities continued to take decisions, but that they should be able to take into account the views of the community and the police in reaching those decisions. While they recognised a right to march, there should be scope for banning marches if there was credible evidence that the march would lead to sectarian violence. This would involve looking at whether the march organisers had convictions related to sectarianism, and reports from the police on the behaviour of march participants during past marches. Local authorities should also have the powers to impose conditions about: the consumption of alcohol; the organisers' stewarding requirements; the times at which music could be played; the need to take routes which avoided residential areas; and banning sectarian singing or chanting. To help inform decision making, the police should file a report after each march detailing the experiences of that march.

Voluntary sector views on numbers and effects on communities

8.97　Two organisations commented. One felt that the no one organisation should have so many marches that it monopolised facilities or resources. Another felt that generally there were too many marches associated with the Orange Order and Republican causes taking place. These types of marches led to sectarian behaviour which intimidated local people and risked violence. They felt that numbers could only be reduced through agreement and consultation and proposed discussion between local authorities, the police and groups organising marches. Should that discussion fail, they thought there should be additional sanctions. To improve behaviour at marches, a respondent suggested there should be a code of conduct for organisers and participants. Local authorities or the police should also help organisers train stewards. If there was sectarian behaviour at marches, then the police should consider charging people with a religious aggravation charge.

Voluntary sector views on policing costs

8.98　Three organisations commented on policing costs. One residents' group was concerned about the effects that marches had on the police's ability to carry out their normal day to day duties and feared that community policing suffered as a result. Another residents' group felt that it was wrong for local communities to have to meet the costs of policing for marches which caused disruption and felt that policing costs could be reduced if organisers ensured they had more better trained stewards. However, they did feel that larger marches should be required to meet some of the costs. One organisation recognised that, in a democracy, the costs of marches needed in general to be met by tax payers. They thought that, depending on the nature of the march, there should be limited circumstances in which the police should be able to recover part or all of their costs. In addition, if organisers breached agreed conditions, then local authorities should be able to require organisers to contribute to policing and if, before the march, local authorities felt there was a risk of a breach occurring, they could require organisers to put up a bond against that risk.

A summary of submissions from religious organisations

8.99　I received 12 submissions from religious organisations: five from the Roman Catholic community; four from the Protestant community; two from the Sikh community; and one representing the Jewish community.

Religious organisations' views on the period of notice

8.100　Six respondents commented that seven days was insufficient. It did not allow time for local authorities to consider the notification nor for communities to be informed and have an opportunity to comment. An extended period would allow greater consultation and more in-depth consideration. Two respondents suggested a 28 day notice period and one suggested that there needed to be exceptions to this to ensure non-recurring protest marches in response to issues could take place.

Religious organisations' views on community input

8.101 There was agreement from the six respondents who commented that better consultation with the community was important. One Protestant respondent was cautious and recognised the right of communities to know about marches occurring in their area but feared that in an increasingly secular society, people might want to see all forms of religious expression banned. One Sikh respondent suggested that local authorities should have a single point of contact where information about marches could be accessed. Local people should be contacted and their views sought, but while it was appropriate to consider their views, that should not encourage racial or religious prejudice. One Catholic respondent felt it very important to take community views on marches as they were sought on many other issues.

8.102 Respondents made suggestions as to how the consultation could be achieved. The Jewish respondent suggested that there were mechanisms put in place to consult quickly and effectively when the need arose. There should be adverts in the local media, including community specific media such as the *Jewish Telegraph,* and information available in minority languages. There needed to be clarity on how the views would affect the decision making process. A Catholic respondent suggested that community views could be taken into account by organising polls of the local community. One Protestant respondent suggested that the timing of events should be discussed with communities to minimise disruption and to avoid clashes with religious services, enabling people safe access to their place of worship. A Catholic respondent agreed and also suggested that communities should be able to object to the frequency of marches and negotiate a limit to the numbers of marches which affect their area in a year.

Religious organisations' views on the basis for decision making

8.103 Ten respondents commented. One Protestant respondent made clear that people should be free to march to safeguard the principle of free speech but that this should be subject to appropriate qualifications and should respect the rights of others, although acknowledged that this was a difficult balance to strike. Others shared that view, including two Catholic respondents who accepted marching as an important part of civil liberties which should be protected, and the Jewish respondent who recognised the right to free speech and to holding political opinions but that it was important to balance the rights of one section of the community with the rights of other sections of the community.

8.104 Some respondents commented that decision making should look at the effects of the march. A Sikh respondent said that it was important to allow marches that brought people together but not to allow those which divided society and caused hatred and animosity. A Catholic respondent said that it was important to respect the rights of community to privacy and to a peaceful life and they should be protected from marches which brought disruption, inconvenience and fear. A Protestant respondent recognised the right to march was important but that it should be understood alongside the right of a community to be protected from violence and intimidation. Some marches were used to stir up hatred or promote feeling against a specific part of society. There was a difference between people who were marching as it was the only way to make their views heard and those who marched to demonstrate their strength. The Jewish respondent suggested that it was important to take into account whether the march impinged on the safety and feelings of vulnerability in the various communities affected by the march. Some communities, because of their history of persecution, could feel particularly isolated and uneasy about certain marches.

8.105   Respondents commented on routes. Compromise over routes was important for one Catholic respondent. Another Catholic respondent thought that marches should be confined to certain times and areas to minimise inconvenience, avoiding city centres as far as possible. One Protestant respondent thought that it was important to look at routes to ensure that they were not being chosen to stir up hatred. Sometimes routes were chosen to demonstrate the superiority of the marches over the community they were marching through and care needed to be taken to avoid this. Marchers should not generally march in the face of other's objections or fear. One Catholic respondent wanted to see routes which led to the harassment of particular groups altered to prevent people being afraid for their safety. Others commented on the timing of marches with both Protestant and Catholic respondents suggesting marches should not be held at times when religious services were taking place. Another Protestant respondent suggested that marches should be held at less busy times of the day.

8.106   One Catholic respondent highlighted the problems for local authorities brought by larger marches and felt it could be difficult for them to ensure public safety, given the numbers participating, and that they would need to consider health and safety, issues carefully. One Protestant respondent suggested that restrictions should only be imposed when there were concerns about public safety or where the march would significantly diminish the ability of the general public to go about their business. One Catholic respondent described the other issues that local authorities should be able to take into account as including consideration of: the frequency of marches and enabling communities to negotiate a limit on the numbers taking place in their community; routes that went down the same street twice in the same day should be avoided; clashes with other publicly arranged events such as weddings or masses. It was important that there were serious reasons for marches.

8.107   The Jewish respondent said that the decision making process needed to be transparent to those people who were not used to the political process.

Religious organisations' views on numbers and effects on communities

8.108 Ten people commented on the numbers and effects on communities. The behaviour of marchers was important and one Protestant respondent highlighted some marches caused anxiety in communities, offended or intimidated residents and the march should be conducted in a way that was sensitive to the concerns of the community. A Catholic respondent agreed, highlighting the need to ensure that marchers behaved in a way that minimised disruption, for example ensuring that traffic could flow past the march.

8.109 Both Catholic and Protestant respondents commented on the disruption caused by marches. Two Catholic respondents commented on the disruptive effect marches had on parts of the community, one suggesting that marches can create *'an atmosphere of unease, fear and alarm'*. The timing of marches had meant that church services such as weddings and funerals needed to be changed. They commented on marchers' behaviour. Large marches in small villages could mean that access is disrupted and the village effectively shut off. Two Protestant respondents agreed and drew attention to the considerable disruption caused to those wanting to attend church services if marches were held on a Sunday.

8.110 The behaviour of onlookers also caused concern with one Protestant respondent describing the *'fear, alarm and sometime injury'* caused by onlookers. They felt it important that organisers did not disown responsibility. A Catholic respondent suggested that while it was not fair to hold organisers responsible for individual criminal acts committed by onlookers it was appropriate to take into account such actions in considering future notifications and to ensure that such behaviour could be addressed. Onlookers should not impede the flow of pedestrians and organisers should help to facilitate that.

8.111 Two Catholic respondents also commented on the number of parades taking place. Neither wanted to see any type of parades banned and commented on the importance of ensuring civil liberties but they did think there was scope for reducing the numbers taking place. One suggested regulations about the frequency of marches taking place in the summer. Another suggested that there had been a reduction over the summer of 2004, with fewer causing less trouble, and wanted to see that encouraging start built upon. A Sikh respondent had also felt that the number of marches were reducing in certain parts of Scotland.

Religious organisations' views on policing costs

8.112 Only two respondents commented specifically on policing costs. One thought that it *'would be a disgrace'* if people's rights to march depended on the policing costs of the event. The other agreed, that in general terms, in a democracy organisers should not be required to meet costs. However, if the police were concerned that protecting public order and safety would require disproportionate resources, then that should be taken into account in the decision making process.

A summary of submissions from MSPs

8.113　I met with three MPs and six MSPs. One MSP followed up the meetings with a detailed submission summarised here.

MSP's view on the period of notice

8.114　The MSP felt seven days was too short and should be at least 28 days.

MSP's view on community input

8.115　The MSP thought that there was scope for community consultation. To achieve a balance between the rights of marchers and the rights of communities, the council should hold local meetings between marching organisations, the police and community representatives. This would allow better arrangements for marches which created less hostility and more positive feelings in the community. There was scope to use community planning arrangements to engage the community but councils should ensure that they develop a structure to ensure that relevant groups such as shopkeepers and residents along the route can make their views known.

MSP's view on the basis for decision making

8.116　The MSP thought that councils needed to ensure that notifications were considered in an open way. The local authority should be able to decide on a notification and make changes on the basis of their assessment of the balance of rights, taking into account the number of local marches, whether a march is new or traditional, its past record and the views of local people and the police. As well as practical issues, local authorities should also be able to look at the atmosphere created by the march.

MSP's view on numbers and effects on communities

8.117　The MSP felt that some events were well established annual events but felt that the number of marches were increasing. It would not undermine an organisation's right of peaceful assembly to consider the number of marches it held in the same area or through a residential area or past a building in a manner seen as threatening to many. Feeder marches around a major march contribute to people's perceptions that there are too many marches.

8.118　The MSP commented that most people taking part in the march behaved acceptably, but the behaviour of those following was sometimes at fault, often because of excessive alcohol. Depending on the number of officers present, it was sometimes difficult for the police to address such behaviour effectively, and sometimes meant that this behaviour was not recorded in their report of the conduct of the march, making it difficult for a local authority to assess accurately the trouble which occured at previous marches.

8.119　Pre-march discussions should include behaviour at marches, such as the need to respect the rights of local communities to go about their business and not act in a way that suggests marchers *'own the streets though which they march'*. There was scope for marches to develop into more inclusive community events and turn into *'a fun day in the park'*.

MSP's view on policing costs

8.120　The MSP considered that the Executive should fund police forces to provide enough officers on marches to tackle drunken misbehaviour at marches more vigorously. Policing costs associated with marches was complex. The Executive should look at whether organisers of major events such as large marches or parades, major sporting fixtures and public entertainment should contribute to policing costs to ensure fair treatment.

A summary of submissions from organisations which arrange marches

8.121　I received 12 submissions from organisations which arrange marches. These organisations particularly highlighted the democratic right to march.

Views of organisations which arrange marches on the period of notice

8.122　Nine organisations commented on the period of notice. Six felt the period was too short, one was cautious about the impact on certain types of parades and two felt seven days was about right. The organisations representing Republican groups and the three Loyalist Institutions agreed that the period should be extended although they made clear that they already gave longer than the seven days statutory notice period, months for the larger marches. They suggested 14 days or 28 days would be a better balance and allow local authorities and the police more time to consider and plan. Other groups such as Scottish CND and NUS Scotland agreed that seven days was too short for meaningful consultation. However, they felt it was essential to allow exceptional circumstances for those marches which were organised in response to local, national or international events. The STUC was also concerned about an increased notification period drawing attention to marches arranged at short notice. If the period was increased there needed to be clear guidance on exceptions and, where it was clear that such a march would not cause disruption despite late notification, it should be able to go ahead. Organisers of regular marches should, however, give as much notice as practical. Pride Scotia and the Equality Network felt that seven days was appropriate and that it would be helpful if notifications could be made electronically.

Views of organisations which arrange marches on community input

8.123　Seven organisations commented on community input. Cairde na hÉireann thought that community input should properly come through councillors. The Grand Orange Lodge of Scotland also felt that councillors were the most appropriate route for community views. The Provincial Grand Black Chapter of Scotland thought community views should come through churches, unions and community councils. NUS Scotland suggested extending consultation to take in community councils. The STUC also thought community councils should have a right to be consulted as should resident groups. Communities most regularly affected by march routes should be most regularly consulted.

8.124 In principle, the Apprentice Boys of Derry and the Grand Orange Lodge of Scotland were cautious about the implications of seeking views from the wider community. They were concerned that a vociferous minority might have an input into banning or rerouting parades and thought it was wrong that parades be refused because some members of the community did not like a particular organisation. The Grand Orange Lodge of Scotland was concerned about how wide the consultation needed to be, how long it would last, how the costs would be met and the risk of allowing those with a personal axe to grind to dominate. A democracy needed to tolerate differing views.

8.125 The Equality Network and Pride Scotia agreed with the importance of consulting the community but they saw potential difficulties as some organisations representing particular communities of interest faced discrimination. Such organisations should be allowed to march even if there were lobby campaigns against them or parts of the community felt offended. Decisions needed to respect equality and diversity issues.

8.126 The Apprentice Boys of Derry recognised the importance of ensuring the community received more information about parades in their area. They suggested adverts in the local media would be one way of providing this and were always prepared to meet with members of the community to discuss their concerns. Cairde na hÉireann also wanted to ensure that the community received more information. They provided leaflets to the local community and businesses in advance describing the purpose of a march, its routes and providing contact details for further information. NUS Scotland emphasised they took their responsibility to the community seriously and minimised disruption wherever possible. The STUC suggested that information about marches should be published in a database available on the internet and in libraries, other local authority facilities and through local media.

Views of organisations which arrange marches on the basis for decision making

8.127 Ten organisations commented on the basis for decision making. Cairde na hÉireann, the Apprentice Boys of Derry and Pride Scotia drew attention to the need for councils to deal with notifications more consistently and ensure that all organisations were treated fairly and equally. Cairde na hÉireann said that it should be clearer that local authorities were responsible for taking decisions and that councillors should take and be accountable for those decisions.

8.128   Cairde na hÉireann, the Provincial Grand Black Chapter of Scotland and the Apprentice Boys of Derry specifically highlighted that decisions should primarily be taken on public safety, based on police concerns. For contentious marches, Cairde na hÉireann thought organisers should be required to consult with the local community and, if they were not prepared to do that, then appropriate sanctions could be taken. The Apprentice Boys of Derry thought it important to ensure that organisers were properly involved in the decision making process so that they could work together with the council and the police to avoid bans and to reach amicable decisions.

8.129   The STUC suggested that it was appropriate to take into account the accumulated level of disruption felt by a community when assessing notifications and alternative routes should be considered as an option. The NUS Scotland also felt that it was appropriate to limit the number of marches taking place in any one community. Pride Scotia and the Equality Network felt that passing disruption in itself was not enough to ban a march and the grounds for decisions should be based on legal grounds – for example, the impact on race relations – and ignore personal prejudices.

8.130   The Grand Orange Lodge of Scotland drew attention to organisers' responsibility to ensuring that parades were organised for appropriate reasons and highlighted their own approach which prevented coat trailing parades or inflammatory routes. Organisers also needed to adopt a reasonable attitude when problems arose and said that they would continue to apply 'a co-operative attitude to any legitimate concerns with regard to parade dates, times or routes and to make adjustments where necessary'. Informal discussion and compromise should avoid the need for formal conditions to be set. The Apprentice Boys of Derry also ensured that the governing body looked at notifications before they were submitted to local authorities to ensure that parades were not meaningless and a burden. Cairde na hÉireann agreed organisers had a responsibility to enter into dialogue and minimise the disruption caused by their marches and said that they ensured that they did not organise marches in areas where it would be provocative. They felt organisers should not have several marches taking place within in the same city on the same day.

8.131   While NUS Scotland felt their own marches were unlikely to cause offence to communities, they felt it important that councils take into account the likelihood of a march to threaten public order, cause offence or have a negative or divisive impact on local communities. They were opposed to marches arranged by racist or fascist organisations feeling those marches threatened public safety.

8.132   The Scottish Youth Hostel Association, which organised marches to promote the use of their non-profit making hostels, thought it important that marches should not cause offence to any members of the community and should be conducted in a lawful and peaceful manner. The Scout Association encouraged individual groups of Scouts who had annual parades to their place of worship to liaise with the police and the council well in advance of their event.

8.133   Pride Scotia and the Equality Network felt it important that local authorities did not ban any specific types of marches. Decisions should not be based on prejudice about an organisation and objections founded on prejudice, such as homophobia, should not be considered. They urged caution on setting timing restrictions which would discourage people from participating in marches if they needed to travel some distance. Disruption in itself was not enough to ban a march.

8.134   Pride Scotia and the Equality Network felt that councils should make some practical improvements to the system. For example, keep an overall diary of events to identify possible clashes early on and improve communication between council departments. Making more use of technology would speed up the process.

Views of organisations which arrange marches on numbers and effects on communities

8.135   Eight organisations commented on the numbers and effects on communities. Organisers recognised the importance of their own role in ensuring successful marches and the importance of dialogue with local authorities and the police. Cairde na hÉireann, the Apprentice Boys of Derry and the Grand Orange Lodge of Scotland all had codes of conduct in place for people participating in their marches.

8.136   To avoid marches clashing, Cairde na hÉireann said that they would be happy to meet other organisers, such as the Grand Orange Lodge of Scotland, to discuss their *'respective calendar of events and any issues arising'*.

8.137   Organisers emphasised the importance of effective stewarding to the conduct of marches and already tried to ensure that they had effective stewarding in place. The Apprentice Boys of Derry had piloted training for their stewards with a hierarchy of clearly identified marshals in constant communication during marches and with full marshal briefing meetings beforehand, covering the route and arrangements. This had helped marches to run more smoothly. The Grand Orange Lodge of Scotland also ensured that their parades were properly stewarded, that they would be prepared to develop their expertise with more rigorous training and suggested that it would be helpful to draw on police experience. The Provincial Grand Black Chapter of Scotland also made sure that they had internal stewarding in place. The STUC said that organisers were responsible for ensuring effective stewarding but were not responsible for the behaviour of onlookers, which was the responsibility of the police. The STUC had developed detailed knowledge and experience in stewarding and would be happy to share that experience.

8.138   Pride Scotia suggested that clear guidance to organisers would be valuable. Such guidance should cover levels of stewards, the need to take out public liability insurance and health and safety matters. There needed to be more consistency across local authority areas. Cairde na hÉireann wanted to see a code of conduct drawn up for organisers covering the responsibilities and behaviour expected – including bands, stewarding, the notice required – and suggested that organisers should be required to sign a statement renouncing racism (including anti-Irish racism) and sectarianism.

8.139   The Grand Orange Lodge of Scotland raised the issue of public perception which often described all parades organised by the Loyal Institutions as 'Orange' as they were not aware of the differences between the institutions. This was made worse with the more recent phenomenon of band parades which had no connection to the Orange Order and over which the Order had no control.

8.140   Given the purpose behind their marches, Scottish CND commented that they often had established routes and it would be difficult for them to change those routes. The STUC agreed that some routes will see more marches. Some marches did cause discord within communities and did not promote a tolerant and modern Scotland. The Equality Network thought it was important that groups which only organised one or two marches were not squeezed out by groups which organised more frequent parades.

Views of organisations which arrange marches on policing costs

8.141   Eight organisations commented on policing costs. All agreed that it would be inappropriate to require organisers to pay for policing costs. Cairde na hÉireann felt that costs should be met by the state. The Provincial Grand Black Chapter of Scotland agreed and said that marchers already contributed to policing costs through the taxes they paid. The Apprentice Boys of Derry said that they already contributed towards some costs associated with parades such as providing risk assessments, providing toilets and the costs for the cleaning of parks. The Grand Orange Lodge of Scotland said that requiring organisers to pay would be an *'affront to democratic rights and the freedom of speech'*. The NUS said that groups, particularly voluntary groups, should not be required to pay. Pride Scotia and the Equality Network suggested that requiring organisers to pay would mean that parades could not take place. Small community groups would not be able to pay costs. It was clear that some events generated tourism and revenue. The STUC thought that protecting the collective freedom of expression was essential and so organisers should not be required to meet additional costs for policing.

8.142   The level of policing was a concern to some organisers. The Apprentice Boys of Derry suggested that some parades appeared over policed and, with more effective stewarding, the number of police present could be reduced. Cairde na hÉireann felt that local authorities should keep the level of policing under regular review. The Equality Network thought that if there were problems with excessive costs of policing particular marches by certain organisations, that needed to be discussed between the police and the organisers.

A summary of submissions from private individuals

8.143   I received 30 submissions direct from private individuals.

Private individuals' views on the period of notice

8.144 About a third (9) respondents commented on the period of notice. All felt that seven days was insufficient, although two made the case that it would not always be possible for organisers to give more than seven days, depending on the reason for the procession. There were a range of suggestions about what an appropriate timescale should be: from six weeks to match local authority committee cycles to six months for Loyalist and Republican parades which were celebrating long standing traditions and anniversaries. The most popular suggestion was two months.

Private individuals' views on community input

8.145 Just under 30% (8) of respondents expressed a view on community input. They were generally agreed that the community had a right to know about the events taking place in its area and a right to express a view. However, there was some wariness about the level of influence that the community should have over proposed marches. Better awareness should remove 'the element of surprise and the sense of shock' when people do not know about marches in advance.

8.146 There were mixed views on who should be consulted. Suggestions included community councils and groups genuinely representative of the community. Another suggested wider views be sought through MSPs, adverts in newspapers, local libraries, community centres, local authority offices and other public places, as well as consultation with Chambers of Commerce, professional and trade bodies, and any other relevant groups who represented community stakeholders. One respondent thought that local authorities should hold a general referendum to agree their policies on marching, covering who should be able to march and when and where those marches should take place. Others felt it would be difficult to find successful ways of engaging with the community.

8.147 Respondents made practical suggestions on how to ensure that the community got better information and were able to comment. Two people suggested that there should be adverts in local papers supplemented by meetings where organisers, such as the Orange Order, would go an explain the reason for the march. Once the decision had been taken the forthcoming march and its route needed to be well publicised.

Private individuals' views on the basis for decision making

8.148 Most people (over 90%) had views on the basis for taking decisions about marches.

8.149 20% of respondents felt that different types of processions should be treated in different ways, according to the reason for the procession. Generally, those that commented suggested that marches organised by Loyalist Orders or Republican organisations should be treated in one category and political protests and community celebrations in another category. Both types of processions caused disruption, but there was a feeling that communities were more prepared to accept disruption linked to events with community, civic, national or job related reasons. One respondent thought that Loyalist Orders or Republican organisations should hold meetings in special venues to minimise disruption to the wider community. Others thought that street protests in general should be phased out as there were now more effective ways to express opposition and displeasure.

Bans and respecting traditions

8.150 Private individuals had strongly held views about the need to ban certain marches or to ensure traditions were respected. A sizeable minority of respondents suggested that certain kinds of marches should be banned. They described the kinds of marches which should be banned as:
- *'all denominational and religious marches which incite violence and are offensive'*;
- all religious marches which were *'assertive, intolerant and abusive'*;
- Loyalist Orders and Republican marches which were *'a pernicious residue of religious and political feuds which date back many centuries'*;
- Orange Order marches which: *'are a blight to our pluralistic society'*; *'encourage bigotry and prejudice'*; *'promote religious hatred'*; *'cause intimidation and harassment'*; and *'are anti-Catholic'*.

8.151 Other respondents recognised the need to protect people's right of freedom of speech and assembly and suggested this could be respected if they were able to gather in an appropriate venue rather than in the streets. Respondents said that while the rights of people to march needed to be respected, it was also important to respect the rights of communities.

8.152 25% of people were concerned about the prospects of banning Loyalist Order marches. Rather than banning processions, there needed to be better explanation and understanding of why processions were taking place and discussions to promote understanding and tolerance of others' beliefs. Processions should not be banned simply because of the behaviour of opponents. These respondents supported Loyalist Order parades as a way of promoting their Protestant heritage and celebrated historical events which lead to religious and political freedoms. A multi-cultural society needed to respect everyone's rights equally. Banning Loyalist marches would undermine their rights. Most marches were peaceful events *'colourful and musical'*, *'promoting a proud heritage and culture'* with marchers *'acting within the law and dignified at all times'*.

8.153 Respondents made suggestions about the kind of issues which should be taken into account in reaching decisions about the routes of marches. Some suggested it was appropriate only to take into account a narrow range of issues (usually public safety and significant disruption) whereas others were keen to see a much broader range of issues taken into account. Suggestions about the kind of issues that should be considered included where:
- there were concerns about public safety;
- the ability of the general public to go about their business was significantly diminished;
- there would be unacceptable disruption to traffic;
- roads were unsuitable for marches due to traffic controlling measures;

- there would be unacceptable disruption to business;
- there had been incidents at previous marches that suggested that the safety and well-being of the community would not be protected or which had caused offence to the community;
- the date clashed with other events requiring a police presence;
- the likely behaviour of onlookers would be troublesome;
- there was a likely risk of harm to the general public due to protestors; and
- there appeared to be doubts about the risk assessment carried out by the organisers or that they would not conform to the march notification.

8.154 On routes, a number of respondents suggested that marches should generally avoid city centres, main thoroughfares, bus routes, and shopping centres.

8.155 There were some specific suggestions about restrictions for Loyalist Order and Republican marches. These included a suggestion that they should take place in areas which did not interfere with the general community, they should not go past places of worship or residential areas where offence could be caused and intimidation felt. These marches should be rerouted if the community was unhappy that they took place in their area.

Private individuals' views on numbers and effects on communities

8.156 45% of respondents commented on the numbers of marches and the effects on communities. Four people specifically commented on their perceptions that there was a 'surfeit of Orange Order marches' and suggested that some communities were disturbed every weekend over the summer. They felt the frequency of marches was the issue rather than the reason for the marches. They had little warning of the marches and so could not plan around the disruption. Marches could disturb the community from early in the morning to later in the evening. A small number of marchers caused disruption for the wider community. Some respondents thought there should be scope for combining marches, perhaps one parade per lodge or one parade for all lodges.

8.157 Many respondents described the type of personal disruption they had experienced through marches taking place in the community, from the frustration caused by not being able to cross roads and missing trains, to detrimental effects on arrangements for weddings, christenings and funerals. Some marches organised by the Orange Order caused particular concerns in communities, causing fear and division. A couple of people felt that there should be guidelines to cover behaviour at marches, governing behaviour to minimise disruption and offence. Another thought that there needed to be a genuine reason for the march and it should not be on *'a whim'*.

Private individuals' views on policing costs

8.158 45% of respondents commented on policing costs and the scale of police resources at marches. Respondents were divided about whether marchers should be required to pay or not. Almost two thirds of those who expressed a view said that it was wrong to expect people to pay as it was their right to march. They felt that peaceful marches incurred limited costs, and in a democracy, policing costs should be met by the government and marchers were already making a contribution through general taxation.

8.159   Others thought that some marchers should be required to meet charges. They suggested that Loyalist and Republican marches, or those with a commercial intent, should be required to contribute to policing costs. Some thought that to encourage marches away from city centres, there should be a charge for policing in the city centre but no charge outwith the centre. Others felt that organisations such as the Orange Order, which organised a large number of parades a year, should be allowed a number free of charge and then would be required to contribute for additional parades.

8.160   Some respondents had views on the scale of policing, particularly at Orange Order marches. Given the Orange Order ensured that their marches were effectively stewarded, there should be scope to scale down the police presence and have officers on standby instead. The police were there to supervise the onlookers and direct traffic as the marches were generally well behaved, meeting their own codes of conduct.

A summary of standard letters

8.161   A number of people also submitted their views using the template of a standard letter. I received 216 versions of three slightly different letters.

8.162   187 people wrote in support of everyone's right to peaceful assembly to allow them to celebrate their history and traditions. They felt that society was enriched through a greater understanding and tolerance of all its components. They thought the notification period should be extended to 28 days. They believed that only processions which posed a threat to public safety or contravened the Terrorism Act 2000 should be banned. They did not think that it was appropriate to require organisers of any procession to meet policing costs.

8.163   21 people wrote to support the democratic right to march. They felt that a two month notice period was more appropriate. They thought that community input could best be ensured through educating and informing people. Decisions on restrictions or refusing parades should only be made when there was sufficient information regarding the likelihood of serious trouble at parades. They commented that most parades passed without any trouble and had little effect on most communities. They did not think that it would be appropriate to charge marches for policing costs, as most would be taxpayers and marching organisations did put money back into the economy.

8.164   Eight people wrote expressing their belief that everyone had the democratic right to march as long as they were law abiding. They suggested an extension of the notification period to one month. They felt that community input into decisions could be made by ensuring communities had the right to object. They believed that the police had sufficient information on parades to recommend if they should be rerouted or cancelled. They commented that most parades passed with little or no effect on community life and greater tolerance and understanding of different viewpoints would be helpful in improving community relations. They did not think it was right to charge people for exercising their right to march and felt it would be an infringement of their civil rights.

A summary of responses forwarded from the Scottish Executive

8.165   The Scottish Executive drew my attention to relevant views that had been expressed to it during the course of the Review.

8.166   They had received 18 letters commenting specifically on Orange walks. The majority (two thirds) of those who wrote about Orange walks were strongly opposed to these events seeing them as divisive and having a detrimental effect on Scotland's image. They felt that they lead to sectarian behaviour which should not be tolerated. A couple of people objected that some of the flags flown at marches were inappropriate. Some respondents described their experiences in Glasgow when Orange walks were being held and recorded disruption (being prevented from going about their daily business such as visiting a cemetery, crossing the road, or enjoying a night out) and intimidation (caused by the behaviour of the marchers but particularly the onlookers highlighting sectarian abuse and drunkenness). There was concern about the effects of holding large marches in small towns given the level of disruption. Some people were worried about the impact on police resources. It was felt that most people did not support Orange walks and so they should be banned.

8.167   Other respondents (one sixth) were less opposed to Orange walks and recognised everyone's right to march. However, they felt this needed to be balanced with the rights of the community and suggested that marches take place with limitations. The conditions suggested included: marches should not take place at the same time as church services; routes should not go past churches; fewer marches should be allowed; sectarian music should not be played or bands should not be allowed at all; and organisers should pay towards policing and cleaning up. A national referendum was suggested so that people had a chance to express their views.

8.168   Some people (one sixth) strongly supported Orange walks and did not want to see them banned. They felt that they were an integral part of Scotland's heritage and that the Orange Order was a legitimate organisation with a right to march and a tradition of parading. The marches were lawful. Banning their marches would be more divisive and lead to trouble. It was important to support Protestant traditions as well and, in Scotland, Protestants and Catholics lived side by side.

8.169   Aside from Orange walks, two respondents expressed views relevant to my remit, particularly on the need to ensure that councils could take a wider range of issues into account when reaching decisions. Marches which lead to racial hatred or religious intolerance should be restricted, although freedom of speech needed to be protected. There was also a need to route marches away from areas such as city centres where they caused considerable disruption.

9 A summary of the telephone survey: 'Review of marches and parades: a survey of views across Scotland'

Introduction

9.1 I wanted to make sure that I explored the wide range of views that people had on marches and parades in general and that the Review was informed by those views. I decided the best way to do this was to commission an attitude survey addressing the areas of my remit. TNS Social Research was commissioned, after a selective tendering process, to undertake the survey exploring the views and experiences of a broadly representative sample of the Scottish population. The aims of the survey were to explore:
- individual views on parades and marches;
- individual experiences of parades and marches;
- the impact of parades and marches on individuals and the wider community; and
- views on the five elements of my remit, including how the community should be consulted and engaged in matters relating to the planning of parades and marches.

9.2 This chapter provides a summary of the views and issues which emerged from the telephone survey. The full report 'Review of Marches and Parades: A Survey of Views Across Scotland' has been published separately and is also available at *http://www.scotland.gov.uk/marchesandparades*

Methodology

9.3 Computer-assisted telephone interviews were undertaken with 676 respondents across Scotland during October 2004. Random Digit Dialling was used to achieve a random sample of landline telephone numbers within each of the eight police force areas in Scotland. To allow some analysis of results by police force area, approximately 150 interviews were undertaken in the Strathclyde Police area and 75 interviews in each of the other seven areas. To take account of the geographically disproportionate sampling, the data was then weighted to provide a sample representative of the geographical distribution of the Scottish population. Quotas were set within each police force area in order to achieve a sample broadly representative of the adult population in terms of age, sex and working status.

9.4 The main topics covered in the survey questionnaire were:
- experiences of different kinds of marches or parades as a participant, spectator or as someone 'otherwise affected' (for example, as a passer-by or as someone who lives or works nearby);
- positive and negative impacts of different kinds of march or parade (for example, community spirit, enjoyment, being held up or delayed, feeling angry, upset or offended);
- whether decisions about marches and parades are perceived as an 'issue' in respondents' local communities;
- views on what should be taken into account when making decisions about marches and parades;
- the amount of notice which should be required from march organisers;
- who should be involved in decisions about marches and parades; and
- views on whether organisers should contribute to costs.

9.5 The full text of the questionnaire is at Appendix B.

Experiences of marches and parades

9.6 Respondents were asked about their experiences of different sorts of marches and parades, including gala day parades, political protests, and Orange walks and Republican marches. A sizeable proportion of the Scottish population has been involved in, or affected by, some form of march or parade. The table below illustrates experiences of the different types of march.

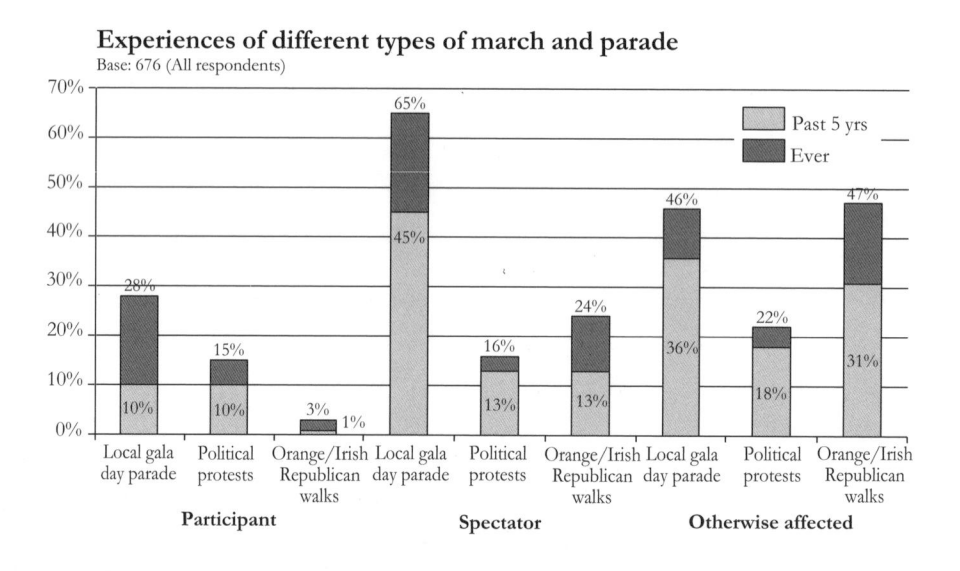

Experiences of different types of march and parade
Base: 676 (All respondents)

	Local gala day parade	Political protests	Orange/Irish Republican walks
Participant (Past 5 yrs / Ever)	10% / 28%	10% / 15%	3% / 1%
Spectator (Past 5 yrs / Ever)	45% / 65%	13% / 16%	13% / 24%
Otherwise affected (Past 5 yrs / Ever)	36% / 46%	18% / 22%	31% / 47%

9.7 Much of the experience has been of local gala day parades, carnivals with floats, student rag week and similar parades – two thirds have been spectators at these kinds of parade, over a quarter have been participants and almost half have been 'otherwise affected' (that is, not participants or spectators but affected in some way by the march, for example, as passers-by or because they live or work nearby). Although few have been participants in Orange Order, Irish Republican walks, a quarter have been spectators and approaching half have been 'otherwise affected'. Around one in seven people have been participants in a political protest or demonstration, a similar proportion have been spectators and a fifth say they have been 'otherwise affected' by this kind of march. Experiences of political protests tended to be more recent than experiences of other types of marches.

Impact of marches and parades

9.8 Respondents were asked about the impact of each type of procession they had been involved in. It is clear that many people felt they had gained positive experiences from marches and parades – enjoyment, feelings of community spirit, feeling involved in something important and feeling that they were making a difference.

9.9 Not surprisingly, participants and spectators are more likely to report positive experiences than those 'otherwise affected' because they are passers-by, or because they live or work nearby. Nonetheless, even some of this latter group report positive experiences – for example, 44% 'otherwise affected' by political protests say they experienced feelings of community spirit. However, there are also a number of problems associated with marches. Some disruption is caused by local gala day parades: around one in three of those involved or affected say they have been held up or delayed, and around one in six say they have been prevented from going somewhere they wanted to go. The following table illustrates some of the impact of different kinds of procession.

Impact of different kinds of procession

Bases: 374 (Local gala day parades) 160 (Political protests) 188 (Orange Order/Irish Republican) (All those who have been a participant, spectator or 'otherwise affected' in past five years)

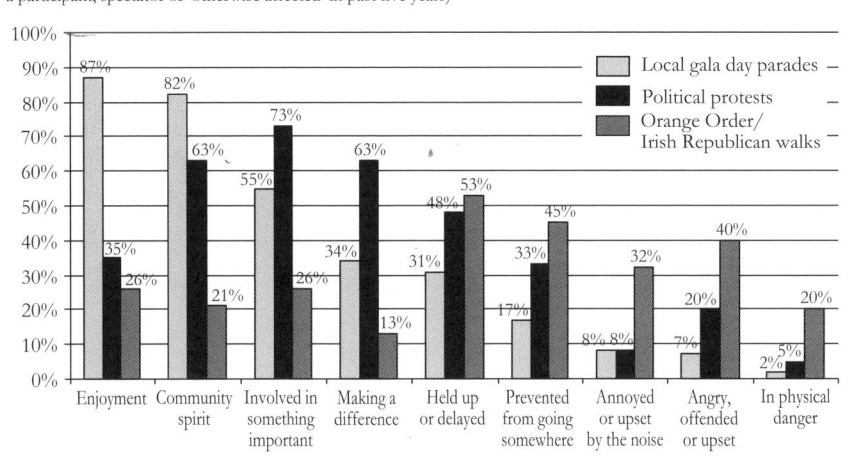

	Local gala day parades	Political protests	Orange Order/Irish Republican walks
Enjoyment	87%	35%	26%
Community spirit	82%	63%	21%
Involved in something important	55%	73%	26%
Making a difference	34%	63%	13%
Held up or delayed	31%	48%	53%
Prevented from going somewhere	17%	33%	45%
Annoyed or upset by the noise	8%	8%	32%
Angry, offended or upset	7%	20%	40%
In physical danger	2%	5%	20%

9.10 Respondents identified more disruption associated with political protests and Orange Order/Irish Republican walks. In each case, of those who were not participants or spectators but were 'otherwise affected', roughly half said they were prevented from going somewhere and roughly six in ten said they were held up or delayed. In relation to Orange Order/Irish Republican walks, four in ten of those 'otherwise affected' said they were annoyed or upset by the noise and around half reported feeling angry, offended or upset. Moreover, a quarter of those 'otherwise affected' said they had felt they were in physical danger.

9.11 Half of respondents agreed that 'Overall, marches and parades benefit my local community' but almost as many felt that 'Overall, marches and parades cause divisions in my local community'. Respondents in the Northern Constabulary area were more likely to feel that marches benefited their community, while those in Strathclyde were more likely to feel that they caused divisions.

The extent to which decisions about marches are an issue

9.12 Respondents were asked two questions about how much of an 'issue' decisions about marches were in their area. Overall, around two thirds of respondents indicated that decisions about marches were 'not really an issue' or 'not an issue at all' in their area. The remaining third said that they were either a 'big issue' or 'something of an issue'. Of this third who thought they were a big issue/something of an issue, the majority (around 15% of *all* respondents) said this in relation to Orange Order walks.

9.13 The extent to which marches are seen as an issue because of disruption (for example, because of disruption to traffic or business, or the mess created) is very similar to the extent they are seen as an issue because of their nature or purpose. This suggests that the two are closely linked and that marches that are an issue because of their nature are also an issue because of disruption.

Type of march that is an issue (among respondents who think that marches are an issue)

Base: 179 (All those saying decisions about marches were an issue or something of an issue)

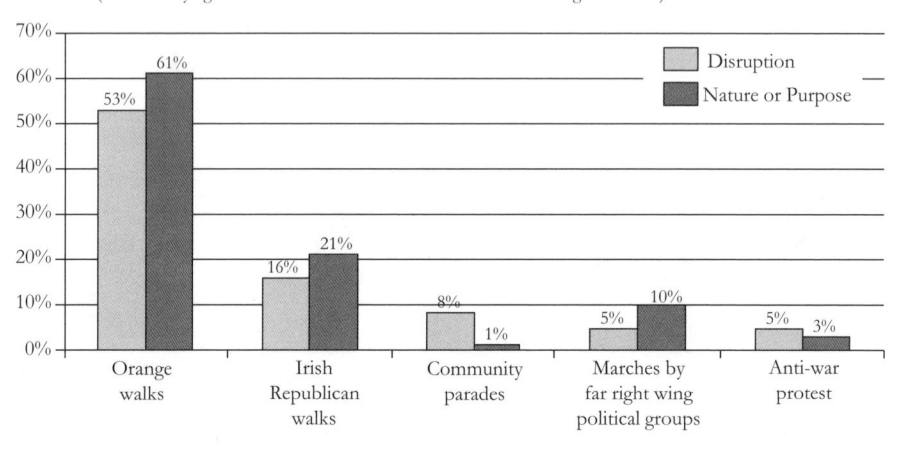

Type of march	Disruption	Nature or Purpose
Orange walks	53%	61%
Irish Republican walks	16%	21%
Community parades	8%	1%
Marches by far right wing political groups	5%	10%
Anti-war protest	5%	3%

What should be taken into account when making decisions

9.14 Respondents were asked about how important it was to take a variety of issues into account when local authorities took decision about march notifications. It was clear that they thought that a wide range of issues should be taken into account when making decisions about whether marches should go ahead, or where and when they should take place. Overall, the most important considerations were the risk to public safety, the protection of freedom of speech, the risk of serious damage to property, and the cost of policing and clearing up afterwards. Views differed slightly in relation to Orange Order/Irish Republican walks, where more importance was placed on the risk of offending or upsetting people and relatively less importance was placed on freedom of speech (although, in absolute terms, freedom of speech was still seen as important).

9.15 The following table illustrates the responses using mean scores. Respondents were asked whether an issue was 'very important', 'quite important', 'not very important' or 'not at all important'. If everyone said the issue was 'not at all important' the mean score would be 1 and if everyone said that the issue was 'very important' the mean score would be 4. The higher the mean score, the more importance was placed on that issue.

How important is it to take into account…? (Mean scores)
Base: 676 (All respondents)

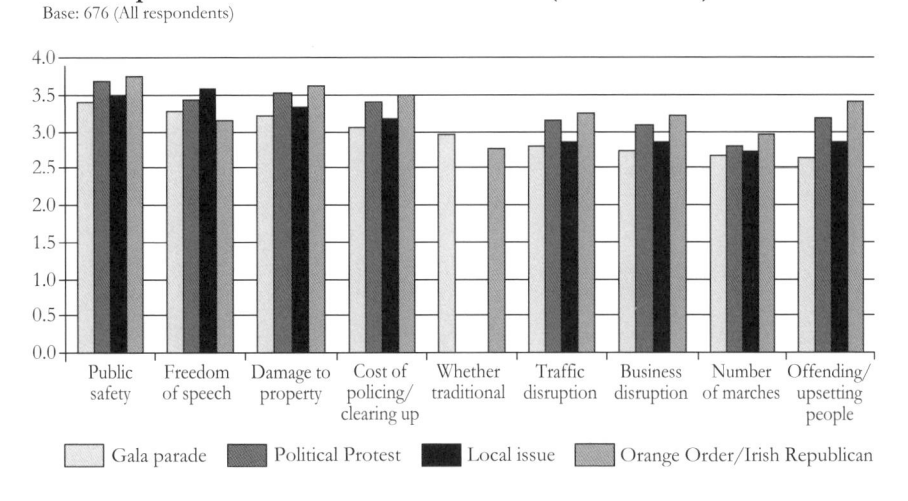

9.16 One of the key difficulties in making decisions about marches is striking a balance between considerations which are seen as important but are not always compatible. This issue was highlighted by responses to some statements on general principles. While two thirds agree that 'Freedom of speech is more important than whether someone is angered or offended by a march', and three quarters agree that 'As a general rule, all marches should be allowed unless there is a serious risk to public safety', three quarters also agree that 'Marches which are likely to inflame racial or religious tensions should not go ahead'.

Notification and involvement in decisions

9.17 Respondents were asked about the amount of notice organisers of processions should give the local authority and police. Most people agreed that requiring march organisers to provide 28 days notice to the authorities was 'about right', but that exceptions should be allowed in certain circumstances.

9.18 Respondents were asked about who should be involved in the decision making process. A majority thought that the council, the police and the other emergency services should be involved in decisions about marches. In general, the view was that local community groups, residents, businesses and places of worship should be notified about marches in their area but not actually involved in decisions.

9.19 Over a third of respondents said that they, personally, would like to be notified about marches in their area. Their preferred methods of notification were by letter or newspaper advert.

Costs

9.20 Respondents were asked whether they thought march organisers should contribute to the various costs associated with marches. The following table shows the views on whether march organisers should contribute to the various costs associated with marches.

Whether march organisers should contribute to costs
(% respondents saying 'yes' they should contribute)
Base: 676 (All respondents)

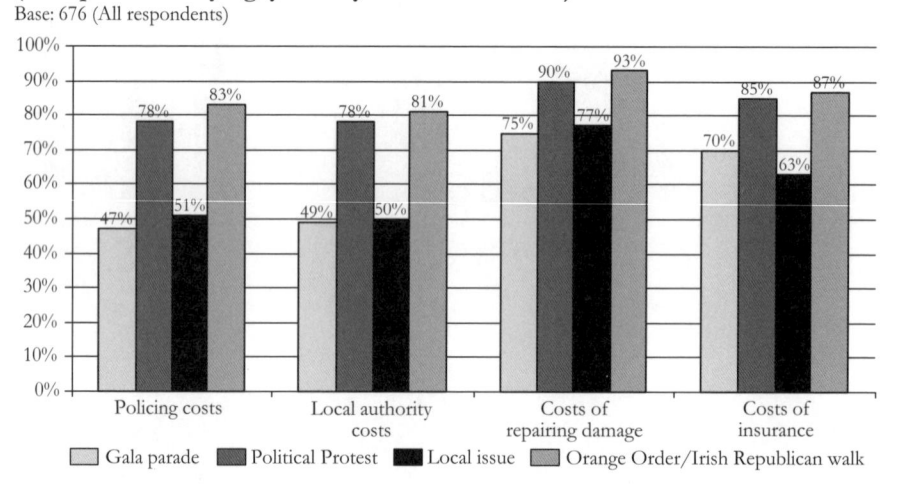

	Gala parade	Political Protest	Local issue	Orange Order/Irish Republican walk
Policing costs	47%	78%	51%	83%
Local authority costs	49%	78%	50%	81%
Costs of repairing damage	75%	90%	77%	93%
Costs of insurance	70%	85%	63%	87%

9.21 Respondents were evenly split on whether organisers of local gala parades and protests about local issues should pay for policing costs and local authority costs. However, in relation to the costs of repairing damage and the costs of insurance, a clear majority thought organisers of these types of parade should contribute.

9.22 In relation to both political protests and to Orange Order and Irish Republican walks, three quarters or more of respondents thought organisers should contribute to policing, local authority and insurance costs, and almost all thought they should contribute towards the costs of repairing damage – 90% thought organisers of political protests should contribute and 93% thought organisers of Orange Order and Irish Republican walks should contribute.

9.23 Interestingly, however, when asked later in the survey how much they agreed with various statements, roughly half of those who thought that organisers of political protests should pay for policing costs agreed that 'Making marchers pay for policing costs limits freedom of speech'.

Conclusions

9.24 It is clear that parades and marches affect a sizeable proportion of the Scottish population. While there are a number of problems associated with marches, there is also evidence that many people gain positive experiences from them. Procedures for authorising parades and marches must therefore attempt to strike a balance – which may be very difficult at times – between minimising the negative impact of marches and maintaining people's freedom to protest, demonstrate and celebrate.

9.25 The survey indicates that there is a consensus on a number of principles – the need to protect freedom of speech, that marches should be allowed unless there is a risk to public safety, and that marches which are likely to inflame racial or religious tensions should not go ahead. Unfortunately, these principles are not always compatible. This again highlights the inherent difficulty in regulating marches and parades – how to balance one individual's right to protest, demonstrate or celebrate with the authorities' responsibilities to ensure public safety, and to allow other individuals to go about their daily business without undue inconvenience or risk of offence.

9.26 Clearly the survey does not provide the Review with any easy answers to this problem. What it does do, however, is confirm that the public wants a range of issues taken into consideration, and a range of organisations and local groups involved in the process.

10 How things are done in England

Introduction

10.1 This section explores the approach South of the Border. I visited London and Merseyside to learn how they handle processions. I gained a valuable insight into their approaches and am grateful for the very open and constructive way they addressed my enquiries. I chose London, given the number and range of processions taking place there, and Liverpool because of that city's historical and cultural links with Scotland and Ireland.

10.2 While neither the legislative background nor the nature of processions in England and Wales is the same as in Scotland, I think there is much to be gained from considering how others approach arrangements for processions. I was particularly impressed by a number of aspects of the approach to processions in both London and Liverpool including:
- a planning process which involved organisers in detailed discussions resulting in an agreed and signed 'statement of intent';
- the expertise built up in specialised planning units both in the police and in local authorities;
- the guidance notes produced to help organisers plan and deliver effective processions; and
- the clear and straightforward planning documents leading to a consistent approach to the handling of all processions ensuring that key issues are not missed.

The legislative position in England – The Public Order Act 1986

10.3 Part II of the Public Order Act 1986 sets out the legal framework for arrangements for processions in England and Wales. The organiser must give six clear days written notice of any proposal to hold a public procession to the police. This is a key difference from Scotland where notice must be given to the local authority. Like Scotland, there is an exception to the notice period for cases where 'it is not reasonably practicable' to give advance notice of the procession. There is also an exception where the 'procession is one commonly or customarily held' although the processions which fall into this category are not defined.

10.4 The chief constable, having considered the notification, including details about the time, place, circumstances and route, can set conditions on the procession. Conditions can be imposed if the chief constable 'reasonably' believes that the procession may result in:

- *'serious public disorder, serious damage to property or serious disruption to the life of the community'*

or that the purpose of the people organising the procession is:

- *'the intimidation of others with a view to compelling them not to do an act they have a right to do, or to do an act they have a right not to do.'*

10.5 These conditions can be imposed in advance of the procession or during the procession itself. The chief constable has similar powers under this section in Scotland, but only when people are assembling to take part in a procession and during the procession itself. Those powers do not cover setting conditions in advance of the procession. In Scotland, any advance conditions are imposed by the local authority, after consultation with the chief constable.

10.6 The Public Order Act also gives the chief constable powers to prohibit public processions if he reasonably believes that the procession will lead to serious public disorder and he has insufficient powers to impose conditions to prevent the disorder. The chief constable has to make an application to ban all processions or a class of processions throughout the area or in a part of the area. He cannot ban a single procession. The application is made to the local authority who may approve a prohibition banning order with the consent of the Secretary of State. In London, local authorities are not involved, and the Commissioners of the City of London Police or of the Metropolitan Police can make an order direct with the consent of the Secretary of State. Orders have a maximum duration of three months. This power has been used, for example, to ban processions relating to Northern Ireland in certain parts of central London and to ban assemblies within a four mile radius from the junctions of roads adjoining Stonehenge Monument for four days around the summer solstice.

10.7 The Act creates particular offences if appropriate notice is not given, if any conditions imposed are not followed or if prohibition orders are not followed.

10.8 There are separate provisions about public assemblies (defined as an assembly of 20 or more people in a public place which is wholly or partly open to the air). There is no requirement for advance notice. The police can, however, impose conditions on the same basis as those for a procession. Conditions can be imposed about the place the assembly is to be held, its maximum duration or the maximum number of people participating. The police can also apply to the council to prohibit trespassory assemblies on land where the public has limited right of access.

Processions in London

10.9 The Metropolitan Police and the City of London Police are responsible for handling the arrangements for processions taking place in London. They work very closely together under agreed protocols to ensure effective coordinated planning and policing for processions which have the potential to impact on more than one force. The police forces have developed expertise in dealing with processions and specific units deal with notifications. In the City of London Police, the Operational Planning Unit deals with all processions in the City area and have developed detailed protocols for dealing with the various kinds of processions that take place. In the Metropolitan Police area, the Public Order Branch coordinates arrangements, involving local police stations in meetings with organisers. They also liaise closely with local authorities, particularly with the Special Events Group in the City of Westminster Council. As well as effective planning, processions are policed by trained and experienced staff. That experience is gained by working on operations and shadowing others. Having in place a well organised command and leadership structure contributes to successfully policed processions.

Giving notification of the intention to process

10.10 Organisers are required to complete a signed notification form giving some basic details about the procession including: the name of the organisation; the name, address and telephone number of the organiser; the details of the event (including date, time and place); the proposed route; the numbers likely to attend; and the dates the organiser is available for further meetings.

Planning meetings

10.11 Once the initial notification form has been received, there is a clearly nominated lead officer in the police who is responsible for taking forward all the event planning, consulting and coordinating information as appropriate. There is a meeting between the event planning team which is minuted. The meeting gives the police and the organisers a chance to discuss the proposed procession in detail. In the Metropolitan Police area, this meeting also involves someone from Westminster Council's Special Events Group. They discuss the proposed route, likely disruption and other practical issues. Depending on the scale of the procession, the initial meeting is followed up with a series of other meetings.

'Statement of Intent'

10.12 At the initial planning meeting, a 'Statement of Intent' is signed between the organiser and the police. While this is not a legally binding document, it is very helpful in setting out what has been agreed and the respective roles and responsibilities of the police and the organiser. The role of the police is to prevent or stop breaches of the peace and to prevent the commission of criminal offences. The police will intervene in the event of breaches of the criminal law, breaches of the peace or if a situation arises where they anticipate there will be an imminent breach of the peace. The role of the organiser is to take all reasonable steps to ensure the safety of those involved in or affected by the event, to avoid the risk of damage to property, to avoid frightening or alarming the public, to minimise any adverse effect of the event on the local community and to preserve good order.

10.13 The 'Statement of Intent' records details of the organisers, the purpose of the event, its route, its start and finish time, and assembly and dispersal arrangements. It looks at conditions relating to banners, leaflets, collection, floats, vehicles, stalls, music, address systems and requirements relating to traffic management and disruption. The organisers' arrangements for public safety are set out, as are the provisions around stewarding, the numbers, the chief stewards, the head steward, communication and identification. There is a section which sets out possible contingencies – for example, if there needs to be a delayed start, if the event needs to be discontinued, if there needs to be emergency changes to the route, or in the event of bad weather.

Guidance for Organisers

10.14 The police have prepared some straightforward guidance to organisers which they are given at the initial planning meeting. This explains the respective roles and responsibilities. It also makes clear that while the freedom to process is important, so too is the freedom of people to go about their normal business with the minimum of disruption, and there is a need to strike a balance. The guidance looks at the organisers' responsibility. In addition to carrying moral and social responsibilities, it makes clear that organisers have civil, common and criminal law responsibilities for which they may have to answer in the courts. Organisers may be liable for the consequences when things go wrong, particularly if there are defects in the planning or control of the event. This is more likely to happen if other interested parties are not consulted or if their advice is ignored. The guidance draws organisers' attention to the provisions in the Public Order Act 1986 and the need to get permission where necessary for assembly and dispersal points. It makes clear that the organiser has primary responsibility for public safety, both those taking part and those affected by it. This responsibility extends to avoiding damage to property, fear or alarm to the public or disruption to the local community.

10.15 The guidance also considers stewarding arrangements to ensure that organisers can keep control throughout the event. There should be sufficient stewards and while requirements vary considerably according to the particular procession, the guidance recommends that there should be at least one steward for every 50 participants. Stewards should be properly briefed with a head steward to liaise with the police. The overall stewarding should be broken down into sections and a chief steward appointed to be responsible for groups of stewards. Stewards need to be fitted, both physically and temperamentally, for their role. They need to be easily identifiable and in communication with the organisers throughout the event. They should inform the

10.16 Other practical issues are covered in the guidance. Participants should be encouraged to use public transport. Vehicles and animals should not be used. Leaflets associated with the purpose of the procession should be distributed separately. Prior notice should be given for petitions, to allow arrangements with their intended recipient. Collections should not usually be made at processions, and if they are there needs to be a separate application for a licence. Banners need to be properly designed with a hole to reduce danger if they are used in high winds. The use of public address systems should be controlled to minimise disruption to the local community. Children under 16 need to be accompanied by a responsible adult and kept away from the edge of a procession adjoining moving traffic. Organisers also need to consider provisions for first aid.

10.17 Finally, the guidance looks at debriefing and suggests that organisers make sure that stewards and safety officers are debriefed so that useful information for the organisers and the police may be gathered. The organisers should liaise with the police after the event to exchange and discuss information.

Police actions

10.18 Following the initial meeting with organisers, the police then consider the notification to develop their strategy for handling the procession. They develop an event strategy and complete a health and safety risk assessment. This results in an operation order for the event which will cover all aspects, including liaising with traffic management.

Debriefing

10.19 Immediately after the event, those involved complete a debriefing process, recording what happened at the procession. This includes a log of any damage, injury and prisoners as well as other incidents and general views on the effectiveness of arrangements. The police are able to review their systems to identify good practice and where improvements can be made to assist in future planning.

Commissioner's Directions

10.20 In considering how processions are policed in London, I should mention Commissioner's Directions, although these are unique to London. Under Section 52 of the Metropolitan Police Act 1839 and Section 22 of the City Police Act 1937, the Commissioners of the City of London and Metropolitan Police Forces have particular powers to make directions relating to the handling of processions to ensure public order and to prevent obstruction of thoroughfares. These powers are used for events of an extraordinary nature, such as marches and demonstrations, and are only applicable for so long as conditions render them necessary. Amongst other things, Commissioner's Directions can close streets to traffic, restrict parking and authorise the removal of vehicles. For pre-planned events the traffic management can be done through the Road Traffic Regulation Act 1984, the Road Traffic Regulation (Special Events) Act 1994 and the London Local Authorities Act 1995. Commissioner's Directions are useful for extraordinary events giving a degree of flexibility.

Communication with the community

10.21 In the Metropolitan Police area, the police inform large institutions (such as hotels and offices) on the route of forthcoming marches to ensure that they are aware of possible disruption. In return, those organisations share information about events they have on, for example, weddings. Depending on the size of the march, the Metropolitan Police Media and Information Section puts out information. They also make use of their website and keep a rolling notice of events which show road closures and disruptions. If the route of the march means it is in a confined area which would restrict access, the police inform the local community. Westminster Council also provide a basic public event listing on their website. They complement this, for internal planning purposes, with a more detailed database drawing on information through liaison with other London authorities, the police, industry, representative groups and local residents to ensure they have a full picture of events occurring within their area.

10.22 There is a similar approach in the City of London Police area. They have developed an email system to inform the business community of any processions and disruption that would impact on the City. An initial email is sent out a week before the procession, with information about the route, time and road closures and, a reminder email was sent out closer to the time of the procession. There is also a pager system to send out alerts outside office hours and companies pay the pager company a small fee. This means that over 1,500 companies receive regular information about processions. For larger events, the City of London Police inform the Corporation of the City of London who notify the wider community through their website.

Special Events Group, City of Westminster Council

10.23 As well as a wide range of processions, there is a wide range of special events taking place in London, as Westminster's streets form an important national showcase for large and small events. It is the workplace for nearly 500,000 people and is also the home of nearly 275,000 residents. Westminster Council needs to strike a balance between competing demands and has developed some general principles to enable it to do so. It has set up a discrete unit to coordinate all events and filming which take place in Westminster, including coordinating with the police relative to arrangements for special events and processions. They have built up a great deal of experience over the five years they have now been in existence. They deal with around 390 events and 1,500 filming days. The variety of events include: one off events such as the Rugby World Cup Parade and the Golden Jubilee Celebrations; annual events such as the New Year's Day Parade, the Chinese New Year, the London Marathon and the Pride March;

community street festivals; and protest marches such as Stop the War, the Countryside Alliance and Fuel Price Protests.

10.24 There are, of course, differences in the way that special events and processions are handled, but there are some important similarities in the process. The planning process always involves at least the organiser, the Westminster City Council and the Metropolitan Police Service. For special events, Westminster City Council Special Events Group makes sure that there is a robust process in place for risk assessment and the health and safety of the public. The group represents a wide range of council interests, including refuse collection, highways panning, parks and gardens, and parking. Large events are planned in partnership through an Operational and Safety Planning Group, chaired by the local authority bringing together key agencies and ensuring that there is an audit trail for decisions.

10.25 The Special Events Group has produced guidance notes for major special events. Much of it draws on the guidance issued by the police for processions. However, it also looks at wider issues. The Group provides a helpful events planning checklist of what needs to be considered in arranging an event and what the Council will consider in assessing applications. Some of the key issues it covers include risk assessment, stewarding and control management, parking and traffic arrangements, first aid and emergency access, and contingency arrangements. The council also provides additional advice on risk management. Other factors which the council will take into account in reaching a decision include: the area and capacity of the immediate surroundings to the event; the likely disruption to traffic; the level and nature of noise; the overall time taken to set up and dismantle the event; other demands likely to be made on the area during the event; the frequency of events in the location; plans to clear litter; assessments of the risk of street crime; damage to the street environment or private property or injury to people; organisers' insurance cover; and provisions for first aid.

10.26 Organisers of events are required to indemnify the council against any claims or proceedings in respect of any injury to people or damage to property. Organisers are required to take out liability insurance with a limit of not less than £1,000,000. There is provision made to ensure that certain people are notified in writing of the proposals for the event. These include: people who own premises with frontage on the event, including residents and businesses; those likely to be materially affected by the event; all residents affected either directly or indirectly by the event; and local associations in the immediate vicinity of the event. The Council requires evidence that this consultation has taken place.

10.27 In reaching decisions, the Council always takes close notice of police views of the event. They sometimes consult elected members whose wards are affected, emergency services, public utilities and the Westminster Safety Committee. The council charges a fee in some cases, to cover closing streets, for licenses for refreshment stalls and requires a deposit from the event organisers to offset any losses, for example if additional cleaning is required or there is damage caused.

Processions in Merseyside

10.28 Merseyside Police is responsible for handling all processions in Merseyside. They work closely with the five local authorities areas they cover: Wirral; Sefton; Knowsley; St Helens; and Liverpool. Liverpool Council has also established a Cultural Events Unit to encourage events to Liverpool and to ensure that the community is involved in events happening in and around the city. The Cultural Events Unit coordinates arrangements for those events and has expertise in the necessary technical and health and safety infrastructure.

Planning meetings with organisers

10.29 As in London, Merseyside Police see early discussions with organisers of processions as an essential part of the planning process, ensuring that they run effectively. These meetings include local authorities, as appropriate. The police have developed good working relationships with the organisers of marches, over time, who are generally receptive to open discussion and the need to act responsibly. One example of this has been the Orange Order which reacted positively to concerns about the numbers of feeder marches that took place at the annual walk to commemorate the Battle of the Boyne and worked with the police to reduce the numbers of separate marches. The police welcomed this as evidence of the Order's willingness to reach appropriate compromise and exercise self regulation. The Orange Order has also been happy to provide as much advance notice of their proposed marches as possible, allowing the police to improve their advance planning. Through the better working relations and trust built up through these planning meetings, the police have been able to work with the Orange Order to help them to develop more effective stewarding.

10.30 The planning meetings give the police an opportunity to emphasise to organisers the extent of their responsibilities to those on their marches. They make clear that, at the very least, organisers have a moral obligation for the safety of the people on their march. They encourage organisers to take out public liability insurance so that they have cover should people get hurt on their march. The police also take time to explain other possible obligations under health and safety legislation.

The police planning process

10.31 I was interested to see the effective operational planning system that Merseyside Police has developed which is supported by a very useful Operational Planning Handbook (the 'Cops Core Package'). This helps to ensure a consistency of approach across the Merseyside Police area. The approach is applied to all operational policing and, I think, the steps it sets out are particularly relevant in the handling of arrangements for processions. This approach means that there is a standard planning process for all operations. The level of detail depends on the nature of the operation but the standardised approach ensures a consistent approach and that aspects of planning are not overlooked.

The 'Cops Core Package'

10.32　The 'Cops Core Package' sets out very clearly the 15 key elements of operational planning that should be brought together in a comprehensive plan:

- **Command Structure** – this section describes who is responsible for the operation and each element within it to ensure that people know their role and the extent of their responsibilities;
- **Outline of Operation** – this section gives an overview of the operation (when, where, how, why and timeline) to provide a quick reference for what is being done and how it will be carried out;
- **Preparatory Actions** – this section provides a log of events in the planning process with a chronological table to ensure there is a record of what was done;
- **Significant Locations** – this section identifies all locations important before, during and after the operation to ensure everyone knows where the operation is to take place;
- **Communications** – this section looks at operational communication and external communication, and public impact strategy to ensure effective communication and information;
- **Objectives** – this section gives a description of what success will look like for each aspect of operation to guide and direct action during the operation;
- **Resources and Responsibilities** – this section paints a picture of the scale of total staff and other resources being used in the operation;
- **Equipment** – this section gives an overview of the logistic needs of the operation and how equipment is to be managed;
- **Policy** – this section includes a broad statement of policy issues which will dictate priorities and helps to determine the approach that is expected, providing guidance before they have to act;
- **Administration** – this section provides details of all administrative matters;
- **Contingencies** – this section describes the 'what ifs' that have been identified and a brief detail of the responses that have been planned;
- **Key Briefing Points and Debrief** – this section lists the key points to be included in the briefing and the arrangements for debriefing;
- **Assessment of Risk Impact** – this section provides an operational risk assessment in a set format looking at the health and safety implications of an operation, identifying risks and consequences, how likely they are; what needs to be done to reduce risk and who will do it;
- **Gathering Information** – this section provides a checklist of information used as the basis of risk assessment to provide an audit trail; and
- **External Agencies and Organisations** – this section includes an overview of role and contacts of other agencies and organisations involved.

10.33 I consider that there are a number of aspects of this approach which are particularly relevant to the handling of processions. It is important in including other agencies such as local authorities and commercial companies, as a standard part of the planning process. It helps to identify that interaction with other partners is essential to achieving smooth planning and is identified in advance of the operation. Thinking about other partners and their roles needs to become a standard way of working. I was also interested in the detailed risk assessment carried out which allows advance and focused consideration of the risks and the impact and the action that will be taken in various situations. It ensures that there is a consistent approach to risk assessment. It also means that possible risks, for example of flash points and pinch points during a procession, have been analysed and the proposed responses thought about well in advance.

Communication with the community

10.34 Merseyside Police has also developed structured techniques to allow them to analyse the impact of any event on their local community. They consult with a wide range of individuals and agencies, using already established networks in the community. It helps the police to understand better the needs of communities and the feelings within that community of the effects of their actions and of other incidents. It helps to analyse objectively any factors which might impact on community tranquillity and confidence and the specific needs of groups or of 'at risk' communities. There is much valuable information to be gained from a wide range of sources. It allows the police to scan who is affected, analyse how likely something is to happen and its impact, identify options for a response and assess its impact. Community impact assessments will, of course, be used in relation to many different incidents which have an effect on a community, but having systems like this in place is helpful in looking at the impact of any particularly contentious march on the community or parts of the community.

10.35 The local authorities ensure that the community has access to events happening within the Merseyside area. Sefton Council provides a four monthly plan of events on its website and is looking at a publishing it in the local media. The Cultural Events Unit in Liverpool City Council also keeps a rolling programme of events on its website.

11 How things are done in Northern Ireland

Introduction

11.1 This section looks at the Northern Ireland experience. I visited Belfast and spent time with the Parades Commission, Mediation Northern Ireland and the Police Service in Northern Ireland. Again, I welcomed the very open way they received me and my questions. The processes in Northern Ireland are unique in that decisions on the 3,000 or so processions are now taken by a body independent of the police and of local authorities, the Parades Commission. While what has developed in Northern Ireland clearly reflects their own history and particular circumstances, it is worth considering what we in Scotland can learn from aspects of their approach.

Processions in Northern Ireland

Background to the creation of the Parades Commission.

11.2 Until the creation of the Parades Commission in 1998, decisions on processions were taken by the police force under the Public Order (Northern Ireland) Order 1987. In his review of parades and marches, Sir Peter North described the main criticisms of that Order. In summary, he recorded that:
- it was felt to be too focused on public order, not recognising the rights of peaceful assembly or the rights of those in an area through which a parade passes, or those of the wider community;
- it placed a premium on threats of disorder; and
- it had been implemented inconsistently with a lack of transparency and rigour.

The Creation of the Parades Commission – The Independent Review of Parades and Marches, 'The North Review'

11.3 In August 1996, the Secretary of State for Northern Ireland (Sir Patrick Mayhew) commissioned Sir Peter North to review the arrangements for processions in Northern Ireland and associated public order issues and to make recommendations for the future conduct and regulation of processions. He took evidence from a wide range of interests, receiving 300 written submissions and letters and holding a series of 93 meetings involving more than 270 people. This was supplemented by a detailed attitude survey.

11.4 The review was prompted by the various serious disputes over the summer of 1996 between the Loyal orders and Nationalist resident groups, which required major intervention by the police under public order legislation, and by the general dissatisfaction with the exiting legislation. Sir Peter North, in his report, estimated the major costs to Northern Ireland of that disruption: two deaths and a significant number of injuries, the polarisation between two parts of the community, damage to the relationship between the police and the community, public expenditure costs apparently in excess of £30 million and losses to trade, tourism and inward investment.

11.5 The Report of the Independent Review of Parades and Marches (the North Report), was published in January 1997 and made 43 main recommendations. It identified a number of key principles which were to inform and underlie the development of processes and procedures to address the issue of conflict over parades, including:
- the right to peaceful free assembly should (subject to certain qualifications) be protected;
- the exercise of that right brings with it certain responsibilities, in particular those seeking to exercise that right should take account of the likely effect of doing so on their relationships with other parts of the community and be prepared to temper their approach accordingly;
- all those involved should work toward the resolution of difficulties through local accommodation;
- in the exercise of their rights and responsibilities, those involved must neither commit nor condone criminal acts or offensive behaviour;
- the legislation must comply with the United Kingdom's obligations under international law and provide no encouragement for those who seek to promote disorder;
- the structure for and process of adjudication of disputes over individual parades should be clear and applied consistently with as much openness as possible; and
- any procedures for handling disputes over parades and the enforcement of subsequent decisions should be proportional to the issues at stake.

11.6 The most fundamental of North's recommendations was the creation of a new independent body, the Parades Commission, that would:
- allow interested parties to put their views forward about proposed parades;
- encourage them to settle difficulties locally; and, where that became impossible
- itself to come to a view on what, if any, conditions should be imposed on contentious parades after an appropriately transparent process of examination of all the relevant issues against the background of reformed legal provisions.

11.7 In creating a new body, responsibility for making decisions about disputed parades passed from the police to the Parades Commission. North's other recommendations proposed a remit for the Commission; proposed guidelines be developed on how it should operate and that a code of conduct with statutory force be drafted for participants; proposed a longer period of notice than the existing seven days be given and suggested the way in which notice should be given; made provision for the continuing role of the Police Service of Northern Ireland; and suggested a registration scheme for bands.

The Parades Commission

11.8 The Parades Commission, recommended by Sir Peter North, was established in 1998. It is an independent, quasi-judicial body and its determinations are legally binding. The Commission is made up of a Chairman and six members. They are appointed by the Secretary of State for Northern Ireland, usually for a term of three years. The current Commission has been extended while the findings of the Quigley Review are considered. The members are from a variety of backgrounds: legal, business, community relations, the Presbyterian church and farming. Members had experience in facilitating, for example at the Dumcree talks and in community relations. The Commission is supported by a full time Secretariat with a permanent Secretary and two geographic case workers as well as administrative support. It has an annual budget of around £1.2 million.

Powers and duties of the Parades Commission

11.9 The powers and duties of the Parades Commission are set out in the Public Processions (Northern Ireland) Act 1998. The Act sets out the functions and powers of the Commission, the powers of the Secretary of State to review the Commission's determinations and to prohibit processions, makes provision about the time period for advance notice for processions (28 days) and protest meetings related to processions (14 days). It also makes provisions to enable a band registration scheme to be developed and provisions about the control of alcohol. Under the Act, the Commission was required to develop three documents: procedural rules explaining how it will exercise its functions; guidelines about how it will reach decisions on its determinations setting conditions on parades; and a Code of Conduct for participants in the parade.

Functions of the Parades Commission

11.10 The legislation sets out the key functions of the Commission as being to:
- promote greater understanding by the general public of issues concerning public processions;
- promote and facilitate mediation as a means of resolving disputes concerning public processions; and
- keep itself generally informed as to the conduct of processions and protest meetings.

Authorised Officers

11.11 To assist with mediation, the Parades Commission funds a team of 12 Authorised Officers who work on the ground throughout Northern Ireland, normally in teams of two. They are not members of the Commission staff but are self employed and contracted to provide services. Their job is to understand the issues and concerns raised by the various interest groups in relation to any parade and to seek to find ways towards a local consensus or mediated accommodation about parades at a local level. They are an important source of advice to the Commission, providing an invaluable perspective of realities within individual communities. For example, they will, in the run-up to a contentious parade, talk to many of the stakeholders in the area to establish what, if any, progress has been made on the ground in recent months; they will examine the prospects for dialogue and seek to facilitate the setting up of meetings where this is possible between the parties; they will discuss with parade organisers, residents, local clergy, community leaders and politicians the grass root sensitivities and feelings; and they will explore the potential for proposals to take into account the concerns of those living in the area. These insights, in turn, provide the Commission with valuable additional knowledge to that which is presented to them in the more formal advice and evidence gathering exercise, which is part of the procedure leading to a determination.

Monitors

11.12 The Parades Commission also uses monitors to observe parades and protest meetings to help in its duty to 'keep itself generally informed', of the conduct of public processions and protest meetings. Monitors, who are all volunteers, are trained with the assistance of Mediation Network for Northern Ireland. They are briefed before they attend a parade and are likely to be briefed to focus only on certain aspects of a parade, rather than attempt to observe and report on everything that happens. They carry identification cards for the purpose of making themselves known to the police and others. However, monitors are not otherwise publicly identifiable. Monitors' reports are based on what they see and hear as neutral observers and they work to a code of principles which emphasises their independence from the Commission when it comes to monitoring and reporting on parades.

Parades Commission's powers to set conditions on processions

11.13 The legislation gives the Parades Commission the power to impose conditions on public processions. This is a general power, but conditions could include provisions as to the route or prohibiting it from entering any place. The legislation required the Commission to set out guidelines on how it will reach its determinations (the second document required by legislation). They ensure that the Commission's processes are transparent, making sure there is consistency but also a degree of flexibility and discretion so that each case is looked at individually. Its guidelines set out the issues it will consider in reaching its determination. The guidelines and the Act require them to have regard to:
- *public disorder or damage to property which may result from the procession* – in doing so the Commission will seek and consider advice from the Police Service of Northern Ireland;

- *any disruption to the life of the community which the procession might cause* – including the restriction of freedom of movement by local residents, the restriction of normal commercial activity, the restriction of access to public amenities such as hospitals, the restriction of access to places of worship, and the duration of the procession;
- *any impact that the procession might have on relationships within the community considering:*
  - the location and route and the extent to which the route comprises residential or commercial property, the demographic balance of residents, the presence of monuments or churches, the purpose of the parade and the availability of other non controversial routes;
  - the type and frequency of parades, the purpose of the parade, the numbers notified to take part, the past experience of parades, the regalia associated with the parade, the nature and number of bands and the frequency;
  - communication with the local community and whether the organisers have been in contact with local community to address any genuine, relevant concerns; and
  - the broader context including any history of conflict associated with a parade and the impact for relationships within the wider Northern Ireland community.
- *Compliance with the code of conduct and the steps that organisers have taken to meet its requirements;* and
- *the desirability of allowing a procession customarily held along a particular route to continue be held along that route.*

Overturning the Parade Commission's determinations

11.14   The legislation makes provision for the Commission's determinations to be reviewed in certain circumstances. The Commission can look itself at its determination in light of new evidence or information brought to its attention. The chief constable can apply to the Secretary of State for a review of a decision, explaining his reasons for his concern and making recommendations about a preferred course of action. The Secretary of State can then confirm, amend or overturn the decision or prohibit a public procession or the holding of a series of processions in an area. The Secretary of State can also prohibit a procession or a series of processions if he is of the opinion that it could result in:
- any serious public disorder or serious damage to property;
- any serious disruption to the life of the community;
- any serious impact which the procession may have on relationships within the community; and
- any undue demands which the procession may cause to be made on the police or the military forces.

Process for giving notice of public processions

11.14   There is a prescribed form that organisers must complete to give advance notice of their intention to organise a procession. They must submit the form at least 28 days before the proposed date of the procession, to the police station nearest the start of the procession. The form requires details of the organiser, the purpose, the size, the route and the names of any bands taking part. When the police receive the form they forward it to the Commission, usually within 24 hours of having received it, stating whether it refers to an annual procession, whether the procession had been contentious in the past, whether there was any reason to believe the procession will be contentious and any other views of the police.

11.15   Before making a decision on a parade, the Commission also gathers a wide range of information from the police, the organiser, residents groups, elected representatives and other interested people or bodies. The Commission has detailed procedural rules on how it will exercise its functions (the first document required by legislation). The rules explain how it will gather information about past history, the demographic mix of the local community, the local area and key points on the route. The Commission may request a further, fuller police report. The report covers recent parading history at the venue, compliance with the Code of Conduct, public disorder or damage which has occurred, a community impact assessment, disruption to the life of the community and assessments under the Human Rights Act. The Authorised Officers have an important role in gathering information, sometimes supplemented by additional research and the Commissioners visiting the location of the parade. The Commission can also hold formal evidence gathering sessions in order to hear views and clarify issues. The evidence gathering sessions are recorded. In addition to these sessions, the Commission also receives information and representations from any interested party or organisation at any time prior to the date of the parade. All the information gathered by the Commission is treated as confidential and only for the use of the Commission. However, the Parades Commission will, if requested, advise the organiser of the nature of any objections to the parade (without revealing who has made objections) and give the organiser an opportunity to respond to those concerns.

11.16   The Commission recognises explicitly that disputes about parades are best resolved locally. If accommodation cannot be reached locally, the Commission takes into account all available evidence of the steps taken by any of the parties to secure accommodation. Once the Commission has the evidence it requires, it meets to consider whether to issue a legally binding determination on the parade. The decision is taken by majority vote. The Commission aims to make its decision five working days in advance of the date of the parade. It will provide written notification of its decision to the organiser, the Secretary of State for Northern Ireland, the Chief Constable and other concerned parties. The Commission issued 130 determinations in 2003. Its determinations include setting conditions on routes with restrictions or prohibitions on where the march could go, on the bands which can participate, on starting and dispersal times, on the playing of music or the sorts of music that could be played and stops along the route.

Code of Conduct

11.17　The third document the Commission was required to prepared by the legislation (as well as its Guidelines and procedural rules) was a Code providing guidance to people organising a public procession or protest meetings and regulating the conduct of people participating. It is designed to assist organisers by providing a checklist of the points they will need to cover and the issues they will need to address in planning and on the day. It aims to strike a balance to ensure that people can participate in parades while minimising disruption to those who work or live on the routes. The Commission takes into account compliance with the Code when considering whether or not to impose conditions on a parade.

11.18　The Code covers:
- *routes* – it requires the organiser to consider factors about the route including:
the level of commercial activity to ensure that the organisers give notice to businesses through flysheets, posters or a public notice in a newspaper so that they can make alternative arrangements where necessary;
whether the routes pass places of worship to determine whether any services are taking place at the time of the parade;
whether the route passes through a residential area and the organiser is required to let the local people know and, if the majority population are of a different tradition or interface area the organiser must establish a line of communication;
whether the route passes along a main road as this will require traffic diversions and stewards briefed about the safety issues involved.
- *Timing* – the code makes clear the timings notified must be definitive and that parades in the dark pose health and safety issues;
- *Bands* – the code emphasises the need to establish and enforce high standards with bands and to ensure that these are reflected in their contracts;
- *Stewarding* – the code reinforces the importance of properly trained stewards who are aware of their responsibilities and how to react in unforeseen circumstances. The number will vary according to the size of the parade, the length and nature of the route. They must be clearly identified and have an effective means of communication;
- *Giving notice* – the Code explains that the statutory notice period is 28 days but encourages organisers to give more notice if possible to help effective planning; and
- *Preparation* – the Code emphasises the importance of good preparation to ensure a successful event.

11.19　The other key area on which the Code provides guidance is on the behaviour of those participating. It provides that:

Behaviour – All participants in parades should:
- behave with due regard for the rights, traditions and feeling of others in the vicinity;
- refrain from using words or behaviour which could reasonably be perceived as being intentionally sectarian, provocative, threatening, abusive, insulting or lewd;

- obey the lawful directions of parade organisers and stewards at all times, from assembly to dispersal;
- abide by the conditions of this Code of Conduct; and
- comply with police directions and in accordance with legislation.

Dress – No paramilitary-style clothing is to be worn at any time during a parade.

Parade – Whenever possible, the parade should be positioned on one side of the carriageway so as to allow for the free flow of traffic, or as otherwise stipulated by police.

Route – Participants should keep to the designated route as directed by the police.

Alcohol – Alcohol should not be consumed immediately prior to, or during a parade. An organiser or steward, who believes a participant to be under the influence of alcohol, should take the necessary measures to remove that person from the parade.

Bands and Music – Each band must clearly display its name. Restrictions on the playing of music will be in accordance with the conditions as set out in Appendix B of the Code. No musical instrument will bear any inscription or mark of a proscribed organisation.

Flags etc – Flags and other displays often have a legitimate historical significance, but in no circumstances should such items relating to a proscribed organisation be displayed.

Stewards – The names of stewards will have been notified to the police and the Parades Commission at the time of notifying the proposed parade. Stewards should:
- be properly trained;
- be briefed by the organisers prior to the parade;
- carry proof of their status at all times during the event, and provide this information to police on request;
- be fully aware of their responsibilities and role;
- be highly visible by means of jackets, singlets, armbands, etc.;
- not consume alcohol before or during the parade;
- cooperate with the police; and
- be prepared to identify to the police any persons in the parade who may be committing any offence against criminal law.

Policing – Organisers of parades must cooperate with the police from the time of submission of the notice of intention to parade until the parade disperses.

Dispersal – When a parade has concluded, all those taking part must disperse immediately. It will be the responsibility of the organisers to ensure compliance with instructions in this regard.

Abiding by Conditions – Organisers must ensure that all participants in any parade have been informed of any conditions imposed. As a general principle, the organiser is responsible for the behaviour of all participants and for ensuring compliance with the Code of Conduct.

11.20 The Code also provides additional guidance for those participating in parades in the vicinity of sensitive locations:

Places of Worship – Only hymn tunes should be played; when church services are taking place, no music should be played; there should be no irreverent behaviour; and marching should be dignified.

War Memorials and Cemeteries – Only hymn tunes should be played; behaviour should be respectful; and marching should be dignified.

Where the Majority Population of the Vicinity are of a Different Tradition, and in Interface Areas – behaviour should be respectful; there should be no excessively loud drumming; participants should refrain from conduct, words, music or behaviour which could reasonably be perceived as intentionally sectarian, provocative, threatening, abusive, insulting or lewd; and marching should be dignified.

The Police and the Parades Commission

11.21 The Police have appointed a full time liaison officer to work with the Commission to provide a link between the police districts and the Commission. In evidence to the Northern Ireland Affairs Committee, the Assistant Chief Constable said that *'we have built up a very professional working relationship and we hope we are able to iron out any or all the issues or any problems that potentially come about and there have not been all that many.'* He noted that *'The Commission has dealt very professionally with the police, treating all of our correspondence with confidentiality, and this trust we feel has been very important…'* The Police and the Commission hold a joint seminar annually to allow the exchange of views and have joint protocols in place to promote better coordination and understanding which set out clearly the respective responsibilities at every stage of the parades process. Sometimes the Commission reject the police's advice about the public order implications of a parade, but this is normally resolved through negotiation and the police have never asked the Secretary of State to consider overturning a determination.

After the parade

11.22 The Police complete a report on the conduct of the parade. These reports are collated centrally by the police officer who liaises with the Parades Commission.

Protest meetings

11.23 The arrangements for protest meetings related to parades are different. Here organisers need to give 14 days notice to the police on a prescribed form. These forms are copied to the Parades Commission, but the police are responsible for making decisions and placing any conditions on the protest.

Review of the Operation of the Parades Commission, 'The Quigley Review'

11.24 Sir George Quigley was appointed by the Secretary of State for Northern Ireland (Dr John Reid) in November 2001 to review the operation of the Parades Commission and the legislation under which it was established and to consider whether there were any changes which could promote further public confidence on all sides, respects for the rights of all and the peaceful resolution of disputes on parades. He wrote to a wide range of organisations and individuals inviting views and received 104 written submissions and supplemented this in depth discussion with some 60 individuals and representatives of organisations.

11.25 Quigley's report summarised the evidence he had heard. He recorded that there was support for a proactive, mediation-type function to try and achieve local settlement without the need for formal determination. If a formal determination was needed, people wanted to understand better why decisions had been reached and wanted a more open and transparent process. There was also broad acceptance that parades needed to be managed more effectively and organisers should accept their responsibility and be made more accountable for their events. There was a general acceptance that independent third party regulatory machinery was necessary, even amongst those who were critical of the operation of the Parades Commission.

11.26 In his options for the future, Quigley recommended that there was a need to build on the work of the Parades Commission to accelerate the trend towards local accommodation so that fewer cases would require formal determination and outcomes achieved within a framework that was transparently fair and recognised as such. Quigley wanted to see a stronger and more structured role for facilitation, with the establishment of a function charged with facilitating settlement set within the regulatory machinery. He felt there should be a separate rights-based judicial tribunal for making determinations. Where determinations were necessary he thought there should be more clarity about the process which resulted in the determination. He was concerned by the Commission's confidentiality rule surrounding evidence given to it and wanted organisers to be aware of objections and meet to discuss those objections. He wanted to see a much longer notification period of at least six months, with most notifications being submitted in the October before the parade was to take place. He wanted to see better organised parades based on a revised Code of Conduct to emphasise the organisers' responsibilities. Finally, he recommended that a band registration scheme be set up for those bands which did not subscribe to other appropriate codes of conduct.

11.27 Sir George Quigley's Report was submitted to the Secretary of State for Northern Ireland on 27 September 2002 and issued for public consultation on 7 November 2002. Following representations from both sides of the community, including the Orange Order, it became apparent that many organisations would benefit from some extra time in order to come to a clear view on the report. Therefore, on 6 February 2002 the consultation period was extended in order to give key groups time to respond to the consultation.

Northern Ireland Affairs Committee Inquiry

11.28 The Northern Ireland Affairs Committee (NIAC) announced that it was to conduct an inquiry into the Parades Commission and the Public Processions (Northern Ireland) Act 1998 in September 2003. The review took as its starting point the Quigley Report. The Committee's primary concern was to examine:
- the response by Government and other interested parties to the Quigley Review;
- the case for implementing key recommendations of the Quigley Review; and
- the legislative (or other) steps necessary to implement such recommendations, if appropriate.

11.29 The Committee heard from key stakeholders during 2004 and its findings were published on 10 January 2005. When giving evidence to the Committee, the Minister of State in the Northern Ireland Office responsible for parades committed to responding to NIAC's report after it was published.

Numbers of Parades in Northern Ireland

11.30 The following table summarises the numbers of parades taking place in Northern Ireland. The Parades Commission issue determinations on a small proportion (under 4%) of parades considered to be 'contentious'.

	2001	2002	2003	Mid Sept 2004
Total Parades Notified	3,400	3,300	3,270	2,962
Total Contentious	230	225	200	187
Determinations Issued	170	160	130	136
Associated Disorder	6	28	26	22

Policing Costs of Parades in Northern Ireland.

11.31 The police estimate that for the marching season of 2001-02 policing costs were in the region of £22.5 million, in 2002-03 £28.3 million (an increase reflecting a particular dispute) and in 2003-04 £18 million.

Part Three: Recommendations

Introduction to part three

1. There were five elements to my remit and I have grouped my recommendations in line with those five elements:

    Chapter 12 – Period of Notice – recommendations 1 – 8;
    Chapter 13 – Informing and Involving the Community – recommendations 9 – 14;
    Chapter 14 – Decision making – recommendation 15 to 23;
    Chapter 15 – Numbers and effects on communities – recommendations 24 – 35; and
    Chapter 16 – Police costs – recommendations 36 – 38.

    There is, of course, an interaction and interdependence between them and it is best if my recommendations are viewed as a package which, if implemented, should lead to a modernised and professional decision making process which will improve people's experiences of processions. They should ensure better organised processions, minimising unnecessary disruption. My recommendations aim to strike a balance between the rights of those who want to march and the rights of communities to go about their daily business undisturbed.

2. My recommendations for improvements are made to the Scottish Executive and it will be for them to decide to accept or reject them. It will also be for them to consider how my recommendations can best be implemented to ensure they achieve the intended purpose. It is likely, however, that some of my recommendations will require changes to legislation and may take time to effect. Others might be able to be taken forward without such legislative changes. Successful implementation is likely to require the commitment of all involved in processions, including the Scottish Executive, local authorities and the police as well as the commitment of organisers.

12 Recommendations on first element of remit – the period of notice

Introduction and summary

12.1 This chapter makes recommendations on the first element of my remit, the period of notice organisers are required to give to local authorities and the police. It also makes recommendations on some related issues, such as the processes I consider should be followed during the notification period and which organisations should be required to give notice.

12.2 My recommendations propose that organisers in general give 28 days notice of their intention to hold a procession, although this timescale should be waived in certain limited circumstances. No one should be exempt from this requirement. Local authorities and the police should develop expertise in dealing with notifications through putting in place 'single gateways'. There should be clear steps to be taken during the extended notice period. As part of the process of considering a notification, local authorities should complete risk assessments and impact analyses on notifications. To ensure that the recommendations are being followed, there should be effective monitoring systems put in place. The development and sharing of good practice should also be supported.

Recommendations

Extending the period of notice

12.3 Under the Civic Government (Scotland) Act 1982, organisers are only required to give local authorities and the police seven days notice of their intention to hold a procession. While this is similar to the requirement in England and Wales, it is much shorter than the 28 day notification required in Northern Ireland. Local authorities then have only seven days to consider the application and are required to give the organiser their decision on the notice as early as possible and wherever it is practical at least two days before the procession is due to take place. Seven days notice clearly allows local authorities time only to give notifications the most cursory of consideration and it is difficult for them to do anything other than seek a view from the police, to inform the local councillor of the proposal and to consider appropriate

12.4 The information I have collected during the Review and views expressed to me suggest that the current system only seems to work because most organisers act responsibly and give as much notice as they can, in many cases at least a month and sometimes considerably longer. A large majority of people supported an extension of the notification period. They had varying views about how long an extended period should be from a small increase to 14 days, through 28 days to two months and, in some cases, considerably longer. A longer notification period would: enable local authorities to consider the notification in more detail; help more effective planning of police resources; and ensure that communities have more notice of proposed processions in their areas and an opportunity to express their views. I consider 28 days represented a more appropriate notification period.

12.5 I recommend that organisers, in the majority of cases, be required to give the local authority and the police at least 28 days notice. As at present, where organisers can give longer notice they should do so.

Recommendation 1

- Organisers should give 28 days notice to local authorities and the police of their intention to hold a procession.

Exceptions to the 28 day period

12.6 The Civic Government (Scotland) Act 1982 provides for local authorities to dispense with the seven day notification period. I think it is important to ensure that provision for an exemption to the notification period continues and recommend that local authorities should be able to waive the notification period in certain circumstances, for example, where the reason for the procession could not have reasonably been foreseen. This would cover processions that take place as a result of a political announcement, an economic announcement (for example to close a factory), a local decision (for example to close a hospital), or a sporting achievement. Where the notification period is shorter than the general 28 day period, certain of the key steps outlined under recommendation 5 might need to be missed out. However, wherever possible organisers should ensure they give at least 28 days notice.

Recommendation 2

- In certain circumstances, where processions are arranged in response to unforeseen events, the 28 days notification period should be waived and organisers should be able to give less notice.

Exempt organisations

12.7 The current legislation enables local authorities to exempt organisers from giving notice to them of their intention to hold a procession. To do this, local authorities need to make an order listing the exempt groups. It is clear that this power has been differently interpreted across local authorities with some authorities having very few exempt organisations and others having upwards of 300. In many cases, these organisations will currently need to notify the police to ensure that there is appropriate policing for their processions. Many exempt organisations already notify the council and are often separately in contact with various departments of the council to discuss traffic management arrangements or possible licensing requirements. The legislation also exempts organisers of processions commonly or customarily held from notifying local authorities, although again these organisers will in many cases inform the police. The provision for exempt organisations means that local authorities will never the have full picture of the events taking place in their area nor can communities be aware of all the processions that may affect them.

12.8 I recommend that all organisations be required to inform local authorities of their intention to hold a procession, although there might be scope for certain organisations to be exempt from some of the other requirements which I later recommend. This is a different approach from that currently adopted but I think it is important that there is a more consistent approach. Notification should not be an onerous requirement, as exempt groups organising processions currently contact the police and are very often in contact with the council. It should not discourage small, community groups from holding processions. It will add a small additional step to their planning process. However, it will ensure that local authorities and communities have the full picture of processions taking place in their areas and the possible disruption that might be caused. It will help to identify possible clashes in times and routes between processions being organised.

Recommendation 3

- All organisers should notify their intention to march to local authorities and the police.

A 'single gateway' in local authorities and the police

12.9 Organisers currently send their notifications to a variety of local authority departments such as the council solicitor, the chief executive's department or the clerk of the licensing committee. Depending on the nature of their notification, organisers may then have contact with a wide range of council officials from those dealing with transport and traffic management to those dealing with entertainment licensing. In day to day dealings with the police, organisers also report contact with a number of different officers. The range of contact points can be confusing for organisers. Some organisers have pointed out the difficulty of identifying an appropriate contact point or from where they can obtain advice. There is also a risk of organisers being given inconsistent advice from different parts of organisations.

12.10 I have seen good practice in some authorities in helping organisers take forward their planning where specialised units coordinating arrangements for processions and other events have been developed. This allows expertise to develop and also ensures that organisers get consistent, expert advice. It also allows good networks of contacts to be built up and good practice to be developed. I think that a more coordinated approach would be helpful to local authorities, the police and to organisers and recommend that local authorities and the police establish a 'single gateway' within their respective organisations to coordinate notifications for processions.

Recommendation 4
- Local authorities and the police should set up 'single gateways' within their organisations to deal with procession notifications.

Action by local authorities during the 28 day notification period

12.11 The current legislation allows little time for notifications to be considered and local authorities and the police have developed, over time, their own systems to ensure that they are meeting the statutory timetable and requirements. These systems differ across Scotland, reflecting in part different local circumstances, but also leading to a lack of consistency in the way that notifications are handled. A longer notification period will allow more time for notifications to be analysed in greater detail. While it is important to ensure there is space for local discretion, it is also important to ensure that there is a more consistent approach with some key standard steps taken in all local authorities and police forces.

12.12 I recommend that there be some standard key steps, agreed with local authorities and the police, to be taken in the 28 day notification period. This will be helpful in setting out clearly to all involved how the notification will be considered. There should be a clear timetable for the key steps that need to be taken in the assessment process. It will ensure a more consistent and professional approach to assessments and will also ensure that the procedures for taking decisions are transparent to organisers and communities. There could be exemptions from some of these key steps for certain organisations and processions where the 28 day notification period has been waived.

12.13 I consider that the key steps to be taken should include:

Week one
- Organiser submits signed notification to local authority and to police;
- Local authority and police acknowledge receipt of notification;
- Local authority makes arrangements with organiser and police and, depending on nature of procession being notified, other groups (for example, other emergency services, the health service, community groups) for a meeting to discuss the notification;

	• Local authority publicises the notification according to its agreed procedures giving two weeks for views to be submitted and explaining how those views will be taken into account; and
• Local authority provides information to its 'opt-in list' (for example business organisations, churches, community councils) about notification giving two weeks for views.
Week two	• Meeting takes place with organiser, police and local authority to discuss the notification which is recorded with an agreed outcome agreement;
• Local authority carries out risk assessment and impact analysis together with a critical consideration of the notification; and
• Police carry out own risk assessment to inform operational policing plan.
Week three	• Views from public submitted by given deadline;
• Views from opt-in list submitted by given deadline;
• Views from police submitted; and
• Risk assessment and risk analysis completed. Depending on the outcome of the risk assessment, organisers might be encouraged to take out insurance if they have not already done so or provide a behaviour bond.
Week four	• Information reviewed to ensure that circumstances have not changed;
• Local authority considers all information received on the notification according to its agreed procedures (by officials or by committee);
• Local authority makes an order about the procession (if appropriate imposing conditions, prohibitions);
• If necessary, local authority discusses outcome of its consideration of views with organiser;
• Local authority issues organiser with a 'permit to process' outlining what was agreed in the notification, any formal order it has made and the agreed code of conduct; and
• Local authority publicises procession and any possible disruption through its agreed procedures.
After procession	• Procession takes place;
• Debriefing meeting with organiser, police and local authority and if appropriate other groups to discuss experiences and to agree record; and
• Record of procession kept to be taken into account in any future notification.

Recommendation 5

- Local authorities and the police should take certain key steps to assess notifications during the extended notification period.

Risk assessment and impact analysis

12.14 A longer notification period will allow local authorities to complete a more detailed risk assessment and impact analysis of notifications. There is considerable expertise and guidance on how to complete a risk assessment. 'The Event Safety Guide – a guide to health, safety and welfare at music and similar events' produced by the Health and Safety Executive is a key source of advice. It describes the purpose of a risk assessment as being to *'identify hazards which could cause harm, assess the risks which may arise from those hazards and decide on suitable measures to eliminate, or control, the risk.'* 'Hazards' are defined as *'anything which has the potential to cause harm to people'* such as a dangerous property or an item or a substance, a condition, a situation or an activity. 'Risk' is the *'likelihood that the harm from a hazard is realised and the extent of it'*. In risk assessments, risk should reflect both the likelihood that harm will occur and its severity. There are some straightforward steps in risk assessment, deciding what the risks are, deciding what the consequences would be, deciding how likely they are, deciding what needs to be done to negate or reduce the risk and deciding who needs to do it.

12.15 The risk assessment completed by the local authority will highlight issues that it needs to take into account when reaching a decision on a notification. For example, it might show that the route takes the marchers pass a building due for demolition and so an alternative route would need to be considered. A risk assessment will produce good quality factually based material used to inform the decision making process.

12.16 A risk assessment should also be accompanied by an impact analysis. This will enable the local authority to identify systematically the impact a procession might have. The authority could consider the disruption to the life of the community that a procession might cause, for example disruption to traffic, to access, and to business. In analysing the impact they would need to consider whether there were other events taking place that would affect the proposed procession. As part of the impact analysis, local authorities may want to consider the impact that the numbers of parades are having in a particular area. Again, this will produce good quality factually based material that should be used to inform the decision making process.

12.17 These assessments should be done by the 'single gateway' ensuring expertise and a consistency of approach.

12.18 This does not take away from the organisers' own responsibility to carry out their own risk assessment and I look at organisers' responsibility in some detail in Chapter 15 dealing with the fourth element of my remit, looking at the numbers of marches and the effects of processions on communities.

Recommendation 6
- Local authorities should complete risk assessments and impact analyses on notifications to provide good quality, factually based information to inform the decision making process.

Making sure new procedures are implemented effectively

12.19 My recommendations are, in the main, not prescriptive and allow local authorities and the police an appropriate level of discretion to enable them to put in place arrangements which are appropriate for their local circumstances. What is important is that they do put in place effective arrangements so that they follow the key standard steps. To ensure that this happens and the various mechanisms are effective, there needs to be an independent monitoring system. I recommend that the Scottish Executive looks in detail at how this could be achieved. I do not think that this requires a separate body but would hope that this could build on existing monitoring arrangements. It should not be overly burdensome for authorities or the police, or indeed, those carrying out the monitoring.

12.20 Such monitoring could look to local authorities and the police to demonstrate that they had in place effective arrangements for marches and processions in line with the recommended changes to the processes, including having in place effective mechanisms to gather and take into account community views. A regular report should be produced on how the procedures are being implemented and the effects that they are having. The report should be publicly available so that local communities can see how their authorities and police force are implementing the procedures and taking decisions on marches.

Recommendation 7
- The Scottish Executive should ensure that there are effective monitoring arrangements in place to demonstrate that local authorities and the police are implementing the new procedures in a way appropriate to their local circumstances with a regular public report produced.

Sharing good practice

12.21 It is clear that arrangements for handling notifications on processions vary across Scotland. A longer notification period and some standard key steps which need to be taken in assessing notifications will result in a more professional and transparent decision making process.

12.22 I welcomed, during the course of the Review, the good practice developed in some areas, for example in producing clear and straightforward guidance for organisers and in developing coordinating units within local authorities. It is important that the experiences surrounding processions are more widely shared so that those involved can learn from each other. While there will always be differences in authorities' approaches for good reasons, there is scope for sharing experiences and processes. For example, local authorities might want to share information about the variability of conditions they set for marchers' behaviour and on how they take forward community consultation or develop 'How To' guidance for organisers. There is an important role here for local authorities associations and networks (like COSLA and SOLACE) and for police associations (like ACPOS, ASPS and SPF).

Recommendation 8
- Local authority associations and police associations should ensure good practice is shared more widely.

First element of remit: period of notice – summary of recommendations

Recommendation 1
- Organisers should give 28 days notice to local authorities and the police of their intention to hold a procession.

Recommendation 2
- In certain circumstances, where processions are arranged in response to unforeseen events, the 28 days notification period should be waived and organisers should be able to give less notice.

Recommendation 3
- All organisers should notify their intention to march to local authorities and the police.

Recommendation 4
- Local authorities and the police should set up 'single gateways' within their organisations to deal with procession notifications.

Recommendation 5
- Local authorities and the police should take certain key steps to assess notifications during the extended notification period.

Recommendation 6
- Local authorities should complete risk assessments and impact analyses on notifications to provide good quality, factually based information to inform the decision making process.

Recommendation 7
- The Scottish Executive should ensure that there are effective monitoring arrangements in place to demonstrate that local authorities and the police are implementing the new procedures in a way appropriate to their local circumstances with a regular public report produced.

Recommendation 8
- Local authority associations and police associations should ensure good practice is shared more widely.

13 Recommendations on second element of remit – informing and involving the community

Introduction and summary

13.1 The second element of my remit was to look at how the community could input into decisions about marches and parades. I saw two distinct parts to this element of my remit: the first ensuring that the community was better informed; and the second ensuring the community had a way of expressing views about procession notifications.

13.2 A careful balance needs to be struck, between the rights of those who want to exercise their right to peaceful assembly through a procession and the rights of the community to go about their daily lives unhindered and without disruption. Without that balance, the exercise of rights by one section of the community can interfere with the exercise of the rights by another section of the community. It was clear that some people thought that not enough importance was being put on the rights of the community to go about their daily lives unhindered. It was also clear that some people would simply like certain types of marches banned. However, that is not appropriate in a democracy and my recommendations are aimed at striking an appropriate balance. My recommendations addressing the numbers and effects in communities of marches, in Chapter 15 should also be helpful in minimising the disruption felt, so helping communities feel less threatened by some marches and the behaviour they associate with them.

13.3 My recommendations will improve information given to communities by requiring local authorities to prepare and publicise an annual digest of processions, provide up-to-date information about up and coming processions to communities and to an 'opt-in' list of key interests. My recommendations will also ensure that: communities are more involved by requiring local authorities to develop appropriate mechanisms to give communities the opportunity to express their views; local authorities can consider those views as part of their overall assessment of procession notifications; and communities know how their views will be considered.

Recommendations
Informing the community

13.4 I heard many anecdotes over the course of the Review about the effects of processions where communities did not find out about potentially disruptive events until very shortly before they were taking place. That prevented people and businesses from making other arrangements which they could have done had they been told further in advance. This was supported by the telephone survey which showed that almost 40% of people wanted to be told more about processions in their area. It cannot be right that people get minimal or no warning of processions which can cause considerable disruption to their ability to go about their normal daily lives. Greater warning will allow people to make more informed decisions and reduce the irritation they feel at unexpected disruption.

An annual digest

13.5 To ensure that communities get more information about marches well in advance, I recommend that local authorities produce an annual digest of marches at the beginning of every calendar year, up-dated regularly and well publicised. Local authorities should decide the most appropriate way to publicise the digest, perhaps through council newspapers, council websites, having a copy available in council offices and libraries or through circulating to representative groups (for example chambers of commerce or community councils) within the area to allow them to highlight it to their networks. In preparing the digest, local authorities should bring together the organisers of processions, based on their experience and records of events arranged in the previous years. This will help to ensure that there is clarity around the dates for future processions and identify early in the year where there is the potential for clashes. The digest should be updated and recirculated every quarter. The digest should be a comprehensive list of all processions so that communities know well in advance about potential disruption. I am sure that organisers will be receptive to this local discussion. I was pleased to note the offer made by Cairde na hÉireann that they would be prepared to meet with the representatives of the Loyal Orange Institution to discuss the dates of their processions to ensure that clashes could be avoided.

Recommendation 9

- Local authorities should prepare an annual digest of processions with organisers at the beginning of the calendar year and update it every quarter and ensure the digest is well publicised and accessible.

Information about decisions on processions

13.6 An annual digest needs to be supplemented by regular information about processions once decisions are taken on notifications. I recommend that once local authorities have taken their decisions, they publicise the procession widely using the most appropriate medium. Again, I think that it is important that the local authority decides how this is best done in their area. They could, for example, make use of local media (newspapers and radio) to draw attention to the procession, email alerts, websites, posters on routes or in local authority offices or maybe sending letters to those who will be affected. I considered whether publicising processions should be the responsibility of the organiser and, while I would encourage organisers to provide better information and engage with communities, I think the duty to ensure that the community is informed of potential disruption should lie with the local authority.

Recommendation 10
- Local authorities should provide up-to-date information about forthcoming processions to local communities using the most appropriate means.

An 'opt-in' list for information

13.7 It is important for local authorities to ensure that some key groups receive updates about processions. I recommend that each local authority develops an 'opt-in' list so that people can identify if they want to receive further information about processions. For example, churches could opt-in so that they were aware of processions happening in their area so that they could avoid clashes with services such as funerals or draw attention to possible problems with already arranged services such as weddings. Business groups could also opt-in to getting information so that they could rearrange deliveries that were planned at the same time as a procession. Transport operators could also be alerted to allow them to plan altered services where necessary. This opt-in list already operates well in the City of London where businesses receive email alerts of potential disruption caused by processions.

Recommendation 11
- Local authorities should maintain an 'opt-in' list for organisations to receive information about processions.

Involving the community

13.8 Providing improved information about processions is very important but it is not sufficient in itself. People need to be able to express their views about processions and to know what scope they have for influencing the decision making process. Under the current system, local authorities seek the views of the local elected member as representative of their community, as under the statutory timetable, they have little time to do otherwise nor are they required to do more. I also noted a degree of caution in local authorities as to how far it is appropriate for them to take into account wider views, such as those expressed by the community. They drew attention to Sheriff Court judgements concerned about making decisions based on 'emotion or personal feeling' and emphasised that there needed to be substantive information to back up decisions founded on 'public perception'.

13.9   It is important that local authorities do more to ensure that they are aware of public views on a procession. It is also important that the public understands what they can influence. It is clear under human rights legislation that views which differ from the majority view should be heard. Prohibiting a procession simply because the group represents a view that annoys or gives offence to others is inappropriate in a democracy. Local authorities should not be making decisions on what legal organisations stand for but on the risk and impact of the procession. They might conclude that the risk and impact would be mitigated if there was a change to the route or other conditions applied. People need to be clear that simply because they do not personally like an organisation, that is an insufficient reason for a ban. Without that understanding about the context and what they can influence, people will naturally be frustrated if they feel that their views are not being taken into account.

Mechanisms to enable the community and others to express views

13.10   I reflected on whether each local authority should be required to establish a parades panel bringing together a wide range of interests to comment on procession notifications or should hold referendums on processions. I concluded that this would not be appropriate and that views could be sought more effectively in other ways. There is no need for local authorities to create additional mechanisms to do this. Community engagement and consultation is an important cornerstone in the way in which local authorities are required to work and they should build on these existing mechanisms.

13.11   I recommend that during the 28 day notification period, communities are given an opportunity to express their views on procession notifications. The mechanics for doing this will be for the local authority to decide so that views are gathered in a way most appropriate to that authority. The local authority must make clear how the community can make their views heard and publicise notifications appropriately to allow them to put forward views. This will ensure that decisions are not being taken on perception or feeling, but that it is demonstrably evidence based. I would encourage local authorities to take a broad view of who would have an interest in expressing views about notifications.

13.12   There are a variety of mechanisms that might be appropriate in enabling the community to express views. Some obvious ones include views being coordinated through: local elected members; community councils; local area committees; community engagement mechanisms under community planning or local community planning arrangements; other forms of community engagement such as community safety partnerships; or people's panels. Some local authorities may prefer to invite comments to be sent direct to the 'single gateway' by the identified deadline.

13.13   The monitoring system proposed in recommendation 7 could look at whether local authorities have in place effective mechanisms to gather community views.

Recommendation 12

- Local authorities should establish mechanisms appropriate to their areas to ensure that communities are able to express views on processions.

Taking account of community views

13.14 Some local authorities are concerned that the current legislation does not allow them to take into account community views and they can only properly take into account the views of the police in considering procession notifications. This could be regarded by some as a somewhat narrow interpretation of the legislation and of associated sheriff judgements, which seem to suggest that it is hearsay and unsubstantiated perception that should not form the basis for decisions. However, it is important that there is clarity around the views that local authorities can and cannot properly take into account when reaching their decisions. I recommend that it is appropriate that local authorities should take into account a wider range of views than those of the police as part of their consideration of procession notifications. The wider range of views should include community views. This should lead to more informed decision making.

Recommendation 13

- Local authorities should take into account wider views, including community views, when taking decisions on procession notifications.

Procedures to consider the views of communities and others as part of the notification process

13.15 Local authorities should be required to take into account the views of communities and others when deciding on whether or not to prohibit or impose conditions on a procession. Community views will be those expressed through the mechanisms developed under recommendation 12. How they take those views into account will be for local authorities to decide. However, they should ensure that they have transparent procedures in place to enable them to consider community views in a consistent way. They should explain to organisers and to the community how community views will be taken into account alongside the other views and information they have. It will be for local authorities to decide how to do this most appropriately, but they will want to consider how community views will be made available to organisers and whether there is scope for anonymous views to be considered. Local authorities may want to consider developing procedures parallel to the ones they have in place for objections to formal licence applications under the licensing provisions of the Civic Government (Scotland) Act 1982.

13.16 The monitoring system proposed in recommendation 7 could look at whether local authorities had in place effective mechanisms for considering community views.

Recommendation 14

- Local authorities should put in place clear procedures for considering community views.

Second element of remit: informing and involving the community – summary of recommendations

Recommendation 9
- Local authorities should prepare an annual digest of processions with organisers at the beginning of the calendar year and update it every quarter and ensure the digest is well publicised and accessible.

Recommendation 10
- Local authorities should provide up-to-date information about forthcoming processions to local communities using the most appropriate means.

Recommendation 11
- Local authorities should maintain an 'opt-in' list for organisations to receive information about processions.

Recommendation 12
- Local authorities should establish mechanisms appropriate to their areas to ensure that communities are able to express views on processions.

Recommendation 13
- Local authorities should take into account wider views, including community views, when taking decisions on procession notifications.

Recommendation 14
- Local authorities should put in place clear procedures for considering community views.

14 Recommendations on third element of remit – decision making

Introduction and summary

14.1 The third element of my remit was to look at the basis for determining when to restrict, refuse or reroute marches and parades. Local authorities are responsible for taking decisions on procession notifications under the current legislation, after consulting with the police and, if the procession is taking place in a National Park, the National Park authority. The processes for taking decisions vary and there is little time for a detailed analysis of notifications. Local authorities often feel constrained in the issues they can take into account. It is important to modernise and professionalise these arrangements.

14.2 My recommendations aim to improve current decision making processes by providing that local authorities continue to be responsible for taking decisions on notifications. I do not think that creating a new independent body to take decisions on procession notifications is appropriate in Scotland. In reaching decisions, local authorities should be able to take into account a wider range of variables based on evidence. They should be able to impose conditions on processions appropriate to address any concerns about its conduct. These conditions must, of course, comply with the relevant provisions in ECHR and the Human Rights Act 1998.

14.3 Generally, local authorities should respect the importance of traditional dates and organisers should be prepared where necessary to compromise over routes. The local authority should facilitate a meeting at the beginning of the process to discuss the notification with the organiser and the police, resulting in a signed outcome agreement. Local authorities should summarise the discussions, code of conduct and any conditions imposed on the procession in one document, a 'permit to process'. Recorded debriefing should follow processions, providing evidence about what happened, which can be taken into account in future notifications and inform future arrangements.

Recommendations

Who should make decisions?

14.4 Under the Civic Government (Scotland) Act 1982, local authorities are responsible for making decisions about procession notifications, requiring them to consult with the chief constable (and if relevant with a National Park authority). I consider local authorities are best placed to continue to take decisions on processions. Local authorities in Scotland are democratically accountable to their local communities. They take decisions on a wide range of issues for those communities. They are close to their communities and should act in a way that is appropriate to local circumstances, taking into account the views of their communities as they do so.

14.5 Given Scottish circumstances, therefore, I do not think that there is a need to establish an independent body, akin to the Parades Commission for Northern Ireland, for Scotland. The Parades Commission was set up following a detailed review of arrangements for processions in Northern Ireland prompted by various serious disputes in the summer of 1996 which required major intervention by the police. Previously decisions had been taken by the police. With the creation of the Parades Commission in 1998, decision making passed to a new and independent body, creating a distance between the decision making authority and the authority responsible for policing those decisions.

14.6 Clearly, the creation of the Parades Commission reflects circumstances in Northern Ireland. Its role is to make determinations on processions and also to support mediation and promote greater understanding between the different communities. Our history and culture are different. There can be no doubt that certain parades in Scotland, particularly those organised by the Loyalist Institutions, do cause issues for communities. I have heard considerable anecdotal evidence from people who have felt intimidated by parades they describe as 'sectarian' and which they feel 'promote bigotry'. However, we are fortunate that processions in Scotland have never lead to the sort of violence and tension experienced in the past in Northern Ireland. We do not have the same intensity of divisions within our society in this sphere of activity. More practically, organisers here have been receptive to compromise and prepared to enter into discussion with local authorities and the police.

14.7 I consider it would be disproportionate, given the number of processions taking place and the effects they have, to set up new and independent machinery to take decisions on processions. Nor do I think there is a role for a nationally appointed 'Parades Tzar'. Removing decision making from local authorities would lose the importance of a local link with decision making, based where communities are able to influence decisions which impact upon them. I believe it is more important to ensure that existing approaches work more effectively.

14.8 It was suggested by some during the course of the Review that decisions on processions should be taken by the police, as was the case in Northern Ireland and as is the case in England and Wales. The police have an important part to play in the overall decision making process, bringing evidence and information and taking an active part in discussions and planning. I think it is most appropriate that the decision should, however, remain with the locally elected body, as it is currently.

14.9 However, we must improve the way that the current decision making processes are implemented. I have come across too much inconsistency in approach. Local authorities need to exercise their powers responsibly and professionally and be given the right tools to support them in that duty. Organisers too need to ensure they adopt a responsible and professional approach. There are aspects of approaches elsewhere in the UK from which we can learn and we should not shut our minds to that. For example, there are aspects of the operation of the Parades Commission which could be applicable to Scotland: a recognised code of conduct; and transparent guidelines on the decision making process. Similarly, there are aspects of the approach in England, with more regular debriefing, more expert planning and better ways of telling communities that would work well in Scotland. There also needs to be some way of ensuring that an improved approach is being followed and, while I do not think that this is a role for a new national body, there does need to be effective monitoring, which I hope can be built into the responsibilities of existing bodies. I believe that the package of measures I recommend in my report, draws on the strengths of the current Scottish system but learns from others, where it is appropriate.

Recommendation 15
- Local authorities should remain responsible for taking decisions on procession notifications.

Grounds for making decisions on notifications

14.10 The Civic Government (Scotland) Act 1982 empowers local authorities to prohibit or impose conditions on a notified procession after they have consulted with the chief constable. This has seemed to lead to quite a narrow and restrictive interpretation of the legislation. Many local authorities believe it is only appropriate for them to consider public order and public safety issues when reaching decisions on notifications and feel that they are very restricted in the conditions which they can impose.

14.11 The European Convention for the Protection of Human Rights and Freedoms makes clear that the right to peaceful assembly is a qualified one. This recognises that people's rights might be in competition with other people's rights and with the public interest and there may be a need to impose restrictions. The restrictions that can be imposed are those *'prescribed by law and are necessary in a democratic society in the interest of national security or public safety, for the prevention of disorder or crime, for the protection of health or morals or for the protection of rights and freedoms of others'*. To be necessary in a democratic society, a restriction should correspond to a *'pressing social need'* should be proportionate to the aim pursued and should be justified by relevant and sufficient reasons.

14.12 Examples of the kind of restrictions that have been adopted in UK law are set out in the Public Order Act 1986. That Act provides that conditions can be imposed if there is a reasonable belief that the procession would lead to serious public disorder; serious damage to property; serious disruption to the life of the community; or intimidation.

14.13 Against that background, I consider that it is right that local authorities should properly be able to take into account a much wider range of issues than just public order and public safety when reaching their decisions on processions notifications. I think that approach fits well with the tenor of human rights legislation which is clear that the right to peaceful assembly is not an absolute one but a qualified one, where a range of restrictions can be imposed.

14.14 The information I received in written submissions and discussion generally supported me in coming to my conclusion. While considerations of public safety and public security should remain of paramount importance, most people felt there were wider considerations that should be taken into account. I found similar results in the telephone survey.

14.15 I recommend that local authorities should properly be able to take into account a wider range of issues when reaching their decisions about the conditions to be set on marches. There needs to be a consistent approach across Scotland, clarity about what those issues should be and the evidence which can be used to support decisions. A widening of the variables to be taken into account does, of course, need to be appropriate within the context of the ECHR framework.

14.16 The basis of the decision making process needs to be transparent to organisers so that they understand the types of issues that local authorities will properly be taking into account and the evidence they will be using to support the decisions. Local authorities will also need to explain their decisions and the reasons behind them to organisers and ensure that they are justified. It is also important that the decision making process is transparent to the general public so they understand how local authorities take their decisions. A longer notification period with a detailed risk assessment and impact analysis alongside the consideration of any views received from interested parties should produce factual information that can be substantiated and documented. As regular debriefings take place after each event, a record of the behaviour at processions will be built up, again contributing to the evidence base. It should be clear to organisers that the evidence of their behaviour collected as part of the debriefing process will be taken into account in considering notifications.

14.17 Many issues were suggested to me as being appropriate to be considered as part of the decision making process. I consider that it is appropriate for the following issues to be taken into account by local authorities when reaching their decisions about processions:
- the risk of serious public disorder;
- the risk to public safety;
- the risk of serious damage to property;
- the risk of serious disruption to the life of the community;

- the risk of serious disruption to pedestrian and vehicular traffic;
- the risk of serious disruption to business;
- the risk of intimidation;
- the presence of environmental hazards; and
- health and safety issues.

14.18 These variables would allow local authorities to look at a much wider range of issues to consider the effects of a procession and whether imposing conditions could avoid or ameliorate some of the negative effects. For example, it would be appropriate for local authorities to consider:
- under aspects of disruption – whether there were any other events or processions taking place at the same time which would have an impact; whether businesses were having important deliveries being made at the same time; the amount of disruption that numbers of processions along a particular route were regularly causing to the same community;
- under intimidation – whether a route was being chosen to intimidate a particular section of the community, for example a far right group seeking to march through a community which was primarily minority ethnic or a predominantly gay area; whether a march appeared deliberately provocative; whether there were sensitive buildings on the route; or whether the organisers had peaceful intent;
- under environmental hazards – whether there had been changes to road layouts, road works, demolition or building works; or whether the roads were suitable for the march in terms of width or volume of traffic; and
- under aspects of the risk of public disorder – whether the risk assessment had shown a serious risk, perhaps looking at whether the relevant policing costs associated with preventing public disorder were disproportionate.

14.19 I would not expect that widening the range of issues which can be taken into account and ensuring there is clarity about those issues to lead to more bans. Clearly banning processions is a very extreme reaction in a democracy and should only be done in the rarest of circumstances. There still should be the presumption that processions should go ahead. However, I do think that a wider range of variables will allow a better balance to be struck between the rights of marchers and the rights of others. This will allow practical compromise around timings or routes based on sound reasoning and evidence.

Recommendation 16
- Local authorities should be able to take into account a wider range of issues when reaching decisions on notifications. Their decisions should be evidence based and explained to the organisers.

The sorts of conditions that can be imposed?

14.20 Currently, local authorities accept most notifications and do not impose conditions on them through the order making powers they have under the legislation. In many cases, rather than making a formal order under the Act, practical issues are discussed with the police, or sometimes with the roads departments of local authorities, resulting in organisers agreeing changes before conditions need to be imposed. The range of conditions formally imposed through orders have included conditions: to avoid clashes of dates, timing and routes of other processions; to enable proper arrangements to be made for police supervision; for better traffic management; and to make changes to bus services. Orders are usually made based on police concerns although health and safety issues are also taken into account. Some local authorities feel that they are overly limited in the scope of conditions they can set and the control they have on the conduct of processions in their areas. Separately, also, a number of authorities have conditions on the behaviour and conduct of marches which could be seen to be a voluntary code of conduct that organisers follow.

14.21 It is important that local authorities have a degree of flexibility in the conditions they can set on processions. Again, these restrictions should be informed by the requirements of the ECHR framework. Local authorities should not be unduly fettered in the conditions they can set, as long as they can demonstrate that they are proportionate to the aims of the restriction and imposed for a justifiable reason, which is based on evidence, and in response to an issue they have properly taken into account in their decision making process.

Recommendation 17

- Local authorities should have discretion to impose conditions proportionate to the notification and to address the issues upon which it based its decision.

The importance of dates and routes

14.22 There are certain dates that are traditionally very important to various organisations and communities. Many processions very often take place on the same date each year and are an important celebration for that community. It is important that, as far as is possible, local authorities should seek to respect these dates. For these annual events, organisers should be able to give considerably more than 28 days notice and these are the events that could form the backbone of an annual digest of marches discussed at the beginning of each calendar year.

14.23 To allow local authorities to respect the importance of traditional dates, there needs to be discussion and compromise around routes. I was pleased to note that many organisers, particularly those sometimes regarded as being intransigent over routes, recognised the importance of this compromise. For example the Grand Orange Lodge of Scotland made clear in their written submission that they would *'apply a cooperative attitude to any legitimate concerns with regard to parade dates, times or routes and make adjustments where necessary'*.

The Apprentice Boys of Derry gave a similar commitment. Cairde na hÉireann also recognise the need for *'genuine and voluntary negotiation'* and dialogue. It is important that organisers continue to adopt this reasonable approach.

Recommendation 18
- Local authorities should respect key traditional dates but organisers should be prepared to compromise over routes where necessary

Content of the notification

14.24   The current legislation makes provision for what organisers should include in their notification. It must include the date and time when the procession is to be held, its route, the number of people likely to take part, the arrangements for the control of the procession that the organiser is making and the name and address of the person who is holding that procession. Some local authorities provide forms for organisers to complete. The form is helpful in setting out clearly the information required by the authority and it often also sets out the general conditions expected for the conduct of processions. Other local authorities feel that, given the diverse nature of the processions taking place in their area, a standard form is inappropriate and written notice is requested covering the same key details about the procession. To ensure that they are able to reach a fully informed decision on the notification, some local authorities ask for other information to be provided including, the reason for the procession, the nature of the event, a check that the organiser has informed the police, whether it is an annual event, whether there will be a street collection, the assembly and dispersal arrangements, the names of any bands accompanying the procession with the named individual responsible for the band's behaviour as well as any details of a return procession. I consider a written, signed notification to be the key first step. The information in the notification should provide the basis for an initial discussion between the organiser, the local authority and the police.

Recommendation 19
- Organisers should provide a written, signed notification providing the key information required by the local authority.

Discussions before a march takes place

14.25   Once the signed notification has been received, at least 28 days before the intended date of the procession, the local authority should arrange to meet with the organiser, the police and, depending on the nature and size of the procession, any other key groups it considers relevant. Such groups might include, residents associations, community councils, the NHS Health Board, other emergency services, places of worship on the route and business organisations. A wider group will not be necessary for every notification. Currently such precursory discussions only take place between the organiser and the police. As the local authority is responsible for taking the final decision on the notification, they should be facilitating and centrally involved in these early discussions.

14.26 The basis of the precursory discussion should be the signed notification. Each aspect of the notification should be considered confirming the organisers, the purpose of the event, the assembly arrangements, the route of the procession, the timings of the procession and the dispersal arrangements. Such early discussion will uncover any initial practical problems – for example a clash with other arranged events, road works on the proposed route – and allow them to be considered, and if possible addressed. It might be that local authorities require more information from the organisers at this stage. For example, to establish the nature and purpose of the procession, the authority might want to consider the organisation's constitution.

14.27 The precursory meeting will also provide an opportunity to discuss wider issues about the notification, such as:
- the organiser's plans for public safety, such as the arrangements for control and coordination during the procession, whether there are any specific safety provisions and whether they have appointed a specific public safety officer;
- the organiser's plans for stewarding, the level of stewarding, the chief steward, head stewards, numbers of other stewards, their methods of communication, how they will be briefed on their role and their means of identification; and
- the organiser's plans for contingencies, such as the provisions for a delayed start, the provisions for discontinuing the procession, how to communicate any emergency route changes should they be necessary, alternative arrangements in the case of foul weather.

14.28 Clearly, this will require the organiser to have thought carefully about the arrangements for the procession. In most cases, before attending this meeting, the organiser will have completed a risk assessment for the procession which he might want to share with the local authority and the police. The precursory meeting will also give the local authority and the police an opportunity to go through aspects of the code of conduct that will be included as part of the 'permit to process' (see recommendation 21).

14.29 The outcome of the discussion should be agreed by all present and result in a signed agreement so that all are clear about the outcome. Should there be later disputes about what was agreed, this document will provide evidence of what was agreed. The local authority will then be able to consider the agreed record of the discussion as part of their consideration of the notification.

Recommendation 20
- There should be a precursory meeting following the submission of a signed notification facilitated by the local authority, involving at least the organiser and the police, resulting in a signed outcome agreement.

A 'permit to process'

14.30 Under the current legislation, organisers are required to submit a notification of their intention to organise a procession. It is a key principle of the legislation that they are not applying for permission to exercise their right to peaceful assembly but simply notifying the local authority and the police of their intention to do so. I considered whether, in fact, organisers should be applying for permission to process. I concluded, given the framework of the human rights legislation, that it is not appropriate to require people to seek approval from local authorities to exercise their right to peaceful assembly. However, the right it is a qualified one and there has been opinion by the European Commission on Human Rights that states it is appropriate for authorities to set up an authorisation process for processions on the public thoroughfare to ensure that processions are peaceful. The Civic Government (Scotland) Act 1982 sets out that authorisation process in Scotland. My recommendations are designed to improve and refresh that system building on its principles.

14.31 Under the existing legislation, the local authority has the power to accept the notification, set conditions on processions, or to prohibit them. I consider that local authorities should continue to have formal order-making powers to prohibit or impose conditions on processions. The provisions allowing such orders to be varied, revoked or appealed to the sheriff should also continue. However, in the vast majority of cases, the local authority accepts the notification and the procession goes ahead. Some local authorities acknowledge to the organisers that they have considered the notification and do not intend to impose conditions. I have ascertained that some local authorities do not inform organisers who are required to assume that their notification has been considered and accepted as they have not been advised to the contrary. This can be confusing to the organisers. I think that it is important that local authorities inform organisers in all cases that their notification has been considered and of the outcome of that consideration.

14.32 I think it would be helpful to local authorities, the police and to organisers, if the outcome of the consideration of the notification was recorded in a consistent and more standard way. Such a document, which I describe as a 'permit to process', could bring together the key strands of the notification process. The document could record what was agreed following the notification and the precursory meeting and set out the code of conduct that organisers and participants were expected to follow. In the very small minority of cases, where local authorities had exercised their powers to make an order setting formal conditions on the procession, the 'permit' could also record those conditions. This will ensure clarity on what had been agreed and what was expected – in effect, summarising the organisers' responsibilities.

14.33 In implementing this recommendation, further thought will need to be given to how breaches of aspects of the 'permit' (other than the conditions imposed by local authorities order-making powers) should be treated and whether there should be formal sanctions attached to breaches of agreements or the code of conduct. I consider that organisations' willingness to ensure they follow what was agreed and the code of conduct should be one aspect of the debriefing process (see recommendation 23). Local authorities should be able to take into account previous behaviour when considering future applications. Organisers who had not followed the 'permit' should expect to be required to prove for future notifications that they had taken action to address those areas of concern. For example, had the organisers' stewarding not proved effective, they might be expected to demonstrate that they had taken action to improve their arrangements.

Recommendation 21

- Once the notification has been considered by the local authority, the authority should issue organisers with a 'permit to process' outlining what had been agreed and what was expected.

A fee for a 'permit to process'?

14.34 The principle of paying fees for licences from local authorities is a well established one. For example, amongst others, taxis drivers, street traders, marker operators and metal detailers pay a fee for a licence. There are also fees for temporary licences such as for a funfair or public entertainment. The fees are set at a level which covers the application process, including the appeals process. People suggested that organisers of processions should also be required to pay a fee. There is, however, an important principle at stake here and I do not think there is a valid straightforward comparison to be made with the local authority licensing regime. In requiring organisers of processions to pay a fee, there would be a real risk of establishing a two tier system of those who could afford to pay to process and those who could not.

Recommendation 22

- Organisers should not be required to pay a fee for a notification to organise a procession.

Regular debriefing after processions

14.35 Very little regular debriefing involving the police, the local authority and the organiser currently takes place. Some local authorities said that they would only organise a debriefing if something had gone wrong during a procession and that had not yet occurred. One local authority carries out debriefing for larger events, run by a professional events company, such as events around Hogmanay. Some police forces also carry out internal debriefing, requiring the relevant officer to report on events which occurred at a procession, including the number of people arrested or reported, the number of police involved and general comments about the conduct of the procession. These reports are sent to operational planning units to be collated. Occasionally, if particular issues arise, then the police will discuss it locally with the organiser. Copies of the debriefing

14.36 I consider it essential to develop this system of informal debriefing, to formalise and regularise it. Debriefing provides an excellent opportunity for those involved in processions to exchange their experiences of the event from their own perspectives. An open discussion will allow grievances to be aired and successful outcomes to be shared. It allows those involved to consider what went well and what could be improved. Debriefing will also provide valuable information to improve the handling of future processions. However, there should be scope for the local authority, the police and the organiser to agree that no debriefing is necessary. This might be the case for small, annual events where there is little to be learnt or for one off events unlikely to be repeated. In most cases, there should be a presumption towards debriefing taking place.

14.37 Debriefing provides an opportunity to look at the conduct of the procession to see whether the organisers met the agreed conditions as set out in their 'permit to process'. If there were any difficulties associated with the march, it allows those involved to discuss that in detail and identify whether it was the participants involved in the march responsible or whether it was caused by onlookers, not formally participating in the march. There would be an opportunity to examine how that could be addressed in the future – for example, was the stewarding effective and did the police and stewards work cooperatively. It would also allow other issues to be explored. For example, organisers have reported to me that sometimes they feel that events have been over-policed. During a debriefing those concerns could be explored and the reasons for the level of deployed police resources explained. It will then help to inform operational police planning for future processions.

14.38 I would expect a record of the debriefing meeting to be prepared and signed by all those present. It might be necessary to record a divergence of views as those involved could have different perspectives but I would hope that in most cases there will be agreement around what had occurred at the procession.

14.39 Information collected as part of the debriefing process will be helpful in forming an evidence base against which future notifications can be assessed. Building reliable evidence is important to inform local authorities' consideration of future notifications, moving away from relying on anecdote or recollection. Organisers will be clear that that information will be retained and considered in future applications. For organisations which arrange processions in many local authority areas, it might be valuable to share such debriefing reports more widely to allow better planning and preparation. For annual processions, it will help local authorities, the police and organisers to plan more effectively for future events.

Recommendation 23
- Debriefing meetings should be held after processions with the organisers, local authority and the police and other relevant groups resulting in a signed record of what occurred.

Third element of remit: decision making – summary of recommendations

Recommendation 15
- Local authorities should remain responsible for taking decisions on procession notifications.

Recommendation 16
- Local authorities should be able to take into account a wider range of issues when reaching decisions on notifications. Their decisions should be evidence based and explained to the organisers.

Recommendation 17
- Local authorities should have discretion to impose conditions proportionate to the notification and to address the issues upon which it based its decision.

Recommendation 18
- Local authorities should respect key traditional dates but organisers should be prepared to compromise over routes where necessary.

Recommendation 19
- Organisers should provide a written, signed notification providing the key information required by the local authority.

Recommendation 20
- There should be a precursory meeting following the submission of a signed notification facilitated by the local authority, involving at least the organiser and the police, resulting in a signed outcome agreement.

Recommendation 21
- Once the notification has been considered by the local authority, the authority should issue organisers with a 'permit to process' outlining what had been agreed and what was expected.

Recommendation 22
- Organisers should not be required to pay a fee for a notification to organise a procession.

Recommendation 23
- Debriefing meetings should be held after processions with the organisers, local authority and the police and other relevant groups resulting in a signed record of what occurred.

15 Recommendations on fourth element of remit – numbers and effects on communities

Introduction and summary

15.1 The fourth element of my remit was to look at the numbers of processions taking place and the effects on communities. There is a perception that the number of processions is increasing, particularly those organised by the Loyalist Institutions, mainly associated with the Orange Order. The statistics relating to notified processions show that is the case, although not as markedly as might be expected given the very strongly held view that there are more processions taking place than ever before. These statistics are analysed in detail in Chapter 7 – The Number of Marches and Parades in Scotland but, briefly, they show that in 2001 there were 1,577 notified processions; in 2002 there were 1,600 notified processions; in 2003 (which is the year which has the most accurate records) there were 1,712 notified processions; and in the first nine months of 2004 1,428. Statistics from some local authorities show that, while there are more individual processions, overall there are fewer people taking part in those processions. Separately, it has been reported that there is the new phenomenon of band parades taking place, both Loyalist and Catholic or Republican. This has been a tradition in Northern Ireland but has been less traditional in Scotland.

15.2 It is clear that all forms of procession cause a certain degree of disruption to local communities. In views expressed to me, people expressed concern about Orange Order walks which start early in the morning, sometimes feeding into larger processions, returning late in the evening, so that people feel their whole day has been disrupted. Concerns were also raised with me about the frequency of these parades through the same areas, regularly disrupting the same community. People find it difficult to understand why there are so many small processions which seem to mirror each other, each causing their own disruption. Many people have shared with me their experiences of disruption and intimidation which they have felt on march days, including disruption to weddings, to funerals, to travel arrangements and an inability to go about their daily business. Others expressed a general feeling of fear about these processions. However, I was also told about the importance of these parades to members of the Orange Order and other Loyalist Institutions and the key role processions have in

15.3 Organisers have a key role to play in addressing people's perceptions that there are more processions taking place. They also have an important role to play in improving communities' experience of processions, minimising the negative effects that they have and maximising the positive effects that they have. In exercising their duties responsibly, organisers could make a valuable contribution to people's experiences of processions and any associated disruption.

15.4 My recommendations for this aspect of my remit concentrate on three key areas: organisers' responsibility for the numbers of processions being organised; organisers' responsibilities for ensuring processions are properly and professionally planned supported by detailed 'How To' guidance from local authorities; and ways of improving overall behaviour associated with processions. While many of the other areas of my remit require action primarily from local authorities and the police, I believe that organisers have the biggest contribution to make in addressing concerns about the numbers of processions and the effects they have on communities.

15.5 My recommendations encourage organisers to build on and continue to act responsibly in organising processions and consider if various events could be combined. There needs to be better record keeping and I think it is important local authorities and the police keep better statistics about processions. Organisers need to consider taking out public liability insurance and might be required to do so in certain situations or provide a behaviour bond. Local authorities should provide guidance for organisers on all the various aspects of organising a procession, in the form of a 'How To' guide. There should also be a general code of conduct developed and included in the 'permit to process' and organisers should reinforce appropriate behaviour in their own codes of conduct. Organisers need to do what they can to improve the behaviour of onlookers. There needs to be effective stewarding in place to manage processions. Bands engaged in playing in processions need to take responsibility for their own and their followers' behaviour. The police must continue to exercise their enforcement powers appropriately and, where local authorities do not have byelaws in place prohibiting the consumption of alcohol in public places, they should consider them.

Recommendations
Numbers
The number of processions taking place?

15.6 A number of people suggested that there should be quotas of processions established, limiting the number of processions that take place in a community or that are organised by one organisation. I do not support the introduction of quotas, which would result in a first come first serve system. It is fair, however, in coming to decisions about notifications, for local authorities to consider the amount of disruption being experienced by a community and propose alternative routes or times to minimise that

15.7 What remains clear is that people are irritated by the numbers of processions taking place. Organisers need to recognise the degree of irritation communities are feeling. While I do not want to recommend limits on the numbers that take place, it is important that organisers act responsibly and ensure that processions are being organised for appropriate reasons. Some organisations, such as the Grand Orange Lodge of Scotland and the Apprentice Boys of Derry have their own internal guidance on what constitutes an appropriate reason for a procession. It is important that they continue to apply that guidance actively and I commend them for their commitment to doing this. It demonstrates that they are taking their responsibilities to their local communities seriously. Their commitment to ensuring processions take place for the right reasons needs to continue.

15.8 Those responsible for organisations which arrange multiple parades on the same day, celebrating the same event, should look at the scope for combining processions to minimise the disruption caused in an area. In terms of spectacle alone, a larger procession makes more of a visual impact and allows the knock on effects of disruption across a local authority area to be minimised. There have been examples where the overarching organisations have done this and I encourage them to continue to look for these opportunities.

Recommendation 24
- Organisers should continue to act responsibly in ensuring processions are organised for appropriate purposes and consider the scope for combining processions on certain occasions.

Keeping records of the numbers of notified processions taking place

15.9 There is limited, reliable information about the number of processions which have taken place in Scotland in the past. I was grateful to local authorities for providing me with statistics about the numbers of processions being notified and I appreciate for some local authorities this was not an easy exercise to undertake. I recognise that local authorities are improving their record keeping. I recommend that this continues. As part of the monitoring process, local authorities should be required to provide statistics about the numbers of processions that have taken place in their area. The police should also be required to keep statistics about the policing resources required to police processions taking place. Better statistics will enable communities to have more robust information about the numbers of processions taking place in their area and the associated policing costs.

Recommendation 25
- Local authorities and the police should ensure that they keep statistics on the numbers of processions taking place and the associated policing costs.

Organisers' responsibilities in planning a procession

Organisers' responsibilities for insurance

15.10   Organising a procession in the twenty-first century is a considerable responsibility. Organisers have both moral and social responsibilities, as well as civil, common and criminal law responsibilities. In an increasingly litigious age, they may have to answer in the courts when things go wrong, particularly if it is shown that there have been defects in the organisers' planning process. Organisers are responsible for the safety of the public taking part in the procession. They also have some responsibility for the safety of those affected by the procession. Such responsibility would require organisers to avoid damage to property, causing fear or alarm to the public and minimising disruption to the local community. Some local authorities require organisers of events to take out insurance against damage and claims against them. Other authorities require organisers to indemnify the local authority in the event of a claim. Many organisers of various events already routinely take out insurance. It is good practice to consider taking out insurance and I recommend organisers think carefully about the need to do so.

Recommendation 26

- As part of their planning process, organisers should consider whether it is necessary to take out public liability insurance

Guidance for organisers – a 'How To' guide

15.11   Organising any sort of event, including a procession, requires considerable and detailed planning. The planning process, particularly, for larger events needs to be approached in a professional and well organised manner. Organisers need to be aware of the full range of legislation which could apply to their procession, depending on its nature. A non-exhaustive list contains:

- The Health and Safety at Work Act 1974 and its associated Regulations which put a duty on organisers to carry out risk assessments to identify any risk and to reduce it to acceptable levels;
- The Food Safety Act 1990 which applies when food is provided or sold;
- The Occupiers Liability (Scotland) Act 1960;
- Traffic legislation – the Road Traffic Regulation Act 1984 as amended by the Road Traffic (Temporary Restrictions) Act 1991 and the Road Traffic Regulation (Special Events) Act 1994 where there is a requirement for restrictions for road users such as road closures, diversions, signs or cones when a Temporary Traffic Regulations Order may be necessary. There could be a charge;
- The Control of Pollution Act 1974 which makes provision about the use of loud speakers;

- Other licences, permits and certificates could be required depending on the nature of the event or procession. These could include: a public entertainment licence, a liquor licence, a street traders licence, a licence for a use of a park or open space, a lottery permit, a licence for a charitable collection or a market operators licence. There will be a fee associated with some of these licences;
- The Public Order Act 1936 which prohibits the wearing of uniforms signifying association with any proscribed organisation; and
- The Terrorism Act 2000 which prohibits the display of certain symbols associated with any proscribed organisation.

15.12 A number of local authorities in Scotland have already produced guidance for organisers of events. As local authorities establish 'single gateways' to handle notifications of processions, I recommend that they should also give thought to developing guidance for organisers of events including processions drawing on what currently exists appropriate to local circumstances. I am grateful to Scottish Borders Council – 'Organising Events in the Scottish Borders' and to Fife Council for their 'Events Toolkit' and to Edinburgh Council for their 'Planning Guide – Events in Edinburgh'. While this current guidance is aimed at organisers of all events, much of it is applicable to organisers of processions. There is other relevant guidance which local authorities will want to draw upon in developing their own guidance, including the Health and Safety Executive's 'The Event Safety Guide' and 'The Guide to Safety at Sports Grounds'. It has often required a tragedy for safety issues to be given proper consideration. I hope producing straightforward guidance about organising processions would prevent such a tragedy happening on our streets.

15.13 Guidance will be an important source of reference for organisers ensuring all events are organised more professionally and experiences and best practice shared. Clearly there will be much common ground in each set of guidance and local authorities could be supported in preparing this guidance by local authority networks and associations such as COSLA. Appendix I summarises the key elements which could be contained in such a 'How To' guide.

Recommendation 27
- Local authorities should produce 'How To' guides for organisers of processions.

Improving behaviour associated with processions

15.14 My final recommendations aimed at tackling this element of my remit look at how overall behaviour associated with parades can be improved so that people's experience of processions also improves. My recommendations look at both the behaviour of participants and the behaviour of onlookers.

A code of conduct for participants in marches

15.15 Many local authorities and police forces already have a set of standard conditions governing the conduct of those organising and participating in processions. I recommend this approach be formalised and that an agreed code of conduct be set out in the 'permit to process' so that organisers and participants in the procession are clear about the conduct expected of them. As is currently the case, the details of the code of conduct should be for local authorities to decide upon in partnership with the police. However, I consider the following general issues might be covered:

- conditions which ensure that the details of the notification are followed – such as timing, routes, assembly and dispersal arrangements;
- conditions about where participants will march – such as where on the road participants will march and how wide the march will be;
- other conditions to minimise disruption to traffic and pedestrians – such as ensuring processions are split in sections to allow traffic to pass and pedestrians to cross the road;
- conditions about stewarding;
- conditions requiring marchers to obey police instructions;
- conditions relating to organisers' responsibilities – such as the need to liaise with the police and participants;
- conditions about the noise – such as where and when music can be played and loudhailers can be used;
- conditions about what can be carried during a procession – such as no weapons or inflammatory banners; and
- conditions about what can be worn during a procession – such as no paramilitary uniforms.

15.16 Participants' willingness to abide by the code of conduct will be one of the aspects discussed as part of the debriefing system. Breaches, such as playing music before the permitted time or in an area where it was not permitted, would be noted as part of the debriefing record and in making future notifications, organisers would need to be able to demonstrate that they had taken action to ensure that participants would follow the code of conduct. Further thought should be given to whether there should be sanctions attached to serious breaches of the code.

15.17 Such a code should not impose unreasonable requirements on processions nor undermine the purpose of the procession. I consider it would constitute a reasonable standard of conduct for those participating in processions, again striking a balance between those who want to march and those who live in the communities through which they march. It is no more than a charter of civility, that everyone might expect of a good neighbour. I am sure that organisers and participants will want to ensure they meet the code to demonstrate the responsible attitude they take to behaviour at processions.

Recommendation 28

- Local authorities and the police should develop a code of conduct for organisers and participants and this should be set out in the 'permit to process'.

Reinforcing standards of behaviour through organisers' codes of conduct

15.18 Many organisers already have detailed codes of conduct governing the behaviour of their members during processions. The Codes of Conduct of the Grand Orange Lodge of Scotland and the Apprentice Boys of Derry are at Appendix F. These are important in ensuring that participants behave in an appropriate manner. Organisations also take their own sanctions against members who breach their codes of conduct and bring the organisation into disrepute. I recommend organisers ensure that their codes of conduct reinforce the behaviour expected of participants set out in the 'permit to process'.

Recommendation 29

- Organisers should ensure that their existing codes of conduct reinforce the behaviour expected of participants in the 'permit to process'.

A requirement to take out insurance or provide a behaviour bond?

15.19 For most processions, it is right that insurance is not required of an organiser and it is up to the organiser to decide whether or not insurance is necessary given the level of risk posed by the nature of their procession. However, there will be certain processions where the risk of damage is very high. If, having completed a detailed risk assessment following the submission of a notification, the local authority considers the risk of damage to be unduly high, then they should be able to require, as a condition of the procession going ahead, that the organisers take out insurance or provide a behaviour bond. The local authority must be able to demonstrate to the organiser how they reached their conclusion. The terms of the bond must be clear. For example, it would not be appropriate to penalise the organisers for damage caused by those not participating in the procession. The police, together with the organisers' stewards, would need to work closely together so that it can be proved by whom the damage was caused.

Recommendation 30

- In certain circumstances, should the risk assessment demonstrate it is necessary, local authorities should be able to require organisers to take out insurance or provide a behaviour bond.

Organisers' responsibility for the behaviour of onlookers

15.20 It is clear that very often the disruption and feelings of intimidation which are described are caused not by participants in the official march, but by people with no formal connection but who choose to watch the march, either supporting it or opposing it. Some onlookers have genuine motives for watching or following processions, others do not.

15.21 I recognise that the organisers of processions are in a difficult position with regard to onlookers. Many of them feel that they should not be held responsible for the behaviour of onlookers and argue that they have no control over the behaviour of people who have no formal connection with the procession. Organisers feel that their presence and their association in the public mind with the procession can bring their own organisations into disrepute, tarnishing their image. While I have considerable sympathy with that attitude, organisers must recognise that onlookers are there because the procession is taking place and without that procession there would be no reason for them to congregate on the streets.

15.22 There is some action that organisers can take in ensuring that the behaviour of onlookers causes minimum disruption. The first is ensuring that the behaviour of participants does not antagonise difficult situations. Some organisers already require this of their members. For example the Code of Conduct of the Apprentice Boys of Derry makes clear that their members *'shall not even when provoked engage in any action that shames or disgraces the association'*. Where organisers know that the procession will attract followers, for example friends and family of participants, they should make clear the behaviour they expect of those followers, including common sense encouragement not to block the pavement or to react to opponents of the march. Finally, organisers must ensure that their stewards work in cooperation with the police. It is through that effective partnership that prospective trouble can be avoided.

Recommendation 31
- Organisers should recognise the degree of responsibility they have for the behaviour of onlookers and exercise appropriate influence to improve behaviour where they can.

Effective stewarding

15.23 Organisers and the police have a shared responsibility for the conduct and regulation of processions. In general terms, the role of police at processions is to maintain the peace, prevent breaches of the law and the commission of criminal offences and to take action against law breakers. Organisers are responsible for the safety of the public taking part in the procession as well as those affected by it. Clearly these roles are interdependent as guidance from the Metropolitan Police makes clear; *'The organisers' role of maintaining public safety can best be accomplished if there is no crime or disorder taking place. Equally the police role of preventing lawlessness and disorder can best be accomplished when public safety is assured'*.

15.24 One of the key ways in which organisers can ensure that they have control of the procession and ensure it goes according to plan is to have in place an effective system of stewarding and marshalling so that participants abide by what has been agreed and follow the organisers' instructions throughout the procession. If they work in an effective partnership with the police, this will also help to prevent the trouble that is sometimes caused by onlookers.

15.25 In developing their stewarding plans organisers should take some key issues into account:

- Number of stewards – the organiser must ensure that they have enough stewards for the effective management of the procession. There is no exact formula for the numbers of stewards which will be necessary for a march. It will depend on the nature of the procession, previous experience of that procession, where the route is going and whether it is uneven or passes along a busy road. Some local authorities give suggested ratios: a minimum of 4 at a procession, 1:10 to 1:50 or one or more in every coach bringing participants to the procession. The organisers' risk assessment process will help to show how many stewards are necessary and this should be one of the issues discussed at the precursory meeting with the local authority and the police;
- Fitness of stewards – stewards clearly need to be physically fit enough to carry out their role. They also need to have the character and temperament to carry out the duties required of them. Clearly, selecting the right people to act as stewards is important. They need to be firm but tactful, respected by participants and able to deal with difficult situations;
- Identification of stewards – stewards need to be easily identifiable so that participants and others including the police can identify them as stewards. They should wear distinctive clothing such as an armband or a coloured tabard to distinguish them from participants and onlookers;
- Briefing of stewards – stewards need to be effectively briefed. They need to be clear as to the extent of their role. They do not have the same duties, responsibilities or power as the police and they need to be clear about what they are and are not expected to do. Effective briefing will include information about those general requirements, details of the procession and its route, communication, duties before, during and after the procession and any emergency procedures;
- Establishing a chain of command – Sometimes it will be appropriate to establish a chain of command within the stewards with a Head Steward appointed to liaise with the police and to deal with all matters relating to stewards including their briefing. The Head Steward would then liaise with the police officer in charge of the procession during its progress. It is also good practice in appropriate parades to break overall stewarding into sections with a chief steward appointed to be responsible for a group of stewards; and
- Communication – it is essential that stewards are in communication with the organisers and with the police throughout the event. This could be achieved through mobile telephone or radio links. Stewards need to report back to the organisers any relevant developments during the event. They must also report to the police anything they think could lead to a breach of the peace or a breach of the law. This is key when it comes to the behaviour of onlookers. Stewards are well placed to identify those who are not participating in the procession and who are not members of the organisation. By identifying potential difficulties to the police and potential flashpoints for trouble, stewards can help to mitigate the effects.

15.26   I recognise that organisers already work to put in place stewards and are receptive to doing more. I recommend that this continues and is supported by local authorities and the police. There may, for example, be scope for training to be offered to stewards. There is much to be learnt from the experience of football clubs in putting in place effective arrangements for stewarding and ensuring that they are properly trained. I was encouraged that both the Grand Orange Lodge of Scotland and the Apprentice Boys of Derry would be happy to work with the police and local authorities to ensure that their stewards are well trained. The Apprentice Boys of Derry have already piloted a training scheme working with Leeds United Football Club and have seen the quality of stewarding improve and their processions run more smoothly. They have introduced a chain of command, visible clothing, communication systems and briefing meetings before processions. Other organisers such as the Scottish Trades Union Council and the Equality Network have experience in training stewards.

Recommendation 32

- Organisers should ensure that they have effective stewarding arrangements in place for the management of processions, and local authorities and the police consider whether there is appropriate training that can be offered.

Controls on the behaviour of bands and their supporters

15.27   During the course of the Review, people commented about the need to have stricter control on the behaviour of bands and their followers. Bands are a key part of some Orange walks and Catholic or Republican parades. Some bands have a considerable following and bring a number of supporters with them when they play at processions. It is not always clear who is responsible for the bands and who is responsible for their behaviour. Where the band is engaged to play as part of a procession of the Loyal Orange Institution, responsibility lies with the engaging lodge and the lodge member who is identified as the organiser.

15.28   The Grand Orange Lodge of Scotland have suggested, in a written submission to me, that bands should be required to take more responsibility for their own conduct. The Loyal Institutions have a detailed contract of engagement with the bands who are engaged to play. Copies of the contracts of the Grand Orange Lodge of Scotland and the Apprentice Boys of Derry are at Appendix G. The contract sets out standards of expected behaviour including dress, flags and banners to be displayed, drums to be played, music that can be played and prohibitions on the consumption of alcohol. Bands are required to belong to a recognised Band Association. However, responsibility remains with the lodge engaging the band.

15.29   I agree with the suggestion that it is important that the band itself take more direct responsibility for the behaviour of its members and its supporters. I recommend that as part of the notification process the organiser should include the names of the bands who have been engaged to play and the band should stipulate a band member who will be responsible for the band's behaviour. The named person must be present on the day and identify himself as required. That would require the loyal institutions to make changes to their existing contracts. However, it would ensure that bands took more personal responsibility for their conduct. It would also ensure this was the case where the processions were being organised by bands themselves. Any concerns about the behaviour of bands would be highlighted as part of the debriefing process and taken into account in the assessment of future notifications including that band.

15.30 Previous reviews in Northern Ireland have suggested that there be a registration scheme for bands. I do not think this is currently necessary in Scotland. To be engaged by the loyal institutions bands must already be a member of a Band Association recognised by them. All bands engaged for an Orange parade must also be on the approved list of bands operated by the Grand Orange Lodge of Scotland. The Band Associations aim to improve the standard of dress, playing and decorum within member bands. Republican bands are part of the Cairde na hÉireann structure and also have an agreed code of conduct. To take part in a Republican parade, a band must be a member of that structure. However, if the named individual approach does not lead to more personal responsibility being taken, then a registration scheme may be required in the future.

Recommendation 33
- Bands playing at processions should identify a named individual who will be present on the day to be responsible for the conduct of the band and its supporters.

Links with football

15.31 In many people's minds, certain processions, particularly those organised by the Loyal Institutions are associated with football, primarily with Rangers and Celtic football clubs. Onlookers often wear Old Firm football strips. People perceive supporters to be acting in certain ways at processions, including indulging in offensive sectarian behaviour and feel that the clubs do little to address this behaviour in their supporters.

15.32 The Scottish Football Association, with all Premiership and League teams, including Rangers FC and Celtic FC, are working hard to address inappropriate behaviour, including overtly racist and sectarian behaviour amongst supporters at football matches. It might be helpful to highlight some of the initiatives that are in place. The Scottish Football Association's 'National Club Licensing Scheme' accepted by all Premier League Clubs, requires clubs to provide evidence of a clear policy against sectarianism and racism and for those policies to be incorporated in supporters' charters. They have penalties in place for those supporters who are in breach of their policies. They also play their part in promoting the work of 'Show Racism the Red Card' campaign. Football clubs are also taking specific action against supporters who behave in an insulting sectarian way such as excluding them from the ground for one or more matches through the confiscation of season tickets. Clubs publicise the numbers of people who have been warned or suspended or banned from matches as a result of unacceptable behaviour. The police and football clubs are sharing information about supporters who are charged with or convicted of offences at or near football grounds under an agreed protocol. Local authorities ensure that street traders do not sell offensive sectarian material in the vicinity of football grounds.

15.33 Both Rangers FC and Celtic FC have made their position on sectarian behaviour clear. They have clear statements setting out their policy on racism and sectarianism. Rangers FC's 'Pride Over Prejudice' campaign states that the club is a *'multi-cultural, multi-denominational and non-political organisation which promotes social inclusion and encourages tolerance and understanding of the interests of all sectors of the community'*. All Rangers FC season ticket holders receive a Blue Guide which encourages fans to put 'Pride Over Prejudice'. It explains the behaviour expected of fans and sets out the actions which will be taken if fans behave in an inappropriate manner. Celtic FC sets out its position in its 'Social Mission Statement' displayed around the stadium and on each season ticket book. Its 'Social Charter' provides a code of behaviour used in educating youth supporters and which anyone who has caused trouble at a match must sign. A further breach of the Code means dismissal from the ground. The Code also sets out the foundation for the clubs work to on community involvement, charitable giving, work to promote equality and policy on inclusion. Their 'Bhoys against Bigotry' campaign was launched in 1996 to unite fans against sectarianism.

15.34 Rangers FC and Celtic FC also work jointly with Glasgow City Council across a range of issues. They have in place a range of initiatives for young people including 'Old Firm United' 'Football United' and 'Fans United' which challenge issues such as sectarianism, racism and bigotry. Both clubs contribute to 'Sense Over Sectarianism' a multi-agency project which funds community projects in Glasgow, and its travel to work area which encourages inter-cultural understanding, engages with young people and to examine and challenge existing attitudes and empower communities to tackle religious intolerance within their own areas. Projects have included inter-denominational sporting events. Both clubs work on community programmes, such as Rangers FC 'Football in the Community' programme which works to improve the health of future generations of children through exercise, nutrition and lifestyle choices while also addressing truancy and anti-social behaviour and Celtic FC 'community coaching' and 'youth against bigotry' education pack complemented by a 'matchday visit programme'.

15.35 I commend their approach and encourage them to continue to progress this and other work further. Supporters must know that clear racist and sectarian behaviour will not be tolerated.

15.36 Old Firm matches now routinely kick off earlier in the day, leading to fewer incidents. In considering notifications of processions, local authorities should take into account other events and football matches will be one such event. I consider there is little more that the Old Firm can do to address the behaviour of those who choose to wear football colours at processions. It is clear that they are taking measured action to tackle racism and sectarianism amongst their fans.

Police powers of enforcement

15.37 The police already have sufficient powers under common and criminal law to tackle the anti-social, nuisance behaviour sometimes experienced at processions. Common law and criminal offences that are sometimes relevant during processions include: the common law crimes of breach of the peace; minor and major assault; drunk and incapable; and urinating in the street. A majority of local authorities also have byelaws in place prohibiting the consumption of alcohol in a public place, enabling the police to confiscate those in illegal possession of alcohol.

15.38 People have suggested that the police should make more active use of their enforcement powers. However, this is not a simple or straightforward issue and a balance needs to be struck. The police need to exercise careful judgement in exercising their enforcement powers. Ill thought out enforcement action risks leading to an exacerbation of a situation. The nature of processions and associated public order issues are sensitive and the atmosphere potentially tense and volatile. The wrong action can inflame a situation and police officers present must exercise their judgement and police in a sensitive, sensible and appropriate way given the circumstances presented. Cooperation between the police and stewards will help the policing of processions and improve the behaviour of onlookers. Police officers involved in arresting people watching processions will then be abstracted from the route and in the short-term will not be available for continuing procession duties, potentially undermining their ability to police public safety. Careful, commonsense policing should not appear as an abrogation of duty. People watching processions should be expected to meet the same standards of behaviour as they would on any other day.

15.39 Police action should be included in the formal debriefing process following the procession. A review of how the police acted could help inform the policing arrangements for future processions.

Recommendation 34
- The police should exercise their enforcement powers appropriately and, in liaison with stewards, ensure the policing of onlookers is effective and their actions considered as part of the debriefing process.

Sectarian behaviour at processions

15.40 People told me anecdotes over the course of the Review about the sectarian behaviour they experienced during certain processions that they described as 'Orange' covering all processions organised by the Loyalist Institutions. It is clear that what one person sees as bigotry and intimidation another sees as a celebration of a cultural tradition. Whatever the view held, there is no doubt that it is very firmly and genuinely held. We must find a way to come to some sort of understanding or at least accommodation. The Loyalist Institutions, in exercising their rights to peaceful assembly and to process, must therefore take into account the perceived effects they are having on the communities through which they process. Reducing the disruption caused by their processions and improving people's experiences of march days will be a practical step to addressing people's concerns. Communities should in turn recognise others' rights to peaceful assembly.

15.41 If people commit offences which are aggravated by religious prejudice, this can now be taken into account. Section 74 of the Criminal Justice (Scotland) Act 2003 came into force in June 2003 allowing for an offence to be proved to have been aggravated by religious prejudice. To September 2004, 450 charges that included a section 74 aggravation were submitted in reports by the police to Procurators Fiscal. The Crown Office and the Procurator Fiscal Service carried out a detailed review of 108 cases brought in the first six months (June to December 2003). The review showed that in 49% of cases the accused was under the influence of alcohol at the time of the offence, there were twice as many Catholic as Protestant victims, 90% of the accused were male and 15% of cases arose in the context of marches.

The role of alcohol

15.42 Some of the problems associated with behaviour at marches are undoubtedly fuelled by the consumption of alcohol. Most organisers try to control the consumption of alcohol by participants. Their codes of conduct make clear that participants should not consume alcohol before or during processions nor should it be available in coaches taking participants to marches or at assembly points. This aspect of the code of conduct needs to be continued. Organisers' stewards have a role in stopping participants who have clearly been drinking from participating in the march.

15.43 More generally the consumption of alcohol in a public place is prohibited by local authorities who have implemented byelaws. Since the pilot project in 1993, some 27 local authorities have byelaws in place. These byelaws cover more than 450 towns and villages across Scotland, together with areas within the cities of Glasgow, Dundee and Aberdeen. Aberdeenshire, Edinburgh, Orkney, the Scottish Borders and Shetland do not have byelaws in place. Byelaws can be targeted at known trouble spots such as particular streets or localities. The byelaws have reportedly been successful in reducing the nuisance and disorder associated with public drinking. People have told me that the byelaws have reduced the trouble caused by drinking on march days, although some feel that they are not enforced strongly enough. They give the police powers to seize and dispose of alcohol which helps to prevent later trouble caused by people who have drunk too much or who are already drunk and incapable. I recommend that those authorities that do not have byelaws in place consider introducing them or at least look at other ways of tackling the nuisance caused by inappropriate public drinking, for example through civic codes.

Recommendation 35
- Local authorities without byelaws prohibiting the consumption of alcohol in public places should consider putting them in place.

Fourth element of remit: numbers and effects on communities – summary of recommendations

Recommendation 24
- Organisers should continue to act responsibly in ensuring processions are organised for appropriate purposes and consider the scope for combining processions on certain occasions.

Recommendation 25
- Local authorities and the police should ensure that they keep statistics on the numbers of processions taking place and the associated policing costs.

Recommendation 26
- As part of their planning process, organisers should consider whether it is necessary to take out public liability insurance.

Recommendation 27
- Local authorities should produce 'How To' guides for organisers of processions.

Recommendation 28
- Local authorities and the police should develop a code of conduct for organisers and participants and this should be set out in the 'permit to process'.

Recommendation 29
- Organisers should ensure that their existing codes of conduct reinforce the behaviour expected of participants in the 'permit to process'.

Recommendation 30
- In certain circumstances, should the risk assessment demonstrate it is necessary, local authorities should be able to require organisers to take out insurance or provide a behaviour bond.

Recommendation 31
- Organisers should recognise the degree of responsibility they have for the behaviour of onlookers and exercise appropriate influence to improve behaviour where they can.

Recommendation 32
- Organisers should ensure that they have effective stewarding arrangements in place for the management of processions, and local authorities and the police consider whether there is appropriate training that can be offered.

Recommendation 33
- Bands playing at processions should identify a named individual who will be present on the day to be responsible for the conduct of the band and its supporters.

Recommendation 34
- The police should exercise their enforcement powers appropriately and, in liaison with stewards, ensure the policing of onlookers is effective and their actions considered as part of the debriefing process.

Recommendation 35
- Local authorities without byelaws prohibiting the consumption of alcohol in public places should consider putting them in place.

16 Recommendations on fifth element of remit – police costs

Introduction and summary

16.1 The fifth area of my remit covers police costs associated with policing processions. Those costs have always been felt to be significant and the first part of this chapter looks at what those costs actually are, the level of policing at processions and the impact that policing processions has on policing resources. I also look briefly at the numbers of arrests at marches and complaints about marches.

16.2 This area of my remit lead to some thought provoking discussion during the course of the Review and raised many interesting issues about the principles of whether organisers should be required to meet the costs of policing. I have concluded that it would be inappropriate, for a number of reasons, to require organisers of marches and parades to contribute to policing costs. However, I also recommend that local authorities should be able to take into account police costs when coming to decisions about march notifications although prohibiting processions on grounds of police costs alone is not appropriate. Finally, I look in this section at practical ways of improving police liaison with and understanding of organisations arranging marches to contribute to more effective operational policing.

Recommendations

Police costs

16.3 It has always been felt that policing processions represents a significant cost to police forces in Scotland. Figures supplied by the Association of Chief Police Officers in Scotland (ACPOS) show that the salary costs alone associated with policing over 1,800 processions across Scotland (in 2003/2004) are in the region of £1.5 million. This is the minimum cost to the police service in Scotland. Factoring in employers' pension liability (at 27%) means that police costs for salaries are in the region of £2 million and that figure does not, of course, include additional expenses incurred nor does it cover the costs of incidents arising from processions. If set against the overall annual police budget of £1 billion these figures might not sound all that much. But set in context, £1.5 million would pay for 10,000 days for a constable when that officer could have been involved in other policing duties (although of course, the figure of £1.5 million is made up of the costs of a range of officers). Anecdotally, I am told that policing costs associated with some of the larger marches is the same as the costs of policing an Old Firm game between Rangers and Celtic Football Clubs. The costs of policing such games vary depending on the time, game involved and other external factors at the time, for example a recent game at Hampden cost around £47,000 to police.

16.4 Overall some 62,000 hours (or over 8,200 working days) annually are used in the planning and policing of processions. A wide range of officers are involved, most usually chief inspectors, inspectors, sergeants and constables with occasional involvement from more senior officers. The amount of time necessary to plan and police different sorts of parades varies considerably. On average, an Orange walk or Republican parade might take around 39 hours, a procession by a youth organisation seven hours, a community event (a fête or a gala) 31 hours, a protest (anti-war or a union demonstration) 55 hours and a political march (CND or a far right party) 40 hours. However, the average figures do not do justice to the different levels of resources necessary depending on the size of the procession parade and the assessment of the associated risk to public order and public safety.

16.5 The detailed tables which follow show:
- the overall costs per category of parade – which shows the 700 Orange/Republican parades cost £345,732 to police, the 146 youth parades cost £63,712 to police, the 884 community processions £275,870 to police, the 106 protest processions cost £490,154 to police and the 12 political processions £359,080;
- a force by force breakdown of the total number of parades with which each force has dealt with over the year 1 September 2003 and 1 August 2004 and the number of planning hours which take place in advance of the procession and the actual number of policing hours at each procession – which shows 27,240 policing hours for Orange/Republican parades, 1,047 policing hours for youth parades, 27,449 policing hours for community processions, 5,848 hours for protest processions and 485 hours for political processions; and
- the proportion of parades and policing hours each police force deals with and the proportion of costs for each force based on the hours each force takes – which show Strathclyde Police has 56% of the costs, Lothian and Borders Police 19% of the costs, Fife Constabulary 13% of the costs; Tayside Police 4% of the costs, Northern Constabulary 3% of the costs, Dumfries and Galloway Constabulary with around 2% of the costs, Central Scotland Police with around 1.5% of the costs and Grampian Police with 0.5% of the costs. Percentages have been rounded.

16.6 The statistics relating to the numbers of parades which require police involvement will differ from the figures supplied from local authorities used in Chapter 7 – The Number of Marches and Parades although they are broadly in line with those figures. It is important to note that they have been collected over a different time period. They also relate to all processions which required a policing presence. Local authorities supplied figures relating to the processions notified to them under the Civic Government (Scotland) Act 1982 whereas the police may have been involved in providing policing resources to processions arranged by groups which local authorities treat as exempt.

16.7 The figures must be regarded as an indicative only. They show the processions which had a central planning involvement by forces. There will have been additional instances where processions took place where local officers provided services with minimal abstraction as part of that day's duties and these have not been included in the overall costs.

16.8 Clearly the costs do not fall equally across the eight police forces. The types of processions they deal with and the time associated with them varies considerably. I have broken the costs down according to police force area based on the total policing hours taken up on the policing of parades.

Table to show the overall cost of each category of parade

Category of Parade	Number of Parades	Total Hours Used	Average Hours per Parade	Chief Inspector	Inspector	Sergeant	Constable	Cost per Category
Orange/Republican	700	27,240	39	2,137	17,511	45,485	280,599	345,732
Youth Organisation	146	1,047	7	394	3,227	8,382	51,710	63,712
Community	884	27,449	31	1,705	13,973	36,294	223,899	275,870
Protest	106	5,848	55	3,029	24,826	64,485	397,813	490,154
Political	12	485	40	2,219	18,187	47,241	291,432	359,080
TOTAL	1,848	62,069	34	9,484	77,725	201,887	1,245,453	1,534,549

Notes
- Officers rates are calculated based on annual salaries at September 2004 and are based on internal rates for Strathclyde police and reflect the costs of employing an officer on operation duty;
- There is no employers' pension liability included in these figures – which would add 27%;
- The costs do not include any additional expenses, for example travel costs, incurred;
- The costs do not include any costs related to incidents arising from processions, for example incidents occurring after the procession has finished.

Table showing a force by force breakdown of the number of parades, advance planning hours and policing hours spent at each parade

Numbers per category of parade and number of hours	Dumfries & Galloway Constabulary	Strathclyde Police	Lothian & Borders Police	Central Scotland Police	Fife Constabulary	Tayside Police	Grampian Police	Northern Constabulary	Totals
Number of Orange/Republican	2	565	81	34	11	7	0	0	700
Planning Hours	4	2,694	353	73	138	45	0	0	3,307
Policing Hours	28	21,079	815	218	1,638	155	0	0	23,933
Total Hours	32	23,773	1,168	291	1,776	200	0	0	27,240
Number of youth groups (e.g. Scouts)	0	114	6	12	9	4	0	1	146
Planning Hours	0	139	8	38	16	8	0	1	210
Policing Hours	0	724	8	74	16	7	0	8	837
Total Hours	0	863	16	112	32	15	0	9	1,047
Number of community (e.g. fetes, galas)	43	236	355	33	132	35	10	40	884
Planning Hours	152	695	1,421	116	966	587	3	200	4,140
Policing Hours	1,291	5,001	7,793	302	5,375	1,754	293	1,500	23,309
Total Hours	1,443	5,696	9,214	418	6,341	2,341	296	1,700	27,449
Number of Protest (e.g. anti-war/union)	0	63	34	0	5	2	0	2	106
Planning Hours	0	400	280	0	26	10	0	22	738
Policing Hours	0	3,886	815	0	57	92	0	260	5,110
Total Hours	0	4,286	1,095	0	83	102	0	282	5,848
Number of Political (e.g. CND/BNP)	0	7	4	1	0	0	0	0	12
Planning Hours	0	22	34	4	0	0	0	0	60
Policing Hours	0	286	109	30	0	0	0	0	425
Total Hours	0	308	143	34	0	0	0	0	485
Total Number of Parades	45	985	480	80	157	48	10	43	1,848
Total planning hours	156	3,950	2,096	231	1,146	650	3	223	8,455
Total policing hours	1,319	30,976	9,540	624	7,086	2,008	293	1,768	53,614
Total hours	1,475	34,926	11,636	855	8,232	2,658	296	1,991	62,069

Table showing total proportion of parades in each police force area and proportion of total costs

Numbers per category of parade and number of hours	Dumfries & Galloway Constabulary	Strathclyde Police	Lothian & Borders Police	Central Scotland Police	Fife Constabulary	Tayside Police	Grampian Police	Northern Constabulary	Totals
Proportion of Total Number of Parades	2%	53%	26%	4%	8%	3%	1%	2%	100%
Proportion of Total planning hours	2%	47%	25%	3%	14%	8%	1%	3%	100%
Proportion of Total policing hours	2%	58%	18%	1%	13%	4%	1%	3%	100%
Proportion of Total hours	2%	56%	19%	1.5%	13%	4%	0.5%	3%	100%
Costs based on proportion of hours	£36,467	£863,485	£287,680	£21,138	£203,522	£65,714	£7,318	£49,224	£1,534,549

(Note – percentages rounded)

Level of policing at processions

16.9 The nature of the procession dictates the number of planning hours and policing hours needed to handle the event successfully. Some processions can be easily policed by a couple of officers as part of their duty that day, others take a great number of officers away from their usual duties. A few actual examples of recent processions from Strathclyde Police force help to illustrate the variety of resources required:

- The Scottish Republican Socialist Movement notified their intention to hold a parade to commemorate the memory of John MacLean, a former member of the Socialist Workers Party. The notification was submitted on 14 September giving over six weeks notice of a procession to take place on 27 November which would involve a march and rally of 100 people including a Republican flute band. The supervision of arrangements for the parade was done through a dedicated police officer at the Operational Planning Unit. Policing on the day involved eight officers: an inspector, a sergeant and seven constables. These officers were from the Division and diverted from other operational street duties;
- The Springburn Ulster Defenders organised their annual anniversary parade to take place in the evening starting at 6.30pm on 25 June. The procession involved 100 people accompanied by a Flute band. The procession was escorted by six officers: one sergeant and five constables;
- The County Grand Orange Lodge of Glasgow holds an annual parade to commemorate the Battle of the Boyne. The County Lodge submits at least 18 separate notifications for the various processions which form the annual parade. The notifications are usually submitted months in advance. Through the course of the day some 1500 participants including 15 flute bands march through the streets of the south side of Glasgow. Supervision of the parade is arranged through a number of staff in the Operational Planning Unit and involves weeks of work in advance of the day. On the day itself some 236 officers are involved: six inspectors, 28 sergeants and 202 constables. These officers are from the Division and are diverted from other operational street duties. To ensure that sufficient resources are available for normal policing requirements, other officers have rest days cancelled; and
- The West of Scotland Band Association organised a procession in Wishaw in March 2004. There were 425 officers involved on the day; one superintendent, two chief inspectors, 17 inspectors, 51 sergeants, 354 constables.

16.10 The police deploys officers according to the perceived risk presented by the procession to public safety and to public order based on their risk assessment informing the operational policing plan. It is important that the police have sufficient officers present to deal with any incidents that arise during the procession.

The impact on resources

16.11 The police, like other organisations, have finite resources on which they can draw. They must balance the competing demands on their resources. When a procession poses a high risk to public disorder, the police will need to deploy or have available large numbers of police which can be a burden on budgets and resources. Officers who are detailed on procession duties are accommodated by means of duty, working rest days and overtime. From time to time it means that holidays and rest days need to be cancelled disrupting officers' personal lives. There are added costs if shifts need to be changed at short notice and overtime or disturbance payments incurred. Ensuring there are officers available to police the procession also has implications in abstractions which cannot be calculated financially, as an officer on duty at a procession is not available for other duties. Sometimes for larger parades, officers need to be drawn from other areas. Such abstractions require the realignment of police officers' duties. In extreme circumstances there could be detrimental effects on normal policing levels in communities. There is no doubt that ensuring processions are effectively policed can, on occasion, cause significant operation difficulties in planning to ensure that communities continue to enjoy a consistency of policing cover. The objective for the police is to ensure that there is a continuity of policing across their force area.

Arrests at marches

16.12 In general, the conduct of parades does not cause major concerns for the police. Participants follow the conditions set by many police forces on the conduct of processions. In 2003, ACPOS report that there were 119 arrests at Orange walks and Republican parades, those which are most often perceived by the public to be the most threatening and where most trouble occurs. It appears that the vast majority of these arrests were not of people participating in the parades but of those onlookers following the procession. All but nine of these arrests (which were in Central Police area) took place in Strathclyde. Given the number of marches that take place, that is not a large number of arrests. Most of these arrests are likely to be for minor street disorder offences.

16.13 Recent analysis by the Crown Office and the Procurator Fiscal service looked at 108 arrests that took place between June 2003 and December 2003 for offences aggravated by religious prejudice. In most cases the aggravation was added to offences of breach of the peace and assault. Of those 108 cases, 16 were found to have taken place at marches.

Complaints following marches

16.14 Like local authorities, the police receive very few formal complaints about marches. Following the County Grand Orange Lodge of Glasgow's annual parade in Glasgow in July 2004, the police received a small number of complaints from people who had been shopping in the city centre and who were upset at being held up by the procession. They also received two letters from the public complaining that the parade portrayed a poor image of the City due to its aggressive nature and drunken followers. There were no letters of complaint received following the annual Battle of the Boyne parade which, in 2004, took place in Blantyre involving around 12,000 participants.

Should organisers be required to pay for policing costs?

16.15 This element of my remit prompted an interesting debate about whether organisers should be required to pay for the policing costs associated with their parades. Views were, in general, mixed but strongly held. Some people thought that some organisers should pay or make a contribution to costs or else be allowed a certain number of 'free' parades, meeting the costs once that threshold had been reached. Others felt the principle of requiring people to meet policing costs was entirely wrong in a democratic society and, in effect, required people to pay to exercise their right to freedom of assembly.

16.16 The results of the telephone survey showed that over three quarters of people thought that organisers of political protests, Orange walks and Republican parades should be required to pay police costs and local authority costs. Around half thought organisers of gala events and processions in relation to local issues should also be required to meet those costs. There was general agreement that organisers should be required to meet the costs of repairing damage and the costs of insurance. In contrast, almost 50% thought that requiring people to contribute to costs would limit freedom of speech.

16.17 I do not think that it is appropriate to require people to make a contribution to the policing costs. I believe that policing costs must continue to be met from policing budgets. Any form of charging would undermine an individual's right to the freedom of peaceful assembly and potentially prejudice political freedoms. It would create a two-tier system of those who could afford to pay to process and those who could not. Smaller community groups or small charity or protest groups would not be able to meet those costs. Neither do I support a pro-rata system where organisers contribute if costs are over a certain amount or a quota system allowing a certain number of marches for free and then requiring organisers to contribute. The underlying principle is fundamentally wrong in my view and, in practical terms, it would be extremely difficult to operate. The police must be able to deploy the number of officers they consider appropriate to police the procession. It is important not to restrict that necessary operational policing flexibility by issues about charging. Imposing quotas could quickly lead to unhelpful disputes over policing levels.

16.18 The parallel has been drawn with the requirement on football clubs to pay for policing within their grounds. However, football clubs are commercial organisations which charge their fans an entrance fee to watch games. Police associations have also been looking at charging for police services provided to various events, applying a sliding scale of contributions according to the type of event whether it is commercial (for example pop concerts or sporting events), non-commercial (charity events or community fairs) or national community events (constitutional events). However, I consider there to be a difference in charging for people exercising their right of peaceful assembly. In principle, I think organisers of processions should not be required to meet policing costs.

16.19 Organisers should, however, work with the police to help reduce the policing costs associated with their processions. My recommendations, which look at ensuring effective and cooperative stewarding, Chapter 15 – Numbers and Effects on Communities (recommendation 32) should be helpful in allowing the police to look critically at the resources they need to deploy at processions. Requiring organisers to take out a behaviour bond when the risk assessment shows the possibility of damage to be high should also be helpful in underlining to organisers their responsibility for the conduct of the participants in their procession.

Recommendation 36
- Organisers of processions should not be required to meet policing costs.

Should police costs be taken into account when reaching decisions on processions?

16.20 There will always be competing demands on police resources and some processions demand a very significant burden on those resources. However, the human rights framework requires States to act on occasion to protect people's right to peaceful assembly, ensuring that, in cases where a demonstration could be considered to give offence, action is taken to ensure that participants do not fear that they will be subject to physical violence for holding their views. In itself, I do not think that banning a procession on grounds of cost alone is sufficient, rather it is the implication that the procession has for public order and safety. It is, however, proportionate to consider policing costs in coming to a decision about a notification and whether there are appropriate restrictions that can be imposed to reduce those costs to more proportionate levels. For example, changing the start time of a parade so that it does not clash with other events requiring a police presence, ensuring that it avoids sensitive times of day, or considering whether an alternative route would materially affect the number of police officers necessary and the associated costs.

Recommendation 37
- Local authorities should consider relevant police costs when reaching decisions about march notifications.

Ways of improving police liaison with marching organisations

16.21 The police in Scotland have had a long history of successfully handling the many processions which take place every year. The statistics show that there are few arrests and few formal complaints associated with marches. Operationally policing is both effective and efficient. Over time, the police have developed good relationships with organisers and try as far as possible to reach appropriate accommodations with them.

In turn, organisers respect the police's role and follow what has been agreed and their instructions. That most marches pass off with little incident is testament to the commitment of the police, the organisers and participants. My recommendations should help to reinforce this success by formalising some of the discussions and ensuring there are opportunities to discuss and ease out any difficulties before they become grievances. It is important also that the police continue to learn from previous experiences and to develop their understanding of reasons why people want to march. This will build on initiatives that they already have in place to develop their understanding of different communities, such as Strathclyde Police's campaign 'Understanding Islam' which aims to promote a better appreciation of Islam amongst their officers.

16.22 Current operational briefing, provided for officers involved in processions on the day, is very good at explaining the human rights legislation and other legislation which applies. There is an opportunity to build into the briefing more information about the background culture and specific reasons for the march, ensuring that the police have a more rounded understanding of the marching organisations' perspective. This should help officers better understand likely flashpoints where trouble might occur and the likely potential reactions of onlookers and the community. March organisers have a role to play here too in explaining more about their organisation and the purpose behind the march.

Recommendation 38

- Police forces should ensure that there is appropriate briefing provided for officers policing processions and that it includes information about the reasons for the procession and the relevant background to the organisation involved.

Fifth element of remit: police costs – summary of recommendations

Recommendation 36

- Organisers of processions should not be required to meet policing costs.

Recommendation 37

- Local authorities should consider relevant police costs when reaching decisions about march notifications.

Recommendation 38

- Police forces should ensure that there is appropriate briefing provided for officers policing processions and that it includes information about the reasons for the procession and the relevant background to the organisation involved.

Appendix A

Written submissions

Local Authorities
1. Aberdeen City Council
2. Aberdeenshire Council
3. Angus Council
4. Argyll and Bute Council
5. North Ayrshire Council
6. South Ayrshire Council
7. Clackmannanshire Council
8. Dumfries and Galloway Council
9. West Dunbartonshire Council
10. Dundee City Council
11. City of Edinburgh Council
12. Comahairle nan Eilean Siar
13. Falkirk Council
14. Fife Council
15. Glasgow City Council
16. Highland Council
17. Inverclyde Council
18. North Lanarkshire Council
19. South Lanarkshire Council
20. East Lothian Council
21. West Lothian Council
22. Midlothian Council
23. Moray Council
24. Orkney Islands Council
25. Perth and Kinross Council
26. Renfrewshire Council
27. East Renfrewshire Council
28. Scottish Borders Council

29 Shetland Islands Council
30 Stirling Council
31 COSLA
32 SOLACE

Police Associations
33 Association of Chief Police Officers in Scotland
34 Association of Scottish Police Superintendents
35 Scottish Police Federation

Other Parts of the Public Sector
36 Historic Scotland
37 NHS Ayrshire and Arran
38 NHS Lanarkshire
39 NHS Scotland – Scottish Ambulance Service

Community Councils
40 Ashley and Broomhill Community Council
41 Bellshill Community Council
42 Chryston Community Council
43 Community Council representing Aberdeen City
44 Cove and Altens Community Council
45 Forgewood Community Council
46 Greengairs Community Council
47 Ladywell Community Council
48 Merchant City Community Council
49 Newarthill Community Council
50 Penicuik and District Community Council
51 Shotts Community Council
52 Tillydrone Community Council
53 Association of Scottish Community Councils

Business Organisations
54 Edinburgh Chamber of Commerce
55 Edinburgh City Centre Management Company
56 Glasgow Chamber of Commerce
57 Greater Glasgow and Clyde Valley Tourist Board
58 LaSalle Investment Management
59 Princess Street Association

Transport Organisations
60 Amey Highways
61 Bear Scotland
62 First Scotland East
63 FirstGroup plc
64 Lothian Buses
65 Strathclyde Passenger Transport

Voluntary Sector Organisations
66 Islay and Jura Council of Voluntary Service
67 Milton Community Homes
68 Nil By Mouth
69 Voluntary Action Orkney
70 Wishaw and District Housing Association

Religious Organisations
71 Archbishop of St Andrews and Edinburgh
72 Bishop's Conference of Scotland
73 Church of Our Lady and St Bridget
74 General Assembly of the Church of Scotland, Committee on Church and Nation
75 Member of Sikh Community of Glasgow
76 Minister of Religion, Wishaw
77 Open House Catholic Magazine
78 Parish Church of St Cuthbert
79 Parish of Saint Mary of the Assumption
80 Scottish Council of Jewish Communities
81 Scottish Episcopal Church
82 Sikh Sanjog

MSPs
83 Donald Gorrie MSP, Member for Central Scotland

Organisations which organise marches
84 Apprentice Boys of Derry, Scottish Amalgamated Committee
85 Cairde na hÉireann
86 Equality Network
87 Grand Orange Lodge of Scotland
88 National Union of Students Scotland
89 Pride Scotia (Glasgow)
90 Provincial Grand Black Chapter of Scotland

91 Scotmid Co-operative Party
92 Scottish CND
93 Scottish Trades Union Congress
94 Scottish Youth Hostels Association
95 Scout Association, Scottish Council

Individuals
96 Ted Black
97 Douglas Blaney
98 Carole Cannan
99 Angie Dight
100 M Ferrier
101 Agnes Gunn
102 Alan Gunn
103 Derek Lynn
104 Ian Mcadam
105 A Robert Smith
106 David Stevenson
107 Neal Wade
108 – 125 18 Submissions received in confidence

Standard Submissions from Individuals
126 – 341 I received 216 similar submissions from individuals

Views forwarded via the Scottish Executive
342 – 361 I received 20 submissions in confidence via the Scottish Executive

Appendix B

Script for telephone attitude survey

<INTRO> Good —, my name is — and I'm calling from Taylor Nelson Sofres, an independent research company. We have been commissioned by the Scottish Executive to find out about people's views and experiences of parades and marches, and the impact that they have on local communities. The research covers all sorts of marches, including political protests such as anti-war demonstrations, Orange walks or Irish Republican marches, and local gala day parades. Would you mind answering some questions? It should take around 15 minutes. All your responses will be strictly confidential and nothing that could identify you will be passed on to the Scottish Executive.

<SEX>
Do not ask – Interviewer code sex of respondent

Male	86	1
Female		2

<SLA> Can I just check which local authority area you live in?

Stirling	87	1
Falkirk		2
Clackmannan		3
Dumfries and Galloway		4
Fife		5
Aberdeen City		6
Aberdeenshire		7
Moray		8
Edinburgh City		9
East Lothian		10
Midlothian		11
West Lothian		12
The Borders		13
Highland		14
Orkney		15
Shetland		16

Western Isles	17
Glasgow City	18
Arygll and Bute	19
East Dunbartonshire	20
West Dunbartonshire	21
South Lanarkshire	22
North Lanarkshire	23
East Ayrshire	24
North Ayrshire	25
East Renfrewshire	26
Inverclyde	27
South Ayrshire	28
Renfrewshire	29
Dundee City	30
Angus	31
Perth and Kinross	32
None of these	33

We are interested in speaking to a range of different people in order to get a nationally representative picture. So can I check a few details before we start...?

<AGEQ> And can I check how old you are?
refused -1 or F11d

|__|__|__| + 89

<PAIDEMP> And are you currently in paid employment?

Yes	91	1
No		2

I am going to read out a list of different types of march or parade. For each one, could you tell me whether you have ever been involved in that kind of march, either as a participant, a spectator or as someone otherwise affected by the march (for example as a passer-by, or because you live or work nearby). We're just interested in marches or parades that took place in Scotland, not in parades you might have seen when you were abroad or in other parts of the UK.

<Q1A1> 1.a.1. First of all, thinking about local gala day parades, carnivals with floats, or student rag weeks and that kind of thing. Have you ever been an active participant in that kind of parade?

Yes	92	1
No		2
Don't know/can't remember		3
Refused		4

If Yes at q1a1

<Q1A2> 1.a.2. And roughly when was the last time you were involved?
(Read out if necessary) Was it...?

Within the last year	93	1
More than a year but less than 5 years ago		2
5 years ago or more		3
Don't know/can't remember		4
Refused		5

<Q1B1> 1.b.1. And have you ever been a spectator at that kind of parade?

Yes	94	1
No		2
Don't know/can't remember		3
Refused		4

Yes at q1b1

<Q1B2> 1.b.2. And roughly when was the last time you were a spectator?
(Read out if necessary) Was it...?

Within the last year	95	1
More than a year but less than 5 years ago		2
5 years ago or more		3
Don't know/can't remember		4
Refused		5

<Q1C1> 1.c.1. And, other than being a participant or a spectator, have you ever found yourself near to that kind of parade. For example as a passer-by, or because you live or work nearby?

Yes	96	1
No		2
Don't know/can't remember		3
Refused		4

If Yes at q1c1

<Q1C2> 1.c.2. And roughly when was the last time that happened?
(Read out if necessary) Was it...?

Within the last year	97	1
More than a year but less than 5 years ago		2
5 years ago or more		3
Don't know/can't remember		4
Refused		5

<SUM1> Summary of attendances – at march or parade

you were a participant	98	1
you were a spectator		2
you've found yourself near to that kind of parade		3

If yes at any of a to c, and less than 5 years ago ask

1.d. And thinking about the time or times:
being both a participant and a spectator; or
being both a participant and just finding yourself near to that kind of parade; or
being both a spectator and just finding yourself near to that kind of parade; or
all of those experiences, as a participant, spectator and just finding yourself near to that kind of parade, can you tell me if you experienced any of the following...?

<Q1D1> 1.d Feelings of community spirit

Yes	99	1
No		2
Don't know/can't remember		3
Refused		4

<Q1D2> 1.d Enjoyment

Yes	100	1
No		2
Don't know/can't remember		3
Refused		4

<Q1D3> 1.d Feeling you were making a difference (if necessary explain, we mean did you feel you were changing things for the better or influencing things)

Yes	101	1
No		2
Don't know/can't remember		3
Refused		4

<Q1D4> 1.d Feeling you were involved in something important

Yes	102	1
No		2
Don't know/can't remember		3
Refused		4

<Q1D5> 1.d Being annoyed or upset by the noise

Yes	103	1
No		2
Don't know/can't remember		3
Refused		4

<Q1D6> 1.d Being held up or delayed

Yes	104	1
No		2
Don't know/can't remember		3
Refused		4

<Q1D7> 1.d Feeling angry, offended or upset by the march or marchers

Yes	105	1
No		2
Don't know/can't remember		3
Refused		4

<Q1D8> 1.d Feeling that you were in physical danger

Yes	106	1
No		2
Don't know/can't remember		3
Refused		4

<Q1D9> 1.d Being prevented from going somewhere you wanted to go

Yes	107	1
No		2
Don't know/can't remember		3
Refused		4

Q2 And now thinking about political protests or demonstrations about particular issues, for example local hospital closures, anti-war protests, Countryside Alliance marches, student protests, or trade union demonstrations …

<Q2A1> 2.a.1. Have you ever been an active participant in that kind of demonstration?

Yes	108	1
No		2
Don't know/can't remember		3
Refused		4

If Yes at q2a1

<Q2A1B> Q2.a.1b Would you say that this was a protest about a local or national issue?

Local	109	1
National		2
Both		3
Don't know/can't remember		4
Refused		5

<Q2A2> 2.a.2. And roughly when was the last time you were involved?
(Read out if necessary) Was it...?

Within the last year..	110	1
More than a year but less than 5 years ago.................................		2
5 years ago or more...		3
Don't know/can't remember...		4
Refused...		5

<Q2B1> 2.b.1. And have you ever been a spectator at that kind of demonstration?

Yes..	111	1
No...		2
Don't know/can't remember...		3
Refused...		4

Yes at q2b1

<Q2B1B> Q2.a.1b Would you say that this was a protest about a local or national issue?

Local...	112	1
National..		2
Both..		3
Don't know/can't remember...		4
Refused...		5

<Q2B2> 2.b.2. And roughly when was the last time you were a spectator?
(Read out if necessary) Was it...?

Within the last year..	113	1
More than a year but less than 5 years ago.................................		2
5 years ago or more...		3
Don't know/can't remember...		4
Refused...		5

<Q2C1> 2.c.1. And, other than being a participant or a spectator, have you ever found yourself near to that kind of demonstration. For example as a passerby, or because you live or work nearby?

Yes..	114	1
No...		2
Don't know/can't remember...		3
Refused...		4

If Yes at q2c1

<Q2C1B> Q2.a.1b Would you say that this was a protest about a local or national issue?

Local	115	1
National		2
Both		3
Don't know/can't remember		4
Refused		5

<Q2C2> 2.c.2. And roughly when was the last time that happened? (Read out if necessary) Was it...?

Within the last year	116	1
More than a year but less than 5 years ago		2
5 years ago or more		3
Don't know/can't remember		4
Refused		5

<SUM2> Summary of attendances – at demonstration or protest

you were a participant	117	1
you were a spectator		2
you've found yourself near to that kind of~		3

If yes at any of a to c, and less than 5 years ago ask

2.d. And thinking about the time and times:
being both a participant and a spectator; or
being both a participant and just finding yourself near to that kind of demonstration; or
being both a spectator and just finding yourself near to that kind of demonstration; or
all of those experiences, as a participant, spectator and just finding yourself near to that kind of demonstration, can you tell me if you experienced any of the following...?

<Q2D1> 2.d Feelings of community spirit

Yes	118	1
No		2
Don't know/can't remember		3
Refused		4

<Q2D2> 2.d Enjoyment

Yes	119	1
No		2
Don't know/can't remember		3
Refused		4

<Q2D3> 2.d Feeling you were making a difference (if necessary explain, we mean did you feel you were changing things for the better or influencing things)

Yes	120	1
No		2
Don't know/can't remember		3
Refused		4

<Q2D4> 2.d Feeling you were involved in something important

Yes	121	1
No		2
Don't know/can't remember		3
Refused		4

<Q2D5> 2.d Being annoyed or upset by the noise

Yes	122	1
No		2
Don't know/can't remember		3
Refused		4

<Q2D6> 2.d Being held up or delayed

Yes	123	1
No		2
Don't know/can't remember		3
Refused		4

<Q2D7> 2.d Feeling angry, offended or upset by the march or marchers

Yes	124	1
No		2
Don't know/can't remember		3
Refused		4

<Q2D8> 2.d Feeling that you were in physical danger

Yes	125	1
No		2
Don't know/can't remember		3
Refused		4

<Q2D9> 2.d Being prevented from going somewhere you wanted to go

Yes	126	1
No		2
Don't know/can't remember		3
Refused		4

Appendix B

Q3 And now thinking about Orange Order walks or Irish Republican marches....

<Q3A1> 3.a.1. Have you ever been an active participant in that kind of march?

Yes	127	1
No		2
Don't know/can't remember		3
Refused		4

If Yes at q3a1

<Q3A2> 3.a.2. And roughly when was the last time you were involved?
(Read out if necessary) Was it...?

Within the last year	128	1
More than a year but less than 5 years ago		2
5 years ago or more		3
Don't know/can't remember		4
Refused		5

<Q3B1> 3.b.1. And have you ever been a spectator at that kind of march?

Yes	129	1
No		2
Don't know/can't remember		3
Refused		4

Yes at q3b1

<Q3B2> 3.b.2. And roughly when was the last time you were a spectator?
(Read out if necessary) Was it...?

Within the last year	130	1
More than a year but less than 5 years ago		2
5 years ago or more		3
Don't know/can't remember		4
Refused		5

<Q3C1> 3.c.1. And, other than being a participant or a spectator, have you ever found yourself near to that kind of march. For example as a passer-by, or because you live or work nearby?

Yes	131	1
No		2
Don't know/can't remember		3
Refused		4

If Yes at q3c1

<Q3C2> 3.c.2. And roughly when was the last time that happened?
(Read out if necessary) Was it...?

Within the last year	132	1

More than a year but less than 5 years ago 2
5 years ago or more 3
Don't know/can't remember 4
Refused 5

<SUM3> Summary of attendances – at demonstration or protest
you were a participant 133   1
you were a spectator 2
you've found yourself near to that kind of march 3

If yes at any of a to c, and less than 5 years ago ask 3.d. And thinking about the time and times:
being both a participant and a spectator; or
being both a participant and just finding yourself near to that kind of march; or
being both a spectator and just finding yourself near to that kind of march; or
all of those experiences, as a participant, spectator and just finding yourself near to that kind of march, can you tell me if you experienced any of the following...?

<Q3D1> 3.d Feelings of community spirit
Yes 134   1
No 2
Don't know/can't remember 3
Refused 4

<Q3D2> 3.d Enjoyment
Yes 135   1
No 2
Don't know/can't remember 3
Refused 4

<Q3D3> 3.d Feeling you were making a difference (if necessary explain, we mean did you feel you were changing things for the better or influencing things)
Yes 136   1
No 2
Don't know/can't remember 3
Refused 4

<Q3D4> 3.d Feeling you were involved in something important
Yes 137   1
No 2
Don't know/can't remember 3
Refused 4

Appendix B

<Q3D5> 3.d Being annoyed or upset by the noise
Yes 138   1
No   2
Don't know/can't remember   3
Refused   4

<Q3D6> 3.d Being held up or delayed
Yes 139   1
No   2
Don't know/can't remember   3
Refused   4

<Q3D7> 3.d Feeling angry, offended or upset by the march or marchers
Yes 140   1
No   2
Don't know/can't remember   3
Refused   4

<Q3D8> 3.d Feeling that you were in physical danger
Yes 141   1
No   2
Don't know/can't remember   3
Refused   4

<Q3D9> 3.d Being prevented from going somewhere you wanted to go
Yes 142   1
No   2
Don't know/can't remember   3
Refused   4

<Q4A1> 4.a.1. And have you ever been a participant at any other kind of parade or march in Scotland?
Yes 143   1
No   2
Don't know/can't remember   3
Refused   4

If Yes at q4a1

<Q4A1B> 4a1b. What other kind of march have you participated in?
Do not read out
Youth parade (Scouts, Guides, Boys Brigade) 144   1
Pipe band, marching band, majorette   2
Rememberance day parade   3
Football/rugby/sport victory parade   4

205

Pageant		5
May day parade		6
Common riding		7
Carnival/festival		8
Any political protest/demo		9
Orange Order/Loyalist/Apprentice Boys		10
Catholic/Republican/James Connolly/Hibs		11
Other (specify)		49
None		50
Don't know		51

<Q4A2> 4.a.2. And roughly when was the last time you were involved in any of those kinds of marches (Read out if necessary) Was it...?

Within the last year	145	1
More than a year but less than 5 years ago		2
5 years ago or more		3
Don't know/can't remember		4
Refused		5

<Q4B1> 4.b.1. And have you ever been a spectator at any other kind of parade or march in Scotland?

Yes	146	1
No		2
Don't know/can't remember		3
Refused		4

Yes at q4b1

<Q4B1B> 4a1b. What other kind of march have you been a spectator?
Do not read out

Youth parade (Scouts, Guides, Boys Brigade)	147	1
Pipe band, marching band, majorettes		2
Rememberance day parade		3
Football/rugby/sport victory parade		4
Pageant		5
May day parade		6
Common riding		7
Carnival/festival		8
Any political protest/demo		9
Orange Order/Loyalist/Apprentice Boys		10
Catholic/Republican/James Connolly/Hibs		11
Other (specify)		49
None		50
Don't know		51

<Q4B2> 4.b.2. And roughly when was the last time you were a spectator at any of those kinds of parades? (Read out if necessary) Was it...?

Within the last year	148	1
More than a year but less than 5 years ago		2
5 years ago or more		3
Don't know/can't remember		4
Refused		5

<Q4C1> 4.c.1. And, other than being a participant or a spectator, have you ever found yourself near to any other kind of parade or march in Scotland. (For example as a passer-by, or because you live or work nearby?)

Yes	149	1
No		2
Don't know/can't remember		3
Refused		4

If Yes at q4c1

<Q4C1B> 4a1b. What other kind of march have you found yourself near?
Do not read out

Youth parade (Scouts, Guides, Boys Brigade)	150	1
Pipe band, marching band, majorettes		2
Rememberance day parade		3
Football/rugby/sport victory parade		4
Pageant		5
May day parade		6,
Common riding		7
Carnival/festival		8
Any political protest/demo		9
Orange Order/Loyalist/Apprentice Boys		10
Catholic/Republican/James Connolly/Hibs		11
Other (specify)		49
None		50
Don't know		51

<Q4C2> 4.c.2. And roughly when was the last time that happened? (Read out if necessary) Was it...?

Within the last year	151	1
More than a year but less than 5 years ago		2
5 years ago or more		3
Don't know/can't remember		4
Refused		5

<SUM4> Summary of attendances – at other kind of parade or march in Scotland
you were a participant... 152   1
you were a spectator...   2
you've found yourself near to any other kind of   3

If yes at any of a to c, and less than 5 years ago ask 4.d. And thinking about the time and times:
being both a participant and a spectator; or
being both a participant and just finding yourself near to any other kind of march; or
being both a spectator and just finding yourself near to any other kind of march; or
all of those experiences, as a participant, spectator and just finding yourself near to any other kind of march, can you tell me if you experienced any of the following...?

<Q4D1> 4.d Feelings of community spirit
Yes... 153   1
No...   2
Don't know/can't remember...   3
Refused..   4

<Q4D2> 4.d Enjoyment
Yes... 154   1
No...   2
Don't know/can't remember...   3
Refused..   4

<Q4D3> 4.d Feeling you were making a difference (If necessary, explain we mean did you feel you were changing things for the better, or influencing things)
Yes... 155   1
No...   2
Don't know/can't remember...   3
Refused..   4

<Q4D4> 4.d Feeling you were involved in something important
Yes... 156   1
No...   2
Don't know/can't remember...   3
Refused..   4

<Q4D5> 4.d Being annoyed or upset by the noise

Yes	157	1
No		2
Don't know/can't remember		3
Refused		4

<Q4D6> 4.d Being held up or delayed

Yes	158	1
No		2
Don't know/can't remember		3
Refused		4

<Q4D7> 4.d Feeling angry, offended or upset by the march or marchers

Yes	159	1
No		2
Don't know/can't remember		3
Refused		4

<Q4D8> 4.d Feeling that you were in physical danger

Yes	160	1
No		2
Don't know/can't remember		3
Refused		4

<Q4D9> 4.d Being prevented from going somewhere you wanted to go

Yes	161	1
No		2
Don't know/can't remember		3
Refused		4

<Q5A1A> Q5.1a Thinking now about all kinds of marches and parades. In some places, arrangements for making decisions about marches and parades has become an issue because of the disruption caused by them, for example to traffic or businesses, or because of the mess that they create. Thinking about your local community, how much of an issue would you say this is. Is it...?

Read out

A big issue	162	1
Something of an issue		2
Not really an issue		3
Not an issue at all		4
DK		5
Ref		6

If they say a big issue or something of an issue, ask.

<Q5A1B> Q5.1b What particular kinds marches or parades are the issue in your local community because of the disruption they cause? (If say something about what the problem is e.g. there's too many/they cause trouble, rather than the kind of march, probe: and what types of march are the problem?)

Do not read out, multicode

Orange walks	163	1
Irish Republican/Catholic/James Connolly/Hibs		2
National Front/BNP/extreme-right		3
Anti-war/Peace protest		4
Countryside alliance march		5
Fox hunting (pro or anti)		6
Trade Union march/strikes		7
Other national political issues (e.g.		8
Local political issues (e.g. school and hospital		9
Community parades – (e.g. Gala day parades, Common		10
Community parades – (Youth parades)		11
All kinds/many kinds		12
Other (specify)		49
DK		50
Ref		51

<Q5A2A> Q5.2a And in some places, arrangements for making decisions about marches and parades have become an issue because of controversy about the nature or purpose of the march. Thinking about your local community, how much of an issue would you say this is. Is it...?

Read out

A big issue	164	1
Something of an issue		2
Not really an issue		3
Not an issue at all		4
DK		5
Ref		6

If they say a big issue or something of an issue, ask

<Q5A2B> Q5.2b. What particular kinds marches or parades are the issue in your local community because of the controversy they cause? (If say something about what the problem is e.g. there's too many/they cause trouble, rather than the kind of march, probe: and what types of march are the problem?)

Do not read out, multicode

Orange walks	165	1

Irish Republican/Catholic/James Connolly/Hibs	2
National Front/BNP/extreme-right	3
Anti-war/Peace protest	4
Countryside alliance march	5
Fox hunting (pro or anti)	6
Trade Union march/strikes	7
Other national political issues (e.g.	8
Local political issues (e.g. school and hospital	9
Community parades – (e.g. Gala day parades, Common	10
Community parades – (Youth parades)	11
All kinds/many kinds	12
Other (specify)	49
DK	50
Ref	51

There are a number of the different things which the authorities might take into account when deciding whether a march or parade should be allowed to go ahead, or about when and where it can take place. I am going to ask you what you think should be taken into account when making decisions about different kinds of marches...

Q6a1 Thinking about a local gala day parade with floats, how important do you think it is to take the following things into account; is it very important, quite important, not very important or not important at all...

<Q6A1A> Q6a1 And still thinking about a local gala day parade with floats, how important is it to take into account...

The risk of serious damage to property

Very important	166	1
Quite important		2
Not very important		3
Not at all important		4
Not applicable		5
DK		6
Refused		7

<Q6A1B> Q6a1 And still thinking about a local gala day parade with floats, how important is it to take into account...

The risk to public safety

Very important	167	1
Quite important		2
Not very important		3
Not at all important		4

Not applicable 5
DK 6
Refused 7

<Q6A1C> Q6a1 And still thinking about a local gala day parade with floats, how important is it to take into account...

Likely disruption to businesses
Very important 168   1
Quite important 2
Not very important 3
Not at all important 4
Not applicable 5
DK 6
Refused 7

<Q6A1D> Q6a1 And still thinking about a local gala day parade with floats, how important is it to take into account...

Likely disruption to traffic
Very important 169   1
Quite important 2
Not very important 3
Not at all important 4
Not applicable 5
DK 6
Refused 7

<Q6A1E> Q6a1 And still thinking about a local gala day parade with floats, how important is it to take into account...

The cost of policing and clearing up afterwards
Very important 170   1
Quite important 2
Not very important 3
Not at all important 4
Not applicable 5
DK 6
Refused 7

<Q6A1F> Q6a1 And still thinking about a local gala day parade with floats, how important is it to take into account...

Whether people might be offended or upset by it

Very important	171	1
Quite important		2
Not very important		3
Not at all important		4
Not applicable		5
DK		6
Refused		7

<Q6A1G> Q6a1 And still thinking about a local gala day parade with floats, how important is it to take into account...

Whether it's a traditional march or parade

Very important	172	1
Quite important		2
Not very important		3
Not at all important		4
Not applicable		5
DK		6
Refused		7

<Q6A1H> Q6a1 And still thinking about a local gala day parade with floats, how important is it to take into account...

The number of other marches or parades there have been in the area

Very important	173	1
Quite important		2
Not very important		3
Not at all important		4
Not applicable		5
DK		6
Refused		7

<Q6A1I> Q6a1 And still thinking about a local gala day parade with floats, how important is it to take into account...

Freedom of speech and the right to demonstrate

Very important	174	1
Quite important		2
Not very important		3
Not at all important		4
Not applicable		5
DK		6
Refused		7

<Q6IMPT> Q6 rated at very or quite important

The risk of serious damage to property	175	1
The risk to public safety		2
Likely disruption to businesses		3
Likely disruption to traffic		4
The cost of policing and clearing up afterwards		5
Whether people might be offended or upset by it		6
Whether it's a traditional march or parade		7
The number of other marches or parades there have		8
Freedom of speech and the right to demonstrate		9

<Q6IMPTCK> Q6IMPTCK

Very important	176	1
Quite important		2

All more than one coded very important, or none coded very important but more than one coded quite important.

<Q6A2> Q6a2 Which of those things do you think is the most important consideration? **Read out if necessary**

The risk of serious damage to property	177	1
The risk to public safety		2
Likely disruption to businesses		3
Likely disruption to traffic		4
The cost of policing and clearing up afterwards		5
Whether people might be offended or upset by it		6
Whether it's a traditional march or parade		7
The number of other marches or parades there have		8
Freedom of speech and the right to demonstrate		9
None		10
Don't know		11

Q7 Thinking about a demonstration, parade or march by a political party or protest group such as a trade union, the National Front or the Countryside Alliance, how important do you think it is to take the following things into account, is it very important, quite important, not very important or not important at all...

<Q7A1A> Q7a1 And still thinking about a demonstration, parade or march by a political party or protest group such as a trade union, the National Front or the Countryside Alliance, how important is it to take into account...

The risk of serious damage to property

Very important	178	1
Quite important		2
Not very important		3

Not at all important	4
Not applicable	5
DK	6
Refused	7

<Q7A1B> Q7a1 And still thinking about a demonstration, parade or march by a political party or protest group such as a trade union, the National Front or the Countryside Alliance, how important is it to take into account...

The risk to public safety

Very important	179	1
Quite important		2
Not very important		3
Not at all important		4
Not applicable		5
DK		6
Refused		7

<Q7A1C> Q7a1 And still thinking about a demonstration, parade or march by a political party or protest group such as a trade union, the National Front or the Countryside Alliance, how important is it to take into account...

Likely disruption to businesses

Very important	180	1
Quite important		2
Not very important		3
Not at all important		4
Not applicable		5
DK		6
Refused		7

<Q7A1D> Q7a1 And still thinking about a demonstration, parade or march by a political party or protest group such as a trade union, the National Front or the Countryside Alliance, how important is it to take into account...

Likely disruption to traffic

Very important	181	1
Quite important		2
Not very important		3
Not at all important		4
Not applicable		5
DK		6
Refused		7

<Q7A1E> Q7a1 And still thinking about a demonstration, parade or march by a political party or protest group such as a trade union, the National Front or the Countryside Alliance, how important is it to take into account...

The cost of policing and clearing up afterwards
Very important	182	1
Quite important		2
Not very important		3
Not at all important		4
Not applicable		5
DK		6
Refused		7

<Q7A1F> Q7a1 And still thinking about a demonstration, parade or march by a political party or protest group such as a trade union, the National Front or the Countryside Alliance, how important is it to take into account...

Whether people might be offended or upset by it
Very important	183	1
Quite important		2
Not very important		3
Not at all important		4
Not applicable		5
DK		6
Refused		7

<Q7A1G> Q7a1 And still thinking about a demonstration, parade or march by a political party or protest group such as a trade union, the National Front or the Countryside Alliance, how important is it to take into account...

Whether it's a traditional march or parade
Very important	184	1
Quite important		2
Not very important		3
Not at all important		4
Not applicable		5
DK		6
Refused		7

\<Q7A1H\> Q7a1 And still thinking about a demonstration, parade or march by a political party or protest group such as a trade union, the National Front or the Countryside Alliance, how important is it to take into account...

The number of other marches or parades there have been in the area

Very important	185	1
Quite important		2
Not very important		3
Not at all important		4
Not applicable		5
DK		6
Refused		7

\<Q7A1I\> Q7a1 And still thinking about a demonstration, parade or march by a political party or protest group such as a trade union, the National Front or the Countryside Alliance, how important is it to take into account...

Freedom of speech and the right to demonstrate

Very important	186	1
Quite important		2
Not very important		3
Not at all important		4
Not applicable		5
DK		6
Refused		7

\<Q7IMPT\> Q7 rated at very or quite important

The risk of serious damage to property	187	1
The risk to public safety		2
Likely disruption to businesses		3
Likely disruption to traffic		4
The cost of policing and clearing up afterwards		5
Whether people might be offended or upset by it		6
Whether it's a traditional march or parade		7
The number of other marches or parades there have		8
Freedom of speech and the right to demonstrate		9

\<Q7IMPTCK\> Q7IMPTCK

Very important	188	1
Quite important		2

All more than one coded very important, or none coded very important but more than one coded quite important.

<Q7A2> Q7a2 Which of those things do you think is the most important consideration?
Read out if necessary

The risk of serious damage to property	189	1
The risk to public safety		2
Likely disruption to businesses		3
Likely disruption to traffic		4
The cost of policing and clearing up afterwards		5
Whether people might be offended or upset by it		6
Whether it's a traditional march or parade		7
The number of other marches or parades there have		8
Freedom of speech and the right to demonstrate		9
None		10
Don't know		11

Q8 Thinking about a demonstration, parade or march against a local hospital closure or another local issue. (If respondent doesn't understand. Add... For example, a protest about a school or factory closure new property developments, or road developments). How important do you think it is to take the following things into account; is it very important, quite important, not very important or not important at all...

<Q8A1A> Q8a1 And still thinking about a demonstration, parade or march against a local hospital closure or another local issue, how important is it to take into account...
The risk of serious damage to property

Very important	190	1
Quite important		2
Not very important		3
Not at all important		4
Not applicable		5
DK		6
Refused		7

<Q8A1B> Q8a1 And still thinking about a demonstration, parade or march against a local hospital closure or another local issue, how important is it to take into account...

The risk to public safety

Very important	191	1
Quite important		2
Not very important		3
Not at all important		4
Not applicable		5
DK		6
Refused		7

<Q8A1C> Q8a1 And still thinking about a demonstration, parade or march against a local hospital closure or another local issue, how important is it to take into account...
Likely disruption to businesses

Very important	192	1
Quite important		2
Not very important		3
Not at all important		4
Not applicable		5
DK		6
Refused		7

<Q8A1D> Q8a1 And still thinking about a demonstration, parade or march against a local hospital closure or another local issue, how important is it to take into account...
Likely disruption to traffic

Very important	193	1
Quite important		2
Not very important		3
Not at all important		4
Not applicable		5
DK		6
Refused		7

<Q8A1E> Q8a1 And still thinking about a demonstration, parade or march against a local hospital closure or another local issue, how important is it to take into account...
The cost of policing and clearing up afterwards

Very important	194	1
Quite important		2
Not very important		3
Not at all important		4
Not applicable		5
DK		6
Refused		7

<Q8A1F> Q8a1 And still thinking about a demonstration, parade or march against a local hospital closure or another local issue, how important is it to take into account...

Whether people might be offended or upset by it
Very important..	195	1
Quite important...		2
Not very important..		3
Not at all important...		4
Not applicable...		5
DK...		6
Refused..		7

<Q8A1G> Q8a1 And still thinking about a demonstration, parade or march against a local hospital closure or another local issue, how important is it to take into account...

Whether it's a traditional march or parade
Very important..	196	1
Quite important...		2
Not very important..		3
Not at all important...		4
Not applicable...		5
DK...		6
Refused..		7

<Q8A1H> Q8a1 And still thinking about a demonstration, parade or march against a local hospital closure or another local issue, how important is it to take into account...

The number of other marches or parades there have been in the area
Very important..	197	1
Quite important...		2
Not very important..		3
Not at all important...		4
Not applicable...		5
DK...		6
Refused..		7

<Q8A1I> Q8a1 And still thinking about a demonstration, parade or march against a local hospital closure or another local issue, how important is it to take into account...
Freedom of speech and the right to demonstrate
Very important..	198	1
Quite important...		2
Not very important..		3
Not at all important...		4
Not applicable...		5

DK		6
Refused		7

<Q8IMPT> Q8 rated at very or quite important

The risk of serious damage to property	199	1
The risk to public safety		2
Likely disruption to businesses		3
Likely disruption to traffic		4
The cost of policing and clearing up afterwards		5
Whether people might be offended or upset by it		6
Whether it's a traditional march or parade		7
The number of other marches or parades there have		8
Freedom of speech and the right to demonstrate		9

<Q8IMPTCK> Q8IMPTCK

Very important	200	1
Quite important		2

All more than one coded very important, or none coded very important but more than one coded quite important.

<Q8A2> Q8a2 Which of those things do you think is the most important consideration?

Read out if necessary

The risk of serious damage to property	201	1
The risk to public safety		2
Likely disruption to businesses		3
Likely disruption to traffic		4
The cost of policing and clearing up afterwards		5
Whether people might be offended or upset by it		6
Whether it's a traditional march or parade		7
The number of other marches or parades there have		8
Freedom of speech and the right to demonstrate		9
None		10
Don't know		11

Q9 Thinking about an Irish Republican march or an Orange walk, how important do you think it is to take the following things into account; is it very important, quite important, not very important or not important at all...

<Q9A1A> Q9a1 And still thinking about an Irish Republican march or an Orange walk, how important is it to take into account...

The risk of serious damage to property

Very important	202	1
Quite important		2
Not very important		3
Not at all important		4
Not applicable		5
DK		6
Refused		7

<Q9A1B> Q9a1 And still thinking about an Irish Republican march or an Orange walk, how important is it to take into account...

The risk to public safety

Very important	203	1
Quite important		2
Not very important		3
Not at all important		4
Not applicable		5
DK		6
Refused		7

<Q9A1C> Q9a1 And still thinking about an Irish Republican march or an Orange walk, how important is it to take into account...

Likely disruption to businesses

Very important	204	1
Quite important		2
Not very important		3
Not at all important		4
Not applicable		5
DK		6
Refused		7

<Q9A1D> Q9a1 And still thinking about an Irish Republican march or an Orange walk, how important is it to take into account...

Likely disruption to traffic

Very important	205	1
Quite important		2
Not very important		3
Not at all important		4
Not applicable		5
DK		6
Refused		7

<Q9A1E> Q9a1 And still thinking about an Irish Republican march or an Orange walk, how important is it to take into account...

The cost of policing and clearing up afterwards

Very important	206	1
Quite important		2
Not very important		3
Not at all important		4
Not applicable		5
DK		6
Refused		7

<Q9A1F> Q9a1 And still thinking about an Irish Republican march or an Orange walk, how important is it to take into account...

Whether people might be offended or upset by it

Very important	207	1
Quite important		2
Not very important		3
Not at all important		4
Not applicable		5
DK		6
Refused		7

<Q9A1G> Q9a1 And still thinking about an Irish Republican march or an Orange walk, how important is it to take into account...

Whether it's a traditional march or parade

Very important	208	1
Quite important		2
Not very important		3
Not at all important		4
Not applicable		5
DK		6
Refused		7

<Q9A1H> Q9a1 And still thinking about an Irish Republican march or an Orange walk, how important is it to take into account...

The number of other marches or parades there have been in the area

Very important	209	1
Quite important		2
Not very important		3
Not at all important		4
Not applicable		5
DK		6
Refused		7

<Q9A1I> Q9a1 And still thinking about an Irish Republican march or an Orange walk, how important is it to take into account...

Freedom of speech and the right to demonstrate

Very important	210	1
Quite important		2
Not very important		3
Not at all important		4
Not applicable		5
DK		6
Refused		7

<Q9IMPT> Q9 rated at very or quite important

The risk of serious damage to property	211	1
The risk to public safety		2
Likely disruption to businesses		3
Likely disruption to traffic		4
The cost of policing and clearing up afterwards		5
Whether people might be offended or upset by it		6
Whether it's a traditional march or parade		7
The number of other marches or parades there have		8
Freedom of speech and the right to demonstrate		9

<Q9IMPTCK> Q9IMPTCK

Very important	212	1
Quite important		2

All more than one coded very important, or none coded very important but more than one coded quite important.

Appendix B

<Q9A2> Q9a2 Which of those things do you think is the most important consideration?

Read out if necessary

The risk of serious damage to property	213	1
The risk to public safety		2
Likely disruption to businesses		3
Likely disruption to traffic		4
The cost of policing and clearing up afterwards		5
Whether people might be offended or upset by it		6
Whether it's a traditional march or parade		7
The number of other marches or parades there have		8
Freedom of speech and the right to demonstrate		9
None		10
Don't know		11

<Q10> Q10 Currently, anyone organising a parade or march is required to give the council and the police at least 7 days notice. It has been suggested that they should be required to give 28 days notice. In general, do you think that 28 days notice seems...?

Read out

Too much notice	214	1
Not enough notice		2
or About right		3
Depends		4
DK		5
Ref		6

<Q11> Q11 Do you think there are some types of parades or marches that should be allowed to give less notice than other types? For example, if people wanted to react quickly to a political decision, or if a sports team won a competition and wanted a victory parade? (If necessary, give further example of a factory closure).

Yes/Sometimes allowed/Depends	215	1
No		2
DK		3
Ref		4

Q12 Which of the following groups or organisations should be notified when a march is planned? (If yes ask, and should they be involved in decisions about the march or just notified?)

<Q12A> Q12. The police
If Yes ask, and should they be involved in decisions about the march or just notified?

Yes – notified only...	216	1
Yes – notified and involved in decisions...		2
Not notified...		3
DK...		4
Ref...		5

<Q12B> Q12. Other emergency services
If Yes ask, and should they be involved in decisions about the march or just notified?

Yes – notified only...	217	1
Yes – notified and involved in decisions...		2
Not notified...		3
DK...		4
Ref...		5

<Q12C> Q12. Businesses near the proposed route
If Yes ask, and should they be involved in decisions about the march or just notified?

Yes – notified only...	218	1
Yes – notified and involved in decisions...		2
Not notified...		3
DK...		4
Ref...		5

<Q12D> Q12. Residents near the proposed route
If Yes ask, and should they be involved in decisions about the march or just notified?

Yes – notified only...	219	1
Yes – notified and involved in decisions...		2
Not notified...		3
DK...		4
Ref...		5

<Q12E> Q12. Places of worship near the proposed route
If Yes ask, and should they be involved in decisions about the march or just notified?

Yes – notified only...	220	1
Yes – notified and involved in decisions...		2
Not notified...		3
DK...		4
Ref...		5

Appendix B

<Q12F> Q12. Local community groups
If Yes ask, and should they be involved in decisions about the march or just notified?
Yes – notified only	221	1
Yes – notified and involved in decisions		2
Not notified		3
DK		4
Ref		5

<Q12G> Q12. The council
If Yes ask, and should they be involved in decisions about the march or just notified?
Yes – notified only	222	1
Yes – notified and involved in decisions		2
Not notified		3
DK		4
Ref		5

<Q13A> Q13a Do you, personally, want to be notified about all marches or parades near where you live or work ?
Yes	223	1
No		2
DK		3
Ref		4

Yes at Q13a

<Q13B> Q13b In which of the following ways would you most like to be notified...?
If more than two – **Probe** for which most prefer
Read out
By letter	224	1
By email		2
By a newspaper advert		3
By local radio		4
By the council website		5
By posters on the proposed route		6
Don't know		7
Refused		8

I's like to to ask you some questions about cost.

Q14. Thinking about a local gala day parade with floats, do you think the organisers should contribute towards....

<Q14A> Q14. The policing costs

Yes	225	1
No		2
DK		3
Ref		4

<Q14B> Q14. Local authority costs (if necessary, explain that would include the cost of arranging road closures and clearing up)

Yes	226	1
No		2
DK		3
Ref		4

<Q14C> Q14. Costs of repairing damage

Yes	227	1
No		2
DK		3
Ref		4

<Q14D> Q14. Costs of insurance

Yes	228	1
No		2
DK		3
Ref		4

Q15 Thinking about a demonstration, parade or march by a political party or protest group such as a trade union, the National Front or the Countryside Alliance, do you think the organisers should contribute towards....

<Q15A> Q15. The policing costs

Yes	229	1
No		2
DK		3
Ref		4

<Q15B> Q15. Local authority costs (if necessary, explain that would include the cost of arranging road closures and clearing up)

Yes	230	1
No		2
DK		3
Ref		4

<Q15C> Q15. Costs of repairing damage

Yes	231	1
No		2

DK		3
Ref		4

<Q15D> Q15. Costs of insurance

Yes	232	1
No		2
DK		3
Ref		4

Q16 Thinking about a demonstration, parade or march against a local hospital closure or another local issue. (If respondent doesn't understand. Add... For example, a protest about a school closure, new property developments, or road developments)... do you think the organisers should contribute towards....

<Q16A> Q16. The policing costs

Yes	233	1
No		2
DK		3
Ref		4

<Q16B> Q16. Local authority costs (if necessary, explain that would include the cost of arranging road closures and clearing up)

Yes	234	1
No		2
DK		3
Ref		4

<Q16C> Q16. Costs of repairing damage

Yes	235	1
No		2
DK		3
Ref		4

<Q16D> Q16. Costs of insurance

Yes	236	1
No		2
DK		3
Ref		4

Q17 Thinking of an Orange walk or an Irish Republican march or ... do you think the organisers should contribute towards....

<Q17A> Q17. The policing costs

Yes	237	1
No		2
DK		3
Ref		4

<Q17B> Q17. Local authority costs (if necessary, explain that would include the cost of arranging road closures and clearing up)

Yes	238	1
No		2
DK		3
Ref		4

<Q17C> Q17. Costs of repairing damage

Yes	239	1
No		2
DK		3
Ref		4

<Q17D> Q17. Costs of insurance

Yes	240	1
No		2
DK		3
Ref		4

Q19 I'm now going to read out some statements and for each one I'd like you to tell me how much you agree or disagree....

<Q19A> Q19. As a general rule, all marches should be allowed unless there is a serious risk to public safety

Strongly agree	241	1
Agree a little		2
Neither agree nor disagree		3
Disagree a little		4
Strongly disagree		5
DK		6
Ref		7

<Q19B> Q19. Overall, marches and parades benefit my local community

Strongly agree	242	1
Agree a little		2
Neither agree nor disagree		3
Disagree a little		4
Strongly disagree		5
DK		6
Ref		7

<Q19C> Q19. Overall, marches and parades cause divisions in my local community

Strongly agree	243	1
Agree a little		2
Neither agree nor disagree		3
Disagree a little		4
Strongly disagree		5
DK		6
Ref		7

<Q19D> Q19. Freedom of speech is more important than whether someone is angered or offended by a march

Strongly agree	244	1
Agree a little		2
Neither agree nor disagree		3
Disagree a little		4
Strongly disagree		5
DK		6
Ref		7

<Q19E> Q19. Making marchers pay for policing costs limits freedom of speech

Strongly agree	245	1
Agree a little		2
Neither agree nor disagree		3
Disagree a little		4
Strongly disagree		5
DK		6
Ref		7

<Q19F> Q19. Marches which are likely to inflame racial or religious tensions should not go ahead

Strongly agree	246	1
Agree a little		2
Neither agree nor disagree		3
Disagree a little		4
Strongly disagree		5
DK		6
Ref		7

Can I ask you some questions about yourself. This is just so we can compare answers from different kinds of people in different circumstances. Just to remind you, as with all your answers, this information will be kept in strict confidence and no information which could identify you will be passed on to anyone outside the research team...

<OCC> Can you tell me your occupation, or the occupation of the chief income earner in your household? (Or previous occupation if unemployed for less than six months.) And what type of organisation do you work for (or type of organisation chief income earner work for?
And the position/rank/grade?
Any special qualifications related to occupation?
Remember to check widowed or retired details: Widow with widow's pension only
Widow with private means (specify husband's former occupation)
Retired with state pension only
Retired with state pension **and** occupation pension (specify former occupation)

Occupation	29	
DK	30	

You must enter details in the open ended box

<Work> And what is your work status?
Read out

Self-employed	249	1
Employed full-time		2
Employed part-time		3
Homemaker/Housewife		4
Student		5
Retired		6
Unemployed		7
Refused (**Do not read**)		8

<Q21> Q21 How would you describe where you live? Is it ....
Read out

A city	250	1
A large town		2
A small to medium sized town		3
A village		4
In a rural area		5
DK		6
Ref		7

<Q22> Q22 What religion, if any, were you brought up in? If say 'Christian' ask: which particular church?

Church of Scotland	251	1
Other Protestant (Presbyterian/Free Church of)		2
Roman Catholic		3
Other Christian (specify)		49
Muslim		50

Sikh		51
Hindu		52
Jewish		53
Buddhist		54
Other non Christian (specify)		89
None		90
DK		91
Ref		92

<Q23> Q23 And what is your current religion, if any?

Church of Scotland	252	1
Other Protestant (Presbyterian/Free Church of)		2
Roman Catholic		3
Other Christian (specify)		49
Muslim		50
Sikh		51
Hindu		52
Jewish		53
Buddhist		54
Other non Christian (specify)		89
None		90
DK		91
Ref		92

<Q26> Q26 And finally, is there anything else you would like to say about marches and parades that you think is important?

No	253	1
Write in response		49

<RECONTA – Thank you very much for your help with this research.

CT> Would you be willing to be contacted to take part in future research on this topic – you would, of course, be free to say no at the time?

Yes	254	1
No		2

<Confirm> Thank you very much for your help

Appendix C

Meetings

During the course of the Review, I held 45 meetings with 125 people to collect views and information.

No	Organisation	Names	Date
45	Dr Elinor Kelly	Dr Elinor Kelly	16 November
44	Aberdeen Council	Councillor Kate Dean – Leader Councillor Raymond Hutcheon – Convenor of the Licensing Committee Douglas Paterson – Chief Executive Donald MacLeod – Solicitor	16 November
43	MSP – West Region	Annabel Goldie MSP	10 November
42	Rangers FC	John McClelland	10 November
41	ACPOS	John Vine – Chief Constable Ricky Gray – Deputy Chief Constable	26 October
40	MSP – Glasgow	Patrick Harvie	26 October
39	Grand Orange Lodge of Scotland	13 additional members of the Orange Order	26 October
38	MSP – Glasgow Kelvin	Pauline McNeill MSP	26 October
37	Cairde na hÉireann	Jim Slaven & colleague	20 October
36	Sense Over Sectarianism	11 people involved with work addressing sectarianism	11 October
35	Celtic FC	Ronnie Hawthorn	11 October
34	MSP – Glasgow	Nicola Sturgeon MSP	11 October
33	Apprentice Boys of Derry	John McAvoy – Chairman George Evans – Vice Chairman Craig Stevenson – Assistant Secretary John Coutts – Secretary	11 October

No	Organisation	Names	Date
32	Police Service Northern Ireland	Gary White – Superintendent Mark Hamilton – Chief Inspector Roy Marshall – Chief Inspector Amanda Cooke – Inspector Chris Livingston – Constable	21 September
31	Mediation Northern Ireland	Brendan McAllister	20 September
30	Parades Commission	Peter Osbourne – Commissioner Michael Boyle – Deputy to Secretary	20 September
29	Westminster Council	Tim Owen – Assistant Director, Events Angela Kearly – Deputy Director	15 September
28	Metropolitan Police	Michael Messinger – Commander Malcolm Simpson – Superintendent	15 September
27	City of London Police	James Hart – Commissioner	14 September
26	Southwark Council	Iain Thomas – Chief Superintendent	14 September
25	Glasgow Chambers of Commerce	Kate Sanford – Policy Director Lucy Gardner – Carlton George Hotel/Glasgow Hoteliers Association Khalid Javid – K A Javid & Co Jim McPhie – McPhies Craft Bakers Hamish Millar – Buchanan Galleries Rona Taylor – Glasgow Restaurateurs Association	14 September
24	Merseyside Police Liverpool Council Sefton Council	12 representatives from police and councils	8 September
23	Scottish Human Rights Centre	Rosemarie McIlhwan	7 September
22	STUC	Bill Speirs Dave Moxham	7 September
21	Association of Scottish Police Superintendants	Carol Forfar – General Secretary Clive Murray – Chief Superintendent Tom Buchan – Chief Superintendent Allan McIlervie – Superintendent	1 September
20	MSP – Glasgow	Tommy Sheridan – MSP	1 September

Appendix C

No	Organisation	Names	Date
19	North Lanarkshire Council/ COSLA	Councillor Jim McCabe – Leader Councillor Ernie Holloway – Deputy Convenor Gavin Whitefield – Chief Executive John O'Hagan – Director of Administration Norrie Williamson – COSLA Claire Downs – COSLA	31 August
18	MP – Glasgow Springburn,	Michael Martin	31 August
17	Polmont Young Offenders Institution	Five young people involved in 'A Culture of Two Halves' supported by Youthlink	27 August
16	Church of Scotland	Morag Mylne – Convenor, Church and Nation Committee David Sinclair – Secretary, Church and Nation Committee	24 August
15	South Lanarkshire Council	Councillor Eddie McAvoy – Leader Michael Doherty – Chief Executive	19 August
14	West Lothian Council	Councillor Graham Morice – Leader Councillor Neil Findlay Geraldine McCann – Legal Services	19 August
13	Glasgow City Council	Councillor Jim Coleman Councillor Malcolm Green George Black – Chief Executive Ian Drummond – Legal Services	18 August
12	Sense Over Sectarianism	Alison Logan – Coordinator George Mackie – Education Services, Glasgow City Council	18 August
11	Nil by Mouth	Fred Shedden – Chair of the Trustees Quintin Oliver – Trustee Helen Miller – Coordinator	18 August
10	Edinburgh Council	Councillor Donald Anderson – Leader Tom Aitchison – Chief Executive	17 August
9	Scottish Police Federation	Doug Keil – General Secretary Jim McDonald – Research Officer	17 August
8	Roman Catholic Church, Motherwell Diocese	Bishop Joseph Devine	3 August
7	MP – Glasgow Govan	Mohammad Sarwar MP	3 August

No	Organisation	Names	Date
6	Grand Orange Lodge of Scotland	Ian Wilson – Grand Master Robert McLean – Executive Officer	3 August
5	MP – Motherwell and Wishaw	Frank Roy MP	28 July
4	East Renfrewshire Council	Councillor Owen Taylor – Leader Eamon Dayley – Principal Committee Services Officer	28 July
3	Roman Catholic Church, Chancellor of Archdiocese of Glasgow/Parish Priest	Monsignor Peter Smith	27 July
2	Strathclyde Police	Willie Rae – Chief Constable,	27 July
1	MSP – Central Scotland	Donald Gorrie MSP	21 July

Appendix D

Extracts from Part V of the Civic Government (Scotland) Act 1982

EXTRACTS FROM PART V OF THE CIVIC GOVERNMENT (SCOTLAND) ACT 1982

PART V - PUBLIC PROCESSIONS

Notification of processions.

62.--(1) A person proposing to hold a procession in public shall give written notice of that proposal in accordance with subsections (2) and (3) below:

(a) to the local authority in whose area the procession is to be held, or if it is to be held in the areas of more than one such authority, to each such authority;

(aa) if the procession is to be held to any extent in a National Park, to the National Park authority for the National Park;

and

(b) to the chief constable

(2) Notice shall be given for the purposes of subsection (1) above by--

(*a*) its being posted to the main office of the local authority and (where subsection (1)(aa) above applies) of the National Park Authority and to the office of the chief constable so that in the normal course of post it might be expected to arrive not later than 7 days before the date when the procession is to be held; or

(*b*) its being delivered by hand to those offices not later than 7 days before that date.

(3) The notice to be given under subsection (1) above shall specify-

(*a*) the date and time when the procession is to be held;

(*b*) its route;

(*c*) the number of persons likely to take part in it;

(*d*) the arrangements for its control being made by the person proposing to hold it; and

(*e*) the name and address of that person.

(4) A local authority may, on application in accordance with subsection (5) below by a person proposing to hold a procession in public in their area

(a) made to them;

(aa) if the procession is to be held to any extent in a National Park, intimated to the National Park authority for the National Park;

and

(b) intimated to the chief constable, within the period of 7 days before the date when the procession is to be held, make an order dispensing with the requirements of subsection (2) above in relation to the time limits for the giving of notice of that proposal.

(5) An application under subsection (4) above shall specify the matters mentioned in subsection (3) above and, where an order has been made under the said subsection (4), the application for it shall be treated as notice duly given for the purposes of subsection (1) above.

(6) A local authority may (whether upon application made to them or not) make an order exempting any person proposing to hold any procession in public being a procession specified in the order or one of a class of processions so specified from the requirement under this section to give notice to the authority of the proposal to hold that procession.

(7) This section does not apply in relation to processions commonly or customarily held; but a local authority may, as respects their area, order that it shall apply to any such procession so held or any such class of processions so held as is specified in the order.

(8) An order under subsection (6) or (7) above may-

    (*a*) provide that its application in any case or class of cases is subject to such conditions as may be specified in the order;

    (*b*) classify processions by reference to any factor or factors whatsoever;

    (*c*) be varied or revoked by subsequent order made in like manner.

(9) The local authority shall, before making an order under subsection (4) above or making, varying or revoking an order under subsection (6) or (7) above, consult the chief constable.

(10)..

(11) The local authority shall, as soon as possible after they make, vary or revoke an order under subsection (6) or (7) above, give public notice of that fact in a newspaper or newspapers circulating in their area.

(12) In this section and in sections 63 to 65 of this Act-

"procession in public" means a procession in a public place;

"chief constable" means, in relation to a local authority, the chief constable of the police force for the area which comprises or includes the area of the authority; and

"public place" has the same meaning as in Part II of the Public Order Act 1986.

Functions of local authorities in relation to processions.

63. (1) The local authority may, after consulting the chief constable and (where section 62(1)(aa) of this Act applies) the National Park authority in respect of a procession notice of which has been given or falls to be treated as having been given in accordance with section 62(1) of this Act, make an order-

    (i) prohibiting the holding of the procession; or

(ii) imposing conditions on the holding of it.

(1A) Where notice of a proposal to hold a procession has been given or falls to be treated as having been given in accordance with section 62(1) of this Act –

(a) if a local authority have made an order under subsection (1) above they may at any time thereafter, after consulting the chief constable and (where subsection (1)(aa) of that section applies) the National Park authority, vary or revoke the order and, where they revoke it, make any order which there were empowered to make under that subsection;

(b) if they have decided not to make an order they may at any time thereafter, after consulting with the chief constable and (where subsection 62(1)(aa) applies) the National Park authority and make any order which they were empowered to make under that subsection.

(2) The conditions which may be imposed under subsection (1) or (1A) above on the holding of a procession may include conditions-

(*a*) as to the date, time and duration of the procession;

(*b*) as to the route to be taken by it;

(*c*) prohibiting its entry into any public place specified in the order.

(3) A local authority shall -

(*a*) where notice of a proposal to hold a procession has been given or falls to be treated as having been given in accordance with section 62(1) of this Act, deliver at least 2 days before the date when, in terms of the notice, the procession is to be held, to the person who gave the notice-

(i) where they have made an order under subsection (1) or (1A) above, a copy of it and a written statement of the reasons for it; or

(ii) where they decide not to make such an order under subsection (1) above or to revoke an order already made under subsection (1) or (1A) above, notification of that fact;

(iii) where they have, under subsection (1A) above, varied such an order, a copy of the order as varied and a written statement of the reasons for the variations; and

(*b*) where they have made an order under subsection (1) or (1A) above in relation to a proposal to hold a procession, make such arrangements as will ensure that persons who might take or are taking part in that procession are made aware of the fact that the order has been made and, if the order has been varied under subsection (1A) above, that it has been so varied and of its effect; and

(c). where they have revoked an order made under subsection (1) or (1A) above in relation to a proposal to hold a procession, make such arrangements as will ensure that persons who might take or are taking part in that procession are made aware of the fact that the order has been revoked.

(4) The local authority shall comply with subsection (3) above -

(*a*) as early as possible;

(*b*) only insofar as it is reasonably practicable for them to do so.

Appeal against orders under section 63.

64. (1) An appeal to the sheriff shall lie at the instance of a person who, in accordance with section 62 of this Act, has or falls to be treated as having given notice of a proposal to hold a procession in public against

(a) an order under section 63(1) or (1A) of this Act; or

(b) a variation under section 63(1A) of this Act of an order made under section 63(1) or (1A)

in relation to the procession.

(2) An appeal under this section shall be made by way of summary application and shall be lodged with the sheriff clerk within 14 days from the date on which the copy of the order and statement of reasons were received by the appellant.

(3) On good cause being shown, the sheriff may hear an appeal under this section notwithstanding that it was not lodged within the time mentioned in subsection (2) above.

(4) The sheriff may uphold an appeal under this section only if he considers that the local authority in arriving at their decision to make the order, or as the case may be, to vary the order -

(*a*) erred in law;

(*b*) based their decision on any incorrect material fact;

(*c*) exercised their discretion in an unreasonable manner; or

(*d*) otherwise acted beyond their powers.

(5) In considering an appeal under this section the sheriff may hear evidence by or on behalf of any party to the appeal.

(6) Subject to subsection (7) below, on an appeal under this section, the sheriff may

(*a*) uphold the appeal and-

(i) remit the case, with the reasons for his decision, to the local authority for reconsideration of their decision, or

(ii) if he considers that there is insufficient time for the case to be remitted under sub-paragraph (i) above vary the order which is the subject of the appeal or make any such order as the authority were empowered to make under section 63(1) of this Act; or

(*b*) dismiss the appeal,

and on remitting a case under paragraph (*a*)(i) above, the sheriff may-

> (i) specify a date by which the reconsideration by the authority must take place;
>
> (ii) modify any procedural steps which otherwise would be required to be taken in relation to the matter by or under any enactment (including this Act).

(7) The sheriff shall not exercise any of his powers under subsection (6) above unless he is satisfied that all steps which in the circumstances were reasonable have been taken with a view to securing that notice of the appeal and an opportunity of being heard with respect to it have been given to the authority whose order under section 63 of this Act is the subject of the appeal.

(8) The sheriff may include in his decision on an appeal under this section such order as to the expenses of the appeal as he thinks proper.

(9) Any party to an appeal to the sheriff under this section may appeal on a point of law from the decision of the sheriff to the Court of Session within 28 days from the date of that decision.

Offences and enforcement.

65. (1) Subject to subsection (3) below, a person who holds procession in public-

(*a*) without-

> (i) having given or being a person who is treated as having given notice in accordance with section 62 of this Act of his proposal to do so; and
>
> (ii) there being in force in relation to the procession an exempting order under section 62(6) of this Act;

(*b*) in contravention of an order under section 63(1) or (1A) or 64(6)(*a*)(ii) of this Act prohibiting the holding of it;

(*c*) otherwise than in accordance with a condition imposed by an order under section 63(1) or (1A) or 64(6)(*a*)(ii) of this Act in relation to the procession; or

(*d*) otherwise than in accordance with the particulars of its date, time and route specified -

> (i) in the notice given under section 62(1) to (3) of this Act; or
>
> (ii) where an order has been made under subsection (4) of that section, in the application for the order

except to the extent that a condition referred to in paragraph (*c*) above relates to its date, time or route,

shall be guilty of an offence and liable, on summary conviction, to a fine not exceeding level 4 on the standard scale or to imprisonment for a period not exceeding 3 months or to both.

(2) Subject to subsection (3) below, a person who takes part in a procession in public-

    (*a*) in respect of which-

        (i) notice has not been or is not treated as having been given in accordance with section 62 of this Act; and

        (ii) there is not in force an exempting order under section 62(6) of this Act in relation to the procession;

    (*b*) in relation to which an order has been made under section 63(1) or (1A) or 64(6)(*a*)(ii) of this Act prohibiting the holding of it;

    (*c*) which is held otherwise than in accordance with a condition imposed by an order under section 63(1) or (1A) or 64(6)(*a*)(ii) of this Act in relation to the procession; or

    (*d*) which is held otherwise than in accordance with the particulars of its date, time and route specified-

        (i) in the notice given under section 62(1) to (3) of this Act; or

        (ii) where an order has been made under subsection (4) of that section, in the application for the order

except to the extent that a condition referred to in paragraph (*c*) above relates to its date, time or route

and refuses to desist when required to do so by a constable in uniform shall be guilty of an offence and liable, on summary conviction, to a fine not exceeding level 3 on the standard scale.

(3) This section does not apply to processions commonly or customarily held except that it applies to a procession so held if there is in force in relation to it an order under section 62(7) of this Act.

(4) Subject to subsection (5) below, a constable may arrest without warrant a person whom he reasonably suspects of committing or having committed an offence under this section.

(5) A constable who is not in uniform shall produce his identification if required to do so by any person whom he is arresting under subsection (4) above.

Relationship of sections 62 to 65 with Public Order Act 1986.

66. Sections 62 to 65 of this Act are subject to the Public Order Act 1986; and, without prejudice to that generality-

    (*a*) an order under those sections, so far as relating to the same matters as those to which any directions given section 12 of that Act relate, shall be subject to those directions; and

    (*b*) anything done in conformity with any such directions or omitted, in conformity therewith, to be done shall not be an offence under section 65 of this Act.

Appendix E

Examples of Orders of Exempt organisations made by local authorities

East Ayrshire Council
1. Air Training Corps
2. Antartex Christmas Parade
3. Apostolic Church
4. Argyll and Sutherland Highlanders
5. Army Cadet Force
6. Association of Norwegian Students Abroad
7. Association of St Margaret's Hospice
8. The Baptist Church
9. Bellsbank Festival Society
10. Boys Brigade
11. British Legion
12. British Red Cross
13. British Sailor's Society
14. Boglestone Community Association
15. Cameronians (Scottish Rifles)
16. Campaign for Nuclear Disarmament
17. Christian Brethern
18. Church of God – Young Christian Evangelistic Band
19. Church of Scotland
20. CB Radio Enthusiasts
21. Congregational Church
22. Crosshouse Community Council
23. Dalrymple and District Community Council
24. Dalrymple Gala Organising Committee
25. Darvel Community Council
26. Drongan Gala Committee
27. Dunkirk Veteran's Committee

28. Dunlop and Lugton Community Council
29. Earl Haig Fund (Scotland)
30. Episcopal Church
31. Fenwick Community Association
32. Galston Gala Committee
33. Girl Guides
34. Gospel Hall Christian Brethren
35. Hurlford Community Association
36. Kilmarnock and Loudon Festival of Leisure
37. Kilmaurs Community Association
38. Labour Party – Young Socialists
39. LIFE – West of Scotland
40. Logan Carnival Committee
41. Lowland Volunteers TA
42. Masonic Lodge
43. Mauchline Community Association
44. May Day Procession and Demonstration
45. Muirkirk Community Association Gala Day Committee
46. National Union of Railwaymen
47. National Union of Students
48. New Cumnock Gala Day Committee
49. Newmilns and Greenholm Community Council
50. Normandy Veterans Associations – West of Scotland Branch no 54
51. Patna and District Community Council
52. Pentecostal Church of God
53. Queen's Own Yeomanry 'A' Squadron
54. Royal Scottish Society for the Prevention of Cruelty to Children
55. Roman Catholic Church
56. Round Table
57. Royal Air Force Association
58. Royal British Legion
59. Royal Marines Reserve
60. Royal Pipe Band Association
61. Salvation Army
62. Scottish Ambulance Service
63. Scottish Loyalists
64. Scottish Midland Co-operative Society
65. Scottish National Party
66. Scottish Trade Union Congress
67. Scout Association
68. Sea Cadets

69. Sea Scouts
70. Second City Breakers CB Club
71. Society for the Protection of the Unborn Child
72. Stewarton Bonnet Guild
73. Strathclyde Fire Brigade – Memorial Service
74. Strathclyde Police – Annual Service of Remembrance
75. Territorial Army
76. Unison
77. United Services Clubs
78. Young Men's Christian Association

South Ayrshire Council
1. Air Training Corps
2. Annbank Community Association
3. Antartex Christmas Parade
4. Apostolic Church
5. Argyll and Sutherland Highlanders
6. Army Cadet Force
7. Association of Norwegian Students Abroad
8. Association of St Margaret's Hospice
9. Ayr and District Trades Council
10. Ayr's Ex Servicemen's Club
11. Ayr Pipe Band
12. The Baptist Church
13. Boys Brigade
14. British Legion
15. British Red Cross
16. British Sailor's Society
17. Cameronians (Scottish Rifles)
18. Campaign for Nuclear Disarmament
19. Christian Brethren
20. Church of God – Young Christian Evangelistic Band
21. Church of Scotland
22. CB Radio Enthusiasts
23. Congregational Church
24. Coylton Community Council
25. Dunkirk Veteran's Committee
26. Earl Haig Fund (Scotland)
27. Episcopal Church
28. Girl Guides
29. Girvan and District Tourist and Entertainment Association

30. Girvan Juvenile Pipe Band
31. Gospel Hall Christian Brethren
32. Kirkoswald Community Association
33. Labour Party – Young Socialists
34. LIFE – West of Scotland
35. Lowland Volunteers TA
36. Maidens Community Association
37. Masonic Lodge
38. Maybole Community Association
39. Maybole Community Council
40. May Day Procession and Demonstration
41. National Union of Railwaymen
42. National Union of Students
43. Normandy Veterans Associations – West of Scotland Branch no 54
44. Pentecostal Church of God
45. Queen's Own Yeomanry 'A' Squadron
46. Royal Scottish Society for the Prevention of Cruelty to Children
47. Roman Catholic Church
48. Round Table
49. Royal Air Force Association
50. Royal British Legion
51. Royal Marines Reserve
52. Royal Scottish Pipe Band Association
53. Salvation Army
54. Scottish Ambulance Service
55. Scottish Loyalists
56. Scottish Midland Co-operative Society
57. Scottish National Party
58. Scottish Trade Union Congress
59. Scout Association
60. Sea Cadets
61. Sea Scouts
62. Second City Breakers CB Club
63. Society for the Protection of the Unborn Child
64. Strathclyde Fire Brigade – Memorial Service
65. Strathclyde Police – Annual Service of Remembrance
66. Symington Community Association
67. Tarbolton Gala Committee
68. Territorial Army
69. Unison
70. United Services Clubs

Appendix E

71. Whitlets and Dalmilling Social and Recreation Group
72. Young Men's Christian Association

East Dunbartonshire Council
1. Air Training Corps
2. Antartex Christmas Parade
3. Apostolic Church
4. Argyll and Sutherland Highlanders
5. Army Cadet Force
6. Association of Norwegian Students Abroad
7. Association of St Margaret's Hospice
8. Auchinloch Community Council
9. The Baptist Church
10. Baptist Chirch
11. Bearsden and Milngavie Highland Games Association
12. Bishopbriggs Community Council
13. Bishopbriggs Gala Day
14. Boys Brigade
15. British Legion
16. British Red Cross
17. British Sailor's Society
18. Cameronians (Scottish Rifles)
19. Campaign for Nuclear Disarmament
20. Christian Brethren
21. Church of God – Young Christian Evangelistic Band
22. Church of Scotland
23. CB Radio Enthusiasts
24. Congregational Church
25. Dunkirk Veteran's Committee
26. Earl Haig Fund (Scotland)
27. Episcopal Church
28. Girl Guides
29. Gospel Hall Christian Brethren
30. Kirkintilloch Community Council
31. Labour Party – Young Socialists
32. Lenzie Community Council
33. LIFE – West of Scotland
34. Lowland Volunteers TA
35. Masonic Lodge
36. May Day Procession and Demonstration
37. Milngavie Week

38. Milton Community Project
39. National Union of Railwaymen
40. National Union of Students
41. Normandy Veterans Associations – West of Scotland Branch no 54
42. Pentecostal Church of God
43. Queen's Own Yeomanry 'A' Squadron
44. Royal Scottish Society for the Prevention of Cruelty to Children
45. Roman Catholic Church
46. Round Table
47. Royal Air Force Association
48. Royal British Legion
49. Royal Marines Reserve
50. Royal Scottish Pipe Band Association
51. Salvation Army
52. Scottish Ambulance Service
53. Scottish Loyalists
54. Scottish Midland Co-operative Society
55. Scottish National Party
56. Scottish Trade Union Congress
57. Scout Association
58. Sea Cadets
59. Sea Scouts
60. Second City Breakers CB Club
61. Society for the Protection of the Unborn Child
62. Strathclyde Fire Brigade – Memorial Service
63. Strathclyde Police – Annual Service of Remembrance
65. Territorial Army
66. Torrance Community Council
67. Twechar Community Council Gala Committee
68. Unison
69. United Services Clubs
70. Young Men's Christian Association

West Dunbartonshire Council
1. Association of St Margaret's Hospice
2. Balloch/Eastfield Community Council
3. Balloch Highland Games
4. Bowling Day Committee
5. Brucehill Community Association
6. Clydebank Sheltered Housing (Social Work Department)
7. Dumbarton District Festival Association

8. Dumbarton Pipe Band
9. Dumbarton Lions Club
10. Duntocher & Hardgate Gala Day
11. Faifley Fling Management Committee
12. Linnvale Link Playscheme
13. Old Kilpatrick Community Council – Gala Week Committee
14. Vale of Leven Community Council

Inverclyde Council
1. Air Training Corps
2. Antartex Christmas Parade
3. Apostolic Church
4. Argyll and Sutherland Highlanders
5. Army Cadet Force
6. Association of Norwegian Students Abroad
7. Association of St Margaret's Hospice
8. Boys Brigade
9. British Red Cross
10. British Sailor's Society
11. Cameronians (Scottish Rifles)
12. Campaign for Nuclear Disarmament
13. Christian Brethern
14. Church of God – Young Christian Evangelistic Band
15. Church of Scotland
16. CB Radio Enthusiasts
17. 1820 Commemorating Committee
18. Congregational Church
19. Dunkirk Veteran's Committee
20. Earl Haig Fund (Scotland)
21. Episcopal Church
22. GMB
23. Girls Brigade
24. Girl Guides
25. Gospel Hall Christian Brethren
26. Gourock Ex-Servicemen's Club
27. Greenock and Distric Trade's Council
28. Greenock Ex-Servicemen's Club
29. HMS Dalriada
30. Inverclyde Council
31. Inverclyde Navy Club
32. Kindred Clubs, Port Glasgow

33. Labour Party – Young Socialists
34. LIFE – West of Scotland
35. Lowland Volunteers TA
36. Masonic Lodge
37. May Day Procession and Demonstration
38. Megawatt Limited
39. National Union of Railwaymen
40. National Union of Students
41. Normandy Veterans Associations – West of Scotland Branch no 54
42. Old Gourock and Ashton Youth Organisations
43. Pentecostal Church of God
44. Port Glasgow Old Boys Union
45. Port Glasgow Comet Festival Group
46. Port Glasgow Kindred Clubs Association
47. Queen's Own Yeomanry 'A' Squadron
58. Royal Society for the Prevention of Cruelty to Children
49. Roman Catholic Church
50. Round Table
51. Royal Air Force Association
52. Royal British Legion
53. Royal Marines Reserve
54. Royal Pipe Band Association
55. St Andrews Ambulance Service
56. Salvation Army
57. Scottish Ambulance Service
58. Scottish Loyalists
59. Scottish Midland Co-operative Society
60. Scottish National Party
61. Scottish Trade Union Congress
62. Scout Association
63. Sea Cadets
64. Sea Scouts
65. Second City Breakers CB Club
66. Society for the Protection of the Unborn Child
67. Strathclyde Fire Brigade – Memorial Service
68. Strathclyde Police
69. Territorial Army
70. There is Hope (Christian Evangelical Group)
71. Unison
72. United Services Clubs
73. Young Men's Christian Association

Appendix E

North Lanarkshire Council (adopted former Strathclyde Region List and the same approach is followed by North Ayrshire Council – list therefore covers a range of council areas)

1. Abington Social Club
2. Air Training Corps
3. Allanton and Hartwood Old Folks Gala
4. Annbank Community Association
5. Apostolic Church
6. Arden Tenants Association
7. Arneill Pipe Band, Ardrossan
8. Ardrossan Community Council
9. Ardrossan Highland Games
10. Argyll and Sutherland Highlanders
11. Argyllshire Gathering
12. Army Cadet Force
13. Ashgill Community Council
14. Association of Norwegian Students Abroad
15. Association of St Margaret's Hospice
16. Auchinloch Community Council
17. Auldhouse Chapelton Gala
18. Ayr and District Trades Council
19. Ayr Ex-Servicemen's Club
20. Ayr Pipe Band
21. Babcock Renfrew Club
22. Balloch/Eastfield Community Council (Gala Committee)
23. Balloch Highland Games
24. Banton and Kelvinhead Community Council
25. The Baptist Church
26. Balanark Festival Committee
27. Barrhead and District Gala Committee
28. Beith Community Association
29. Bearsden and Milngavie Highland Games Association
30. Bellsbank Festival Society
31. Biggar Gala Day Committee
32. Bishopbriggs Gala Day
33. Bishopbriggs Community Council
34. Backwood and Kirkmuirhill District Council
35. Blantyre Civic Week Committee
36. Blantyre Miners Welfare Society and Social Club
37. BLCR Community Council

38. Bogeha' Bowling Club
39. Boglestone Community Council
40. Bonnystone Community Council
41. Bothwell Community Council
42. Bowhouse Community Council
43. Bowling Gala Day Committee
44. Boys Brigade
45. British Legion
46. British Red Cross
47. British Sailor's Society
48. Broomhouse Community Council
49. Broomlands and Bourtreehill Gala Committee
50. Brucehill Community Association
51. Bute Highland Games
52. Calderbank Gala Day Committee
53. Caldercruix and District Gala
54. Calder Valley Community Council
55. Calderwood and St Leonards Community Council
56. Cameronians (Scottish Rifles)
57. Campaign for Nuclear Disarmament
58. Campbeltown Festival Week Committee
59. Campbeltown Kintyre Highland Games
60. Campbeltown Pipe Band
61. Cambusland Gala Association
62. Cardross Community Council
63. Carfin Children's Carnival
64. Carluke Community Gala Day
65. Carluke Highland Games Association
66. Carmunnock Community Council
67. Carmyle Residents Association
68. Carnwath Gala Day
69. Carstairs and District Gala Day
70. Castlemilk Fair Week Committee
71. Castlepark and Eglinton Community Association
72. Catholic Mens Society St Patrick's School Shotts
73. Chapelhall Gala Day Committee
74. Christian Brethren
75. Church of God – Young Christian Evangelistic Band
76. Church of Scotland
77. Chryston Community Council
78. CB Radio Enthusiasts

Appendix E

79. Clydebank Sheltered Housing (Social Work Department)
80. Coalburn Miners Welfare
81. Coltness Community Association
82. 1820 Commemorative Committee
83. Condorrat Community Council
84. Congregational Church
85. Corsehill Community Centre Association
86. Cowal Highland Gathering
87. Coylton Community Association
88. Craigend Community Council
89. Craigneuk and Wishaw Gala Day Committee
90. Crawford Gala Day
91. Crosshouse Community Council
92. Croy Gala Committee
93. Cumbernauld Civic Week Committee
94. Dalry Civic Week Committee
95. Dalrymple and District Community Council
96. Dalrymple Gala Organising Committee
97. Darnley Estate Community Council
98. Darvel Community Council
99. Douglas Gala Day Committee
97. Douglas Water and Rigside Committee
98. Dreghorn Gala Committee
99. Drongan Gala Committee
100. Drumchapel Festival Committee
101. Dumbarton District Pipe Band
102. Dumbarton Lions Club
103. Dunkirk Veteran's Committee
104. Dunlop and Lugton Community Council
105. Duntocher and Hardgate Gala Day
106. Earl Haig Fund (Scotland)
107. East End Festival of Fun
108. Easthall Gala Committee
109. East Kilbride District Council
110. East Kilbride Taxi Drivers
111. Eddlewood Community Council
112. Episcopal Church
113. Erskine Community Association
114. Faifley Fling Gala Day Association
115. Fairline Gala Day Association
116. Fenwick Community Association

117. Ferguslie Park Playscheme Park
118. Fernigair Community Council
119. Forgewood Community Council
120. Forth and District Gala Day
121. Forth and District Pipe Band
122. Fullarton Community Council
123. Gallowhill Community Council
124. Galstone Gala Committee
125. Garelochhead Community Council
126. Garrowhill Community Council
127. Garthamlock Community Council
128. Girdletoll Community Association
129. Girvan and District Tourist and Entertainment Association
130. Girvan Juvenile Pipe Band
131. Glasgow Academy
132. Glasgow District Council
133. Glasgow East Community Council
134. Glasgow Jewish Ex-Servicemen
135. Glasgow Junior Chamber of Commerce (Lord Provost's Procession)
136. Glasgow and West of Scotland Dunkirk Veterans Association
137. Glassford Gala Committee
138. Glenmavis Community Council (Gala Day Committee)
139. Glespin Community Council
140. Gorbals Fair Children's Procession
141. Gospel Hall Christian Brethren
142. Gourock Ex-servicemen's Club
143. Govan Fair Association
144. Greegairs Children's Gala Committee
145. Greenhill Tenants Association
146. Greenhills Festival
147. Greenock and District Trades Council
148. Harthill, Eastfield and Greenrigg Children's Gala Day
149. Helensburgh and District Ladies Club
150. 51 Highland Volunteers 3rd Battalion
151. Holytown Gala Day
152. Houston and Killellan Kirk
153. Howwood Road Tenants Association
154. Hurlet Community Council
155. Hurlford Community Association
156. Inchinnan Gala Day Committee
157. Inveraray Highland Games Committee

Appendix E

158. Inverclyde District Council
159. Irvine Carters Society
160. Irvine Harbour Festival
161. Johnstone Community Council
162. Joint Whiteinch and Scotstoun Community Council
163. Kilbarchan Community Council
164. Kilbarchan Primary School Parents Association
165. Kilmarnock and Loudon Festival of Leisure
166. Kilmaurs Community Association
167. Kilsyth Community Council
168. Kilwinning Festival Society
169. Kinning Park Festival Society
170. Kirkenfield Gala Day Committee
171. Kirkintilloch Community Council
172. Kirkeswald Community Centre Gala Day Committee
173. Knightwoods Community Centre Gala Day Committee
174. Kyle and Carrick District Council
175. Labour Party – Young Socialists
176. Lanark Lanimar Committee
177. Largs Brisbane Queen Festival Week Committee
178. Largs Viking Festival
179. Larkhall Community Council
180. Law Community Council
181. Law Gala Day Committee
182. Law OAP Welfare Committee
183. Leadhills Gala Day Committee
184. Lesmahagow Civic Society Fair
185. Lesmahagow Highland Games Society
186. LIFE – West of Scotland
187. Linnvale Link Playscheme
188. Logan Carnival Committee
189. Lowland Volunteers TA
190. Low Waters Residents Association
191. Luss Community Council
192. Maidens Community Association
193. Maryhill Corridor Festival Group
194. Marymass Organising Committee
195. Masonic Lodge
196. Mauchline Community Association
197. Maybole Community Association
198. Maybole Community Council

199. May Day Procession and Demonstration
200. Mearns Centre
201. Mid Argyll Pipe Band
202. Milngavie Week
203. Milton Community Project
204. Monklands Youth Concert Brass
205. Motherwell District Council
206. Mount Vernon Community Council
207. Muirkirk Community Association Gala Day Committee
208. Mull Gathering
209. NALGO (now UNISON)
210. National Union of Railwaymen
211. National Union of Students
212. Netherburn Community Council
213. New Cumnock Gala Day Committee
214. Newmains District Committee
215. Newmilns and Greenholm Community Council
216. Newharthill Children's Gala Day
217. North Motherwell Community Council
218. Oban Pipe Band
219. Old Kilpatrick Community Council – Gala Week Committee
220. Paisley College of Technology Students Association
221. Paisley Junior Chamber
222. Patna and District Community Council
223. Penilee Community Council
224. Pentecostal Church of God
225. Petersburn Gala Committee
226. Plains Gala Committee
227. Pollokshields Community Council
228. Priesthill Tenants Association
229. Queen's Own Yeomanry 'A' Squadron
230. Queenslie Community Council
231. Queenzieburn Community Association
232. Rashielea School Resources Committee
233. Renfrew District Council – Paisley Festival
234. Royal Scottish Society for the Prevention of Cruelty to Children
235. Roman Catholic Church
236. Rosneath and Clynder Community Association
237. Rosneath and Clynder Highland Games
238. Round Table
239. Royal Air Force Association

240. Royal British Legion
241. Royal Scottish Pipe Band Association
242. Ruchill Festival Committee
243. Rutherglen Lanemar Committee
244. Salsburgh Children's Gala Fund
245. Saltcoats Community Council
246. Saltcoats Gala Community
247. Scottish Ambulance Service – dispute
248. Scottish Loyalists
249. Scottish Midland Co-operative Society
250. Scottish National Party
251. Scottish Trade Union Congress
252. Scout Association
253. Sea Cadets
254. Sea Scouts
255. Second City Breakers CB Club
256. Shotts Nan Gaidheal
257. Society for the Protection of the Unborn Child
258. South Cowal Community Council
259. Springburn Community Festival
260. Springside Community Association
261. Stevenston Festival Committee (Gala Day)
262. Stewarton Bonnet Guild
263. Stonehouse Festival Committee
264. Strathaven Gala Day
265. Strathclyde Fire Brigade – Memorial Service
266. Strathclyde Police – Annual Service of Remembrance
267. Strathclyde Regional Council – Department of Education
268. Tarbolton Gala Committee
269. Territorial Army
270. Thornliebank Amateur Accordian Band
271. Thornliebank School Fair
272. Torrance Community Council
273. Townhead and Gartsherrie Community Council
274. Twechar Community Council Gala Committee
275. Uddingston Community Council
276. United Services Clubs
277. Vale of Leven Community Council
278. Viewpark Gala Day
279. West End Social Club
280. Westfield Residents Association

281. Whitehill Gala Committee
282. Whiteinch Scotstoun Community Council
283. Whiteletts and Dalmilling Social and Recreation Group
284. Wishaw and District Ex-Servicemen's Memorial Institue
285. Wishawhill Tenants Association
286. Yoker Gala Committee
287. Yoker Mini-marathon Committee
288. Young Men's Christian Association
289. Bardykes Hourse Show Committee
290. Bellshill and Mossend Community Council
291. Bogelstone Community Association
292. Brisbane Queen Festival Week Committee
293. Daisy Park Gala Committee
294. Edinburgh Military Tattoo Procession
295. Forehill Gala Committee
296. Glasgow Students Charities Appeal
297. Glencairn Community Council
298. Hamilton District Council
299. Highlands and Islands Music and Dance Festival Committee, Oban
300. Kilmarnock and Loudon District Council
301. Lenzie Community Council
302. Oban Charities Day Organising Committee
303. Renfrew Gala Week
304. Shortlees Festival Committee
305. Shotts Highland Games Association
306. South Carntyne Fund Raising Association
307. South Nitshill Festival Week
308. Symington Community Association
309. Thankerton Village Gala Day Committee
310. Tollcross Community Council
311. Taynuilt Highland Games Committee
312. West Kilbride Community Association

Renfrewshire Council
1. Air Training Corps
2. Apostolic Church
3. Argyll and Sutherland Highlanders
4. Army Cadet Force
5. Association of Norwegian Students Abroad
6. Association of St Margaret Hospice
7. Babcock Renfrew Club

Appendix E

8. Baptist Church
9. Boys Brigade
10. British Legion
11. British Red Cross
12. British Sailor's Society
13. Cameronians (Scottish Rifles)
14. Campaign for Nuclear Disarmament
15. Christian Brethern
16. Church of God – Young Christian Evangelistic Band
17. Church of Scotland
18. CB Radio Enthusiasts
19. Congregational Church
20. Dunkirk Veteran's Committee
21. Earl Haig Fund (Scotland)
22. Episcopal Church
23. Erskine Community Association
24. Ferguslie Park Playscheme Forum
25. Gospel Hall Christian Brethren
26. Houston and Killellan Kirk
27. Howwood Tenants Association
28. Inchinnan Gala Day Committee
29. Johnstone Community Council
30. Kilbarchan Community Council
31. Kilbarchan Primary School Parent's Association
32. Labour Party – Young Socialists
33. LIFE – West of Scotland
34. Lowland Volunteers TA
35. Masonic Lodge
36. May Day Procession and Demonstration
37. National Union of Railwaymen
38. National Union of Students
39. Paisley Junior Chamber
40. Pentecostal Church of God
41. Queen's Own Yeomanry 'A' Squadron
42. Renfrew Gala Week
43. RDC Paisley Festival
44. Royal Society for the Prevention of Cruelty to Children
45. Roman Catholic Church
46. Round Table
47. Royal Air Force Association
48. Royal British Legion

49. Royal Pipe Band Association
50. Scottish Ambulance Service
51. Scottish Loyalists
52. Scottish Midland Co-operative Society
53. Scottish National Party
54. Scottish Trade Union Congress
55. Scout Association
56. Sea Cadets
57. Sea Scouts
58. Second City Breakers CB Club
59. Society for the Protection of the Unborn Child
60. Strathclyde Fire Brigade – Memorial Service
61. Strathclyde Police – Annual Service of Remembrance
62. Territorial Army
63. United Services Clubs
64. Young Men's Christian Association

Also treated as exempt:

65. Antartex Christmas Parade
66. Girl Guides
67. Normandy Veterans Association – West of Scotland Branch no 54
68. Royal Marines Reserve
69. Salvation Army
70. UNISON
71. University of Paisley Students Association
72. Renfrew 600

Appendix F

Examples of codes of conduct of marching organisations

Loyal Orange Order – rules governing church parades and demonstrations

1. Orange and Royal Arch Purple Colours only shall be worn at Church Parades and Demonstrations.
2. At all Demonstrations, the Union Jack shall be carried at the head of the procession.
3. No intoxicating liquor will be admitted to the field or park at any time.
4. Bands engaged for Church Parades must give an undertaking that only recognisable Hymn tunes will be played.
5. Ladies shall walk with the male members of their own District at all Church Parades.
6. During the time the public meeting is going on at a Demonstration bands will not play in the park; drumming is also forbidden.
7. A County Grand Lodge, District or Private Lodge traversing any route other than that sanctioned by a local authority will be dealt with by the County Grand Lodge.
8. A District or Private Lodge which is not forward when the procession moves off falls in at the rear. This applies to both inward and outward journeys.
9. Dancing or jazzing with banners is strictly prohibited. An offending lodge will not be permitted to carry its banner for 2 succeeding Demonstrations.
10. No intoxicating liquor shall be consumed while in the ranks or when wearing colours out with the procession and the use of improper language at all time is forbidden.
11. All Bands engaged must sign the Condition of Engagement Form, and adhere strictly to the rules thereon. The District Chief Marshal will be held responsible for any breach of this rule.
12. The instructions of the County and Grand Lodge Marshals must be obeyed at all times.
13. The wearing of favours is strictly forbidden.

14. All Lodges must keep strictly to the left hand of the road, except on one way streets where the right hand side of the road will be traversed and members will march in military formation 3 abreast.
15. Marshals must, with courtesy and attention, give facilities to the general public for entry to stations, buses etc
16. Bands taking part in Orange Church Parades must also attend the Church Services.
17. Juvenile and Juniors will not be permitted to take part in adult demonstrations but Junior can parade where they are parading as a Lodge which has been granted permission by the Grand Lodge or where appropriate, the County Grand Lodge. Juvenile and Junior members may be allowed to take part in adult Church parades held under the auspices of the District to which they belong. Juveniles between the ages of 11 and 15, whose District does not have a Junior Lodge, may carry banner cords wearing colours at demonstrations.
18. Any Band found guilty of improper conduct during an Orange Parade will be dealt with through the agreed procedure.
19. Deacon poles, batons or canes are not allowed to be carried between Marshals or Band Marshals.
20. Members should refrain from smoking while wearing collarettes or chains of Office.
21. District Standards may be carried at Grand Lodge Church Parades.
22. Every member participating in a Church Parade must enter and participate in the Service.

Apprentice Boys of Derry – members' code of conduct

1. All member clubs and their respective members and guests shall not even when provoked, engage in any action that shames or disgraces their club or the association.
2. All member clubs and their respective members and guests shall at all times promote a sense of unity and friendship towards fellow clubs and members.
3. On arrival for a parade no member of a club or guest should leave their mode of transport carrying any form of alcohol.
4. Whilst you are in a marshalling area or on the parade route or at dispersal point of any parade no members or guests of your club shall be seen to be urinating in a public place.
5. When attending the May Rally all member clubs are expected to attend public speeches before departing for their return parades, at the December church service all our member clubs and guests are expected in the church for the service.
6. No member clubs shall have their club colour party or any member or guest of their club dressed in or displaying any paramilitary colours or emblems breaching the Terrorism Act 2000.

Scottish Amalgamated Committee

Review of Marches and Parades in Scotland

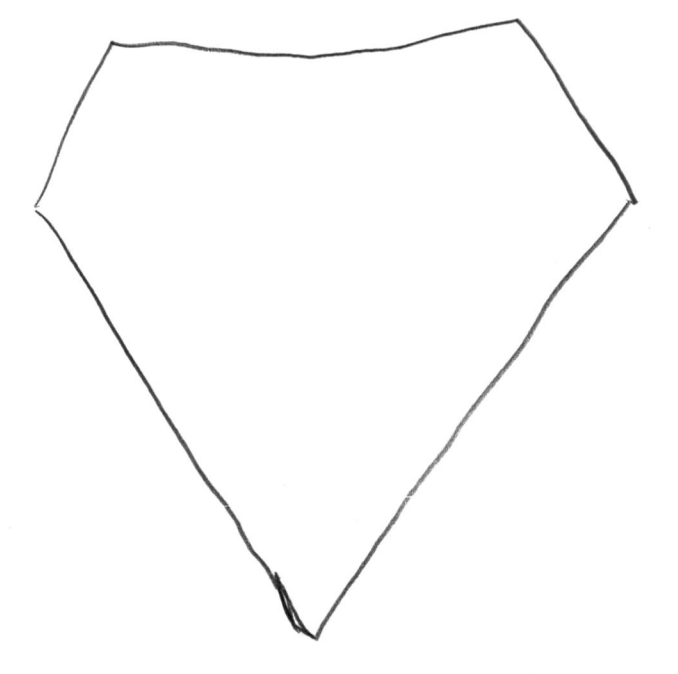

Appendix G

Examples of band contracts of marching organisations

Grand Orange Lodge of Scotland – band contract of engagement

Clause 1

All Bands shall by engaged by a Private Lodge, District Lodge, County Grand Lodge or Grand Lodge of Scotland before they can take part in any parade under the auspices of the Loyal Orange Institution of Scotland and shall be under the jurisdiction of these bodies, singularly or jointly, for the full term of the engagements notified.

All Scottish Flute and Accordion Bands so engaged must belong to a Band Association recognised by the Grand Lodge of Scotland.

Clause 2

No band shall have on parade any member of the Orange Institution who, following the results of disciplinary procedure has been suspended for an offence (other than non-payment of duties) or expelled.

No band shall have on parade former members of a Band which has been debarred from taking part in parades with the Orange Institution by the Grand Lodge of Scotland.

Clause 3

All Band Members must maintain uniformity of dress, reflecting the dignity of the Orange Institution. This will be defined as Full Dress Uniform including cap, or Highland Dress. Bass Drummers only may dispense with the cap and jacket of a full dress uniform and may substitute a single coloured jersey or shirt.

Dispensation to vary the foregoing uniform can only be given by the County Grand Lodge of Association to which the Band belongs or by Grand Lodge of Scotland. The alternative uniform will be subject to inspection before a decision is made.

Clause 4

Only one Adult drum major will be permitted on parade.

Clause 5

No Lambeg Drums shall be permitted as part of a Band's ensemble. Application for the use of a Lambeg Drum, as a single instrument accompanied by one or two 'fifes' can be made by Lodges or District Lodges wishing to hire these directly to their County Grand Lodge, who will consider the application in light of the circumstances pertaining to the parade applied for. An application rejected by the County Grand Lodge is final and without appeal. Grand Lodge of Scotland may also consider applications for parades organised at that level.

Clause 6

A maximum of three flags can be displayed, one of which must be the Union Flag. Bands from within the United Kingdom can additionally display a further two, from the Saltire, St George and Northern Ireland Flags. Bands from outside the United Kingdom may display the Flag of their own Country, provided the total number of flags does not exceed three. Bands may also display a bannerette denoting the Band name only.

Clause 7

Bands must comply with the provisions of Terrorism Act 2000. No paramilitary symbolism or connotation will be displayed on uniforms, drums, flags or bannerettes. This includes a chosen name giving the initials of a proscribed paramilitary organisation or YCV.

Clause 8

Bands will employ regulation step without deviation while on parade. The numbers in each rank of a Band will be determined in accordance with the numbers in the Band but cannot exceed the number laid down in any Local Authority conditions relating to parades/processions. Bands will maintain the predetermined numbers in their ranks at all times during parades, except in cases of emergency.

In respect of Bass Drums, Double drumming (two players on one drum) or Twin drumming (Two Bass Drums) is prohibited.

Shouting or singing on parade is expressly forbidden.

Clause 9

Traditional Orange airs should form the greater part of a Band's repertoire while taking part in Orange Parades. These can be augmented with marches and hymns.

Clause 10

Bands must not play music or indulge in drumming in the Field during Public Meetings associated with the Annual Boyne Celebrations or at any Rally where a Public Meeting forms part of the proceedings.

Clause 11

No alcohol is allowed into a Field where annual Boyne Celebrations or Rallies take place. Under no circumstances should alcohol be consumed in ranks during a parade.

It is strongly recommended that band members refrain from drinking alcohol at all from early morning until the conclusion of evening parades.

Any complaint against, or behaviour by, individual band members which relate to alcohol will have repercussions on the band as a whole.

Clause 12

No Deacon Poles, Batons or canes shall be carried by Band Personnel.

Clause 13

A new band in their inaugural year, must be sponsored by a Private or District Lodge and must actively participate in parades with that Lodge. Sponsorship by a Private Lodge is initially subject to the approval of the District Lodge under whose warrant the Private Lodge operates. All sponsoring of new bands is subject to the ultimate approval of the County Grand Lodge which governs the Private or District Lodge involved in the sponsorship.

A Band, while under sponsorship, may take part in other Parades held under the jurisdiction of the Orange Institution, where the sponsoring Lodge, or representatives of the Trustees of the sponsoring Lodge, also participate.

At the conclusion of all engagements undertaken by a Band in their inaugural year, the sponsoring Lodge are required to submit a report on the Band to their County Grand Lodge, with a copy to their District Lodge if applicable. Should the Band concerned be based within the boundaries of another County Grand Lodge, then a copy of the report should be furnished to that County Grand Lodge, by the County Grand Lodge which initially received it.

Clause 14

Bands must strictly adhere to the conditions relating to parades/processions as laid down by Local Authorities. No member of a Band should approach a Police Officer directly. Should any approach to the Police be deemed necessary, this must be done through an Officer of the Lodge hiring the Band, or through Officers (who will normally be Marshals) of District, County Grand or Grand Lodge.

Clause 15

A minimum of two thirds of the declared Band personnel must be on parade before the fee for an engagement is paid. Non-playing personnel will not be accepted as part of the Band.

Clause 16

The Band Secretary must read the terms and conditions of the Band Contract to a full attendance of Band Members prior to each Parade.

Failure to do so does not absolve the Band, or its members, from the consequences of an infringement of the conditions of the contract.

Clause 17

The fees for all engagements are those agreed between the respective Band Associations and the Grand Orange Lodge of Scotland. These hold from January 2004 for a period of three years and are as follows:

Date of Engagement

Junior and Juvenile Rally – £30

Junior and Juvenile Church Parade – £20

Adult Church Parades – £100

Adult Boyne Celebrations – £350

All other Parades by negotiation.

Meals – Provision of meals to be agreed between the hiring lodge and the band. Where no meal is provided a sum of money per playing member of the Band, including the Drum Major, may be allocated.

Agreement

Name and Number of hiring Lodge –

....

Name of Band –

....

Number of Playing Personnel in Band –

....

Name and Address of Band Secretary –

....

Acknowledgement

I agree to the conditions as stipulated in the Band Contract and, in the event of any violation of these conditions, accept that the Band will be dealt with at the discretion of the Grand Orange Lodge of Scotland, normally, but not confined to, the procedure agreed with the Band Associations.

I understand, however, that for persistent contravention of the conditions of the Band Contract, or behaviour of a manner likely to bring discredit to the Orange Order, while on Parade, the Master of the Lodge organising the Parade, be this Private Lodge, District Lodge, County Grand Lodge or the Grand Orange Lodge of Scotland, is empowered to have the Band removed from the Parade.

Signature of Band Secretary (on behalf of Band) –

....

Signature of Secretary of Jurisdiction Engaging Band –

....

Other Signatures where applicable –

....

In the event of a new band being engaged in their inaugural year by a private lodge, the band contract should be countersigned by the District and County Grand Secretary. The County Grand Secretary should countersign the contract where a district engages a band in this category.

District and Private Lodge Secretaries

Three copies of the band contract should be signed, a copy to be retained by the lodge engaging the band. A copy retained by the band and a copy furnished to the County Grand Secretary or Grand Secretary should the parade involved come under the jurisdiction of Grand Orange Lodge of Scotland.

Bands from outwith Scotland are required to sign a Grand Orange Lodge of Scotland contract, furnish a photograph of their uniform, equipment and standards and forward a letter of approval from a private or district lodge of that area prior to taking part in the parade.

Scottish Amalgamated Committee Band Contract

Conditions of engagements for bands taking part in parades hosted by the Scottish Amalgamated Commitee of the Apprentice Boys of Derry

Clause 1 – All bands shall come under the jurisdiction of the branch club with whom they are parading with and shall at all times obey the instructions of the branch and SAC Marshals when requested to do so.

Clause 2 – all members of the band must maintain uniformity of dress to a standard not reflecting badly on the Apprentice Boys Club of whom they are engaged with.

Clause 3 – No paramilitary symbolism will be displayed on the parade that contravene the Terrorism Act 2000 including flags, uniforms or instruments, a full review of bands will be carried out at the marshalling area prior to parade moving off.

Clause 4 – Shouting or singing for the emphasis of certain tunes is not permitted, regulation step will be maintained and dancing or snaking on the route is forbidden. All bands must stay within white lines and follow marshals instructions at all times.

Clause 5 – Bands must adhere strictly to any conditions laid down by the local authorities in whose area the parade is taking place.

Clause 6 – On the day of the May Rally no bands shall play in the park whilst the speeches are ongoing. Respect must also be shown to fellow bands and no band in fighting will be accepted, bands who are parading in December are expected to attend the service if room is available in the church.

Clause 7 – Whilst bands are in the marshalling area on parade route or at dispersal point no band members shall be seen drinking alcohol or urinating in public, when leaving your mode of transport no alcohol will be displayed.

Clause 8 – the only engagements covered in this contract are the May Rally and December Church Service both of these parades are under the auspices of the Scottish Amalgamated Committee.

Clause 9 – the fees relating to these two parades are as follows:
Annual May Rally – £100.00
December Church Service – £75.00

The above fees are minimum amounts that have to be paid to the band any other band requests get sorted out between club and band being engaged.

Declaration

We agree to the conditions as stated in the band contract and in any event of any violations or breeches of any of the conditions stated that the band will be dealt with by the band association it's a member of and members of the Scottish Amalgamated Executive Committee. Bands who are not members of any band association will be dealt with solely by the members of Executive Committee of the Scottish Amalgamated Committee

It is the duty of the band secretary to read this contract to all members of their band prior to taking part in any parade.

Name of band –
....
Band secretary –
....
Name of club –
....
Club secretary –
....
Date of parade –
....

Note to all club secretaries

Copy of signed contract must be lodged with SAC Secretary at least 6 weeks prior to parade failure to return completed contract and band will be unable to take part in the parade. No copies will be accepted on the day of the parade.

April 2003

Appendix H

Detailed statistics about the number of marches and parades

PROCESSIONS NOTIFIED TO LOCAL AUTHORITIES IN 2001

PROCESSIONS NOTIFIED TO LOCAL AUTHORITIES IN 2001

		Jan	Feb	Mar	Apr	May	June	July	Aug	Sept	Oct	Nov	Dec	Total
Aberdeen	Orange	0	0	0	0	0	0	0	0	1	0	0	0	1
	Catholic	0	0	0	0	0	0	0	0	0	0	0	0	0
	Other	0	0	1	5	2	2	1	3	1	1	3	2	21
	Total	0	0	1	5	2	2	1	3	2	1	3	2	22
Aberdeenshire	Orange	0	0	0	0	0	0	0	0	0	0	0	0	0
(partial figures)	Catholic	0	0	0	0	0	0	0	0	0	0	0	0	0
	Other	0	0	0	0	2	2	3	5	2	1	1	1	17
	Total	0	0	0	0	2	2	3	5	2	1	1	1	17
Angus	Orange	0	0	0	1	0	1	0	0	0	0	0	0	2
	Catholic	0	0	0	1	0	0	0	0	0	0	0	0	1
	Other	0	1	1	0	2	1	1	2	2	0	9	0	19
	Total	0	1	1	2	2	2	1	2	2	0	9	0	22
Argyll and Bute	Orange	0	0	0	0	0	0	0	0	0	0	0	0	0
	Catholic	0	0	0	0	0	0	0	0	0	0	0	0	0
	Other	0	0	0	1	3	1	2	0	0	0	3	0	10
	Total	0	0	0	1	3	1	2	0	0	0	3	0	10
East Ayrshire	Orange	0	0	1	0	1	6	10	1	2	1	2	0	24
	Catholic	0	0	0	0	0	0	0	0	0	0	0	0	0
	Other	0	1	1	0	0	5	0	2	0	1	2	0	12
	Total	0	1	2	0	1	11	10	3	2	2	4	0	36
North Ayrshire	Orange	0	0	0	0	0	0	0	0	0	0	0	0	63
(estimates – 2003	Catholic	0	0	0	0	0	0	0	0	0	0	0	0	0
figures) (no monthly	Other	0	0	0	0	0	0	0	0	0	0	0	0	30
breakdown)	Total	0	0	0	0	0	0	0	0	0	0	0	0	93
South Ayrshire	Orange	0	0	0	0	1	1	1	2	0	0	0	0	5
	Catholic	0	0	0	0	0	0	0	0	0	0	0	0	0
	Other	0	0	0	0	1	11	2	2	1	1	6	0	24
	Total	0	0	0	0	2	12	3	4	1	1	6	0	29
Clackmannanshire	Orange	0	0	0	0	0	2	2	0	0	1	1	1	7
	Catholic	0	0	0	0	0	0	0	0	0	0	0	0	0
	Other	0	0	1	0	2	4	0	0	0	1	0	0	8
	Total	0	0	1	0	2	6	2	0	0	2	1	1	15
Dumfries and	Orange	0	0	0	0	0	0	1	0	1	0	0	0	2
Galloway	Catholic	0	0	0	0	0	0	0	0	0	0	0	0	0
	Other	0	0	1	0	0	0	0	1	0	0	0	0	2
	Total	0	0	1	0	0	0	1	1	1	0	0	0	4
East	Orange	0	0	0	1	0	2	2	0	0	0	0	0	5
Dunbartonshire	Catholic	0	0	0	0	0	0	0	0	0	0	0	0	0
	Other	0	0	0	0	1	1	0	1	0	0	1	0	4
	Total	0	0	0	1	1	3	2	1	0	0	1	0	9

Appendix H

PROCESSIONS NOTIFIED TO LOCAL AUTHORITIES IN 2001

		Jan	Feb	Mar	Apr	May	June	July	Aug	Sept	Oct	Nov	Dec	Total
West Dunbartonshire	Orange	0	0	0	0	0	0	1	0	0	0	0	0	1
	Catholic	0	0	0	0	0	0	0	0	0	0	0	0	0
	Other	0	0	2	4	1	1	1	0	1	0	6	1	17
	Total	0	0	2	4	1	1	2	0	1	0	6	1	18
Dundee	Orange	0	0	0	0	0	1	0	0	0	0	1	0	2
	Catholic	0	0	0	0	0	0	0	0	0	0	0	0	0
	Other	0	0	3	2	1	1	0	2	0	0	3	0	12
	Total	0	0	3	2	1	2	0	2	0	0	4	0	14
Edinburgh	Orange	0	0	0	0	0	2	0	0	0	0	0	0	2
	Catholic	0	0	0	0	0	1	0	0	0	0	0	0	1
	Other	1	0	3	1	10	13	0	6	5	3	9	3	54
	Total	1	0	3	1	10	16	0	6	5	3	9	3	57
Eilean Siar *(all treated as exempt)*	Orange	0	0	0	0	0	0	0	0	0	0	0	0	0
	Catholic	0	0	0	0	0	0	0	0	0	0	0	0	0
	Other	0	0	0	0	0	0	0	0	0	0	0	0	0
	Total	0	0	0	0	0	0	0	0	0	0	0	0	0
Falkirk	Orange	0	0	2	2	3	17	5	2	1	0	1	0	33
	Catholic	0	0	0	0	0	0	0	0	0	0	0	0	0
	Other	0	0	0	1	4	7	4	5	3	0	4	0	28
	Total	0	0	2	3	7	24	9	7	4	0	5	0	61
Fife *(estimates – 2002 figures) (no monthly breakdown)*	Orange	0	0	0	0	0	0	0	0	0	0	0	0	13
	Catholic	0	0	0	0	0	0	0	0	0	0	0	0	0
	Other	0	0	0	0	0	0	0	0	0	0	0	0	132
	Total	0	0	0	0	0	0	0	0	0	0	0	0	145
Glasgow *(estimates - 2002 figures) (no monthly breakdown) (based on 2003 %'s)*	Orange (85%)	0	0	0	0	0	0	0	0	0	0	0	0	257
	Catholic (3%)	0	0	0	0	0	0	0	0	0	0	0	0	9
	Other (12%)	0	0	0	0	0	0	0	0	0	0	0	0	36
	Total	0	0	0	0	0	0	0	0	0	0	0	0	302
Highland *(based on Inverness figures)*	Orange	0	0	0	0	0	0	0	0	0	0	0	0	0
	Catholic	0	0	0	0	0	0	0	0	0	0	0	0	0
	Other	0	0	1	0	0	3	1	3	1	1	1	1	12
	Total	0	0	1	0	0	3	1	3	1	1	1	1	12
Inverclyde	Orange	0	0	0	0	2	4	2	1	1	0	0	0	10
	Catholic	0	1	1	0	1	0	0	1	0	0	0	0	4
	Other	0	1	0	1	0	0	0	3	0	0	3	1	9
	Total	0	2	1	1	3	4	2	5	1	0	3	1	23

Review of Marches and Parades in Scotland

PROCESSIONS NOTIFIED TO LOCAL AUTHORITIES IN 2001

		Jan	Feb	Mar	Apr	May	June	July	Aug	Sept	Oct	Nov	Dec	Total
North Lanarkshire	Orange	0	0	0	0	0	0	0	0	0	0	0	0	157
(estimates - 2003	Catholic	0	0	0	0	0	0	0	0	0	0	0	0	3
figures) (no monthly	Other	0	0	0	0	0	0	0	0	0	0	0	0	0
breakdown)	Total	0	0	0	0	0	0	0	0	0	0	0	0	160
South Lanarkshire	Orange	0	0	0	1	17	18	36	7	1	3	2	2	87
	Catholic	0	0	1	0	0	0	0	0	0	0	0	0	1
	Other	0	1	1	4	5	19	3	4	0	2	9	3	51
	Total	0	1	2	5	22	37	39	11	1	5	11	5	139
East Lothian	Orange	0	0	0	0	0	8	0	0	0	0	0	0	8
	Catholic	0	0	0	0	0	0	0	0	0	0	0	0	0
	Other	0	0	0	7	4	20	5	7	2	1	7	6	59
	Total	0	0	0	7	4	28	5	7	2	1	7	6	67
Midlothian	Orange	0	0	0	0	0	1	0	0	0	0	0	0	1
	Catholic	0	0	0	0	0	0	0	0	0	0	0	0	0
	Other	1	0	0	0	4	5	0	1	1	0	6	0	18
	Total	1	0	0	0	4	6	0	1	1	0	6	0	19
West Lothian	Orange	0	0	2	3	9	39	11	5	1	1	1	0	72
	Catholic	0	0	0	0	0	0	0	0	0	0	0	0	0
	Other	0	0	0	1	1	12	0	1	0	0	6	3	24
	Total	0	0	2	4	10	51	11	6	1	1	7	3	96
Moray	Orange	0	0	0	0	0	0	0	0	0	0	0	0	0
(estimates - 2003	Catholic	0	0	0	0	0	0	0	0	0	0	0	0	0
figures) (no monthly	Other	0	0	0	0	0	0	0	0	0	0	0	0	20
breakdown)	Total	0	0	0	0	0	0	0	0	0	0	0	0	20
Orkney	Orange	0	0	0	0	0	0	0	0	0	0	0	0	0
	Catholic	0	0	0	0	0	0	0	0	0	0	0	0	0
	Other	0	0	0	0	0	0	0	0	0	0	1	7	8
	Total	0	0	0	0	0	0	0	0	0	0	1	7	8
Perth and Kinross	Orange	1	0	0	0	1	0	0	0	0	0	0	1	3
	Catholic	0	0	0	0	0	0	0	0	0	0	0	0	0
	Other	1	0	0	3	3	16	16	15	10	0	3	1	68
	Total	2	0	0	3	4	16	16	15	10	0	3	2	71
East Renfrewshire	Orange	0	0	0	0	1	4	4	0	0	0	0	0	9
	Catholic	0	0	0	0	0	0	0	0	0	0	0	0	0
	Other	0	0	0	3	0	0	0	0	1	1	3	0	8
	Total	0	0	0	3	1	4	4	0	1	1	3	0	17
Renfrewshire	Orange	0	0	0	0	3	5	7	6	5	1	2	1	30
(estimates - 2002	Catholic	0	0	1	0	1	0	0	0	0	0	0	0	2
figures)	Other	0	1	1	3	2	3	2	1	1	1	2	1	18
	Total	0	1	2	3	6	8	9	7	6	2	4	2	50

Appendix H

PROCESSIONS NOTIFIED TO LOCAL AUTHORITIES IN 2001

		Jan	Feb	Mar	Apr	May	June	July	Aug	Sept	Oct	Nov	Dec	Total
Scottish Borders *(estimates - most treated as exempt) (eg common ridings) (no monthly breakdown)*	Orange	0	0	0	0	0	0	0	0	0	0	0	0	0
	Catholic	0	0	0	0	0	0	0	0	0	0	0	0	0
	Other	0	0	0	0	0	0	0	0	0	0	0	0	6
	Total	0	0	0	0	0	0	0	0	0	0	0	0	6
Shetland Islands *(all treated as exempt)*	Orange	0	0	0	0	0	0	0	0	0	0	0	0	0
	Catholic	0	0	0	0	0	0	0	0	0	0	0	0	0
	Other	0	0	0	0	0	0	0	0	0	0	0	0	0
	Total	0	0	0	0	0	0	0	0	0	0	0	0	0
Stirling	Orange	0	0	0	0	2	1	3	0	0	0	0	0	6
	Catholic	0	0	0	0	0	0	0	0	0	0	0	0	0
	Other	0	1	1	1	2	6	4	2	1	1	9	1	29
	Total	0	1	1	1	4	7	7	2	1	1	9	1	35
TOTAL	Orange	1	0	5	8	40	112	85	24	13	7	10	5	800
	Catholic	0	1	3	1	2	1	0	1	0	0	0	0	21
	Other	3	6	17	37	50	133	45	66	32	15	97	31	756
	Total	4	7	25	46	92	246	130	91	45	22	107	36	1577

PROCESSIONS NOTIFIED TO LOCAL AUTHORITIES IN 2001 BY POLICE FORCE AREA

		Jan	Feb	Mar	Apr	May	June	July	Aug	Sept	Oct	Nov	Dec	Total
Central Scotland Police Force Area	Orange	0	0	2	2	5	20	10	2	1	1	2	1	46
	Catholic	0	0	0	0	0	0	0	0	0	0	0	0	0
	Other	0	1	2	2	8	17	8	7	4	2	13	1	65
	Total	0	1	4	4	13	37	18	9	5	3	15	2	111
Dumfries and Galloway Constabulary Area	Orange	0	0	0	0	0	0	1	0	1	0	0	0	2
	Catholic	0	0	0	0	0	0	0	0	0	0	0	0	0
	Other	0	0	1	0	0	0	0	1	0	0	0	0	2
	Total	0	0	1	0	0	0	1	1	1	0	0	0	4
Fife Constabulary Area	Orange	0	0	0	0	0	0	0	0	0	0	0	0	13
	Catholic	0	0	0	0	0	0	0	0	0	0	0	0	0
	Other	0	0	0	0	0	0	0	0	0	0	0	0	132
	Total	0	0	0	0	0	0	0	0	0	0	0	0	145
Grampian Police Area	Orange	0	0	0	0	0	0	0	0	1	0	0	0	1
	Catholic	0	0	0	0	0	0	0	0	0	0	0	0	0
	Other	0	0	1	5	4	4	4	8	3	2	4	3	58
	Total	0	0	1	5	4	4	4	8	4	2	4	3	59
Lothian and Borders Police Area	Orange	0	0	2	3	9	50	11	5	1	1	1	0	83
	Catholic	0	0	0	0	0	1	0	0	0	0	0	0	1
	Other	2	0	3	9	19	50	5	15	8	4	28	12	161
	Total	2	0	5	12	28	101	16	20	9	5	29	12	245
Northern Constabulary Area	Orange	0	0	0	0	0	0	0	0	0	0	0	0	0
	Catholic	0	0	0	0	0	0	0	0	0	0	0	0	0
	Other	0	0	1	0	0	3	1	3	1	1	2	8	20
	Total	0	0	1	0	0	3	1	3	1	1	2	8	20
Strathclyde Police Area	Orange	0	0	1	2	25	40	63	17	9	5	6	3	648
	Catholic	0	1	3	0	2	0	0	1	0	0	0	0	19
	Other	0	4	5	16	13	41	10	13	4	6	35	6	219
	Total	0	5	9	18	40	81	73	31	13	11	41	9	886
Tayside Police Area	Orange	1	0	0	1	1	2	0	0	0	0	1	1	7
	Catholic	0	0	0	1	0	0	0	0	0	0	0	0	1
	Other	1	1	4	5	6	18	17	19	12	0	15	1	99
	Total	2	1	4	7	7	20	17	19	12	0	16	2	107
TOTAL	Orange	1	0	5	8	40	112	85	24	13	7	10	5	800
	Catholic	0	1	3	1	2	1	0	1	0	0	0	0	21
	Other	3	6	17	37	50	133	45	66	32	15	97	31	756
	Total	4	7	25	46	92	246	130	91	45	22	107	36	1577

Appendix H

PROCESSIONS NOTIFIED TO LOCAL AUTHORITIES IN 2002

		Jan	Feb	Mar	Apr	May	June	July	Aug	Sept	Oct	Nov	Dec	Total
Aberdeen	Orange	0	0	0	0	0	0	0	0	0	0	0	0	0
	Catholic	0	0	0	0	0	0	0	0	0	0	0	0	0
	Other	0	0	3	2	4	4	1	0	0	1	3	1	19
	Total	0	0	3	2	4	4	1	0	0	1	3	1	19
Aberdeenshire *(partial figures)*	Orange	0	0	0	0	0	0	0	0	0	0	0	0	0
	Catholic	0	0	0	0	0	0	0	0	0	0	0	0	0
	Other	0	0	0	0	0	4	1	4	1	0	1	1	12
	Total	0	0	0	0	0	4	1	4	1	0	1	1	12
Angus	Orange	0	0	0	1	0	1	0	0	0	0	0	0	2
	Catholic	0	0	0	1	0	0	0	0	0	0	0	0	1
	Other	0	1	3	2	2	3	4	2	2	0	9	0	28
	Total	0	1	3	4	2	4	4	2	2	0	9	0	31
Argyll and Bute	Orange	0	0	0	0	0	0	0	0	0	0	0	0	0
	Catholic	0	0	0	0	0	0	0	0	0	0	0	0	0
	Other	0	0	1	1	3	4	5	4	1	0	3	1	23
	Total	0	0	1	1	3	4	5	4	1	0	3	1	23
East Ayrshire	Orange	0	0	1	0	1	7	4	2	2	0	2	0	19
	Catholic	0	0	0	0	0	0	0	0	0	0	0	0	0
	Other	0	0	0	0	1	8	1	4	1	0	2	2	19
	Total	0	0	1	0	2	15	5	6	3	0	4	2	38
North Ayrshire *(estimates - 2003 figures) (no monthly breakdown)*	Orange	0	0	0	0	0	0	0	0	0	0	0	0	63
	Catholic	0	0	0	0	0	0	0	0	0	0	0	0	0
	Other	0	0	0	0	0	0	0	0	0	0	0	0	30
	Total	0	0	0	0	0	0	0	0	0	0	0	0	93
South Ayrshire	Orange	0	0	0	0	2	2	0	1	1	0	0	0	6
	Catholic	0	0	0	0	0	0	0	0	0	0	0	0	0
	Other	0	0	1	0	3	7	4	1	0	1	5	0	22
	Total	0	0	1	0	5	9	4	2	1	1	5	0	28
Clackmannanshire	Orange	0	0	0	0	1	0	0	0	0	0	0	1	2
	Catholic	0	0	0	0	0	0	0	0	0	0	0	0	0
	Other	1	1	0	1	2	1	1	0	0	0	3	1	11
	Total	1	1	0	1	3	1	1	0	0	0	3	2	13
Dumfries and Galloway	Orange	0	0	0	0	2	0	0	0	0	0	0	0	2
	Catholic	0	0	0	0	0	0	0	0	0	0	0	0	0
	Other	0	0	0	0	0	1	1	0	0	0	0	0	2
	Total	0	0	0	0	2	1	1	0	0	0	0	0	4
East Dunbartonshire	Orange	0	0	0	1	2	4	1	0	0	0	1	0	9
	Catholic	0	0	0	0	0	0	0	0	0	0	0	0	0
	Other	0	1	1	0	0	2	1	0	0	2	2	0	9
	Total	0	1	1	1	2	6	2	0	0	2	3	0	18

PROCESSIONS NOTIFIED TO LOCAL AUTHORITIES IN 2002

		Jan	Feb	Mar	Apr	May	June	July	Aug	Sept	Oct	Nov	Dec	Total
West Dunbartonshire	Orange	0	0	0	0	0	0	1	0	0	0	0	0	1
	Catholic	0	0	0	0	0	0	0	0	0	0	0	0	0
	Other	0	0	0	2	3	1	1	0	0	0	6	1	14
	Total	0	0	0	2	3	1	2	0	0	0	6	1	15
Dundee	Orange	0	0	0	0	0	1	0	0	0	0	1	0	2
	Catholic	0	0	0	0	0	0	0	0	0	0	0	0	0
	Other	0	0	2	2	2	0	0	2	0	1	3	1	13
	Total	0	0	2	2	2	1	0	2	0	1	4	1	15
Edinburgh	Orange	0	0	0	0	0	2	0	0	0	0	0	0	2
	Catholic	0	0	0	0	0	1	0	0	0	0	0	0	1
	Other	1	2	2	3	6	12	3	10	5	3	8	3	58
	Total	1	2	2	3	6	15	3	10	5	3	8	3	61
Eilean Siar *(all treated as exempt)*	Orange	0	0	0	0	0	0	0	0	0	0	0	0	0
	Catholic	0	0	0	0	0	0	0	0	0	0	0	0	0
	Other	0	0	0	0	0	0	0	0	0	0	0	0	0
	Total	0	0	0	0	0	0	0	0	0	0	0	0	0
Falkirk	Orange	0	0	1	2	5	19	3	2	1	1	0	0	34
	Catholic	0	0	0	0	0	0	0	0	0	0	0	0	0
	Other	0	0	0	1	2	8	3	4	2	0	4	1	25
	Total	0	0	1	3	7	27	6	6	3	1	4	1	59
Fife *(no monthly breakdown)*	Orange	0	0	0	0	0	0	0	0	0	0	0	0	13
	Catholic	0	0	0	0	0	0	0	0	0	0	0	0	0
	Other	0	0	0	0	0	0	0	0	0	0	0	0	132
	Total	0	0	0	0	0	0	0	0	0	0	0	0	145
Glasgow *(no monthly breakdown) (split based on 2003 %s)*	Orange (85%)	0	0	0	0	0	0	0	0	0	0	0	0	257
	Catholic (3%)	0	0	0	0	0	0	0	0	0	0	0	0	9
	Other (12%)	0	0	0	0	0	0	0	0	0	0	0	0	36
	Total	0	0	0	0	0	0	0	0	0	0	0	0	302
Highland *(based on Inverness Figures)*	Orange	0	0	0	0	0	0	0	0	0	0	0	0	0
	Catholic	0	0	0	0	0	0	0	0	0	0	0	0	0
	Other	0	0	2	0	0	1	3	1	1	2	1	0	11
	Total	0	0	2	0	0	1	3	1	1	2	1	0	11
Inverclyde	Orange	0	0	0	0	3	3	4	1	0	0	0	0	11
	Catholic	0	0	0	0	0	0	0	1	0	0	0	0	1
	Other	0	0	1	0	0	0	0	0	0	0	0	0	1
	Total	0	0	1	0	3	3	4	2	0	0	0	0	13

Appendix H

PROCESSIONS NOTIFIED TO LOCAL AUTHORITIES IN 2002

		Jan	Feb	Mar	Apr	May	June	July	Aug	Sept	Oct	Nov	Dec	Total
North Lanarkshire (estimates 2003 figures) (no monthly breakdown)	Orange	0	0	0	0	0	0	0	0	0	0	0	0	157
	Catholic	0	0	0	0	0	0	0	0	0	0	0	0	3
	Other	0	0	0	0	0	0	0	0	0	0	0	0	0
	Total	0	0	0	0	0	0	0	0	0	0	0	0	160
South Lanarkshire	Orange	0	0	0	2	19	21	42	9	2	3	4	4	106
	Catholic	0	0	0	0	0	0	0	0	0	0	0	0	0
	Other	0	0	0	0	2	13	3	2	1	1	12	4	38
	Total	0	0	0	2	21	34	45	11	3	4	16	8	144
East Lothian	Orange	0	1	0	0	0	6	0	0	0	0	0	0	7
	Catholic	0	0	0	0	0	0	0	0	0	0	0	0	0
	Other	1	0	1	2	4	15	8	7	4	0	10	6	58
	Total	1	1	1	2	4	21	8	7	4	0	10	6	65
Midlothian	Orange	0	0	0	1	0	3	0	0	0	0	0	0	4
	Catholic	0	0	0	0	0	0	0	0	0	0	0	0	0
	Other	1	0	1	0	4	8	0	2	1	0	5	0	22
	Total	1	0	1	1	4	11	0	2	1	0	5	0	26
West Lothian	Orange	0	0	0	5	10	37	14	10	1	0	0	1	78
	Catholic	0	0	0	0	0	0	0	0	0	0	0	0	0
	Other	0	0	1	0	2	10	0	1	0	0	7	5	26
	Total	0	0	1	5	12	47	14	11	1	0	7	6	104
Moray (estimates - 2003 figures) (no monthly breakdown)	Orange	0	0	0	0	0	0	0	0	0	0	0	0	0
	Catholic	0	0	0	0	0	0	0	0	0	0	0	0	0
	Other	0	0	0	0	0	0	0	0	0	0	0	0	20
	Total	0	0	0	0	0	0	0	0	0	0	0	0	20
Orkney	Orange	0	0	0	0	0	0	0	0	0	0	0	0	0
	Catholic	0	0	0	0	0	0	0	0	0	0	0	0	0
	Other	0	0	0	0	0	3	0	0	0	0	1	2	6
	Total	0	0	0	0	0	3	0	0	0	0	1	2	6
Perth and Kinross	Orange	0	0	0	0	0	2	0	0	0	0	1	0	3
	Catholic	0	0	0	0	0	0	0	0	0	0	0	0	0
	Other	1	1	1	3	5	16	7	7	6	3	7	0	57
	Total	1	1	1	3	5	18	7	7	6	3	8	0	60
East Renfrewshire	Orange	0	0	0	1	3	8	2	0	0	1	2	0	17
	Catholic	0	0	0	0	0	0	0	0	0	0	0	0	0
	Other	0	0	1	3	1	1	0	0	0	2	3	0	11
	Total	0	0	1	4	4	9	2	0	0	3	5	0	28
Renfrewshire	Orange	0	0	0	0	3	5	7	6	5	1	2	1	30
	Catholic	0	0	1	0	1	0	0	0	0	0	0	0	2
	Other	0	1	1	3	2	3	2	1	1	1	2	1	18
	Total	0	1	2	3	6	8	9	7	6	2	4	2	50

PROCESSIONS NOTIFIED TO LOCAL AUTHORITIES IN 2002

		Jan	Feb	Mar	Apr	May	June	July	Aug	Sept	Oct	Nov	Dec	Total
Scottish Borders *(estimates - most treated as exempt) (eg common ridings) (no monthly breakdown)*	Orange	0	0	0	0	0	0	0	0	0	0	0	0	0
	Catholic	0	0	0	0	0	0	0	0	0	0	0	0	0
	Other	0	0	0	0	0	0	0	0	0	0	0	0	6
	Total	0	0	0	0	0	0	0	0	0	0	0	0	6
Shetland Islands *(all treated as exempt)*	Orange	0	0	0	0	0	0	0	0	0	0	0	0	0
	Catholic	0	0	0	0	0	0	0	0	0	0	0	0	0
	Other	0	0	0	0	0	0	0	0	0	0	0	0	0
	Total	0	0	0	0	0	0	0	0	0	0	0	0	0
Stirling	Orange	0	0	0	0	1	3	3	0	0	0	0	0	7
	Catholic	0	0	0	0	0	0	0	0	0	0	0	0	0
	Other	0	0	1	0	2	2	2	4	3	1	8	1	24
	Total	0	0	1	0	3	5	5	4	3	1	8	1	31
TOTAL	Orange	0	1	2	13	52	124	81	31	12	6	13	7	832
	Catholic	0	0	1	1	1	1	0	1	0	0	0	0	17
	Other	5	7	23	25	50	127	51	56	29	18	105	31	751
	Total	5	8	26	39	103	252	132	88	41	24	118	38	1600

Appendix H

PROCESSIONS NOTIFIED TO LOCAL AUTHORITIES IN 2002 BY POLICE FORCE AREA

		Jan	Feb	Mar	Apr	May	June	July	Aug	Sept	Oct	Nov	Dec	Total
Central Scotland Police Force Area	Orange	0	0	1	2	7	22	6	2	1	1	0	1	43
	Catholic	0	0	0	0	0	0	0	0	0	0	0	0	0
	Other	1	1	1	2	6	11	6	8	5	1	15	3	60
	Total	1	1	2	4	13	33	12	10	6	2	15	4	103
Dumfries and Galloway Constabulary Area	Orange	0	0	0	0	2	0	0	0	0	0	0	0	2
	Catholic	0	0	0	0	0	0	0	0	0	0	0	0	0
	Other	0	0	0	0	0	1	1	0	0	0	0	0	2
	Total	0	0	0	0	2	1	1	0	0	0	0	0	4
Fife Constabulary Area	Orange	0	0	0	0	0	0	0	0	0	0	0	0	13
	Catholic	0	0	0	0	0	0	0	0	0	0	0	0	0
	Other	0	0	0	0	0	0	0	0	0	0	0	0	132
	Total	0	0	0	0	0	0	0	0	0	0	0	0	145
Grampian Police Area	Orange	0	0	0	0	0	0	0	0	0	0	0	0	0
	Catholic	0	0	0	0	0	0	0	0	0	0	0	0	0
	Other	0	0	3	2	4	8	2	4	1	1	4	2	51
	Total	0	0	3	2	4	8	2	4	1	1	4	2	51
Lothian and Borders Police Area	Orange	0	1	0	6	10	48	14	10	1	0	0	1	91
	Catholic	0	0	0	0	0	1	0	0	0	0	0	0	1
	Other	3	2	5	5	16	45	11	20	10	3	30	14	170
	Total	3	3	5	11	26	94	25	30	11	3	30	15	262
Northern Constabulary Area	Orange	0	0	0	0	0	0	0	0	0	0	0	0	0
	Catholic	0	0	0	0	0	0	0	0	0	0	0	0	0
	Other	0	0	2	0	0	4	3	1	1	2	2	2	17
	Total	0	0	2	0	0	4	3	1	1	2	2	2	17
Strathclyde Police Area	Orange	0	0	1	4	33	50	61	19	10	5	11	5	676
	Catholic	0	0	1	0	1	0	0	1	0	0	0	0	15
	Other	0	2	6	9	15	39	17	12	4	7	35	9	221
	Total	0	2	8	13	49	89	78	32	14	12	46	14	912
Tayside Police Area	Orange	0	0	0	1	0	4	0	0	0	0	2	0	7
	Catholic	0	0	0	1	0	0	0	0	0	0	0	0	1
	Other	1	2	6	7	9	19	11	11	8	4	19	1	98
	Total	1	2	6	9	9	23	11	11	8	4	21	1	106
TOTAL	Orange	0	1	2	13	52	124	81	31	12	6	13	7	832
	Catholic	0	0	1	1	1	1	0	1	0	0	0	0	17
	Other	5	7	23	25	50	127	51	56	29	18	105	31	751
	Total	5	8	26	39	103	252	132	88	41	24	118	38	1600

Review of Marches and Parades in Scotland

PROCESSIONS NOTIFIED TO LOCAL AUTHORITIES IN 2003

		Jan	Feb	Mar	Apr	May	June	July	Aug	Sept	Oct	Nov	Dec	Total
Aberdeen	Orange	0	0	0	0	0	0	0	0	0	0	0	0	0
	Catholic	0	0	0	0	0	0	0	0	0	0	0	0	0
	Other	0	0	2	4	3	1	1	0	1	0	2	0	14
	Total	0	0	2	4	3	1	1	0	1	0	2	0	14
Aberdeenshire	Orange	0	0	0	0	0	0	0	0	0	0	0	0	0
(partial figures)	Catholic	0	0	0	0	0	0	0	0	0	0	0	0	0
	Other	0	0	0	3	0	5	3	7	0	0	1	1	20
	Total	0	0	0	3	0	5	3	7	0	0	1	1	20
Angus	Orange	0	0	0	0	0	1	0	0	0	0	0	0	1
	Catholic	0	0	0	1	0	0	0	0	0	0	0	0	1
	Other	0	1	2	1	0	1	3	3	2	0	8	0	21
	Total	0	1	2	2	0	2	3	3	2	0	8	0	23
Argyll and Bute	Orange	0	0	0	0	0	0	0	0	0	0	0	0	0
	Catholic	0	0	0	0	0	0	0	0	0	0	0	0	0
	Other	0	0	1	2	4	6	8	10	2	2	5	2	42
	Total	0	0	1	2	4	6	8	10	2	2	5	2	42
East Ayrshire	Orange	0	1	1	1	0	15	2	1	2	2	1	0	26
	Catholic	0	0	0	0	0	0	0	0	0	0	0	0	0
	Other	0	0	0	2	1	4	0	3	1	0	3	0	14
	Total	0	1	1	3	1	19	2	4	3	2	4	0	40
North Ayrshire	Orange	0	0	0	0	0	0	0	0	0	0	0	0	63
(no monthly	Catholic	0	0	0	0	0	0	0	0	0	0	0	0	0
breakdown)	Other	0	0	0	0	0	0	0	0	0	0	0	0	30
	Total	0	0	0	0	0	0	0	0	0	0	0	0	93
South Ayrshire	Orange	0	0	0	1	1	4	0	1	0	1	1	0	9
	Catholic	0	0	0	0	0	0	0	0	0	0	0	0	0
	Other	0	0	1	2	2	5	2	2	1	2	5	0	22
	Total	0	0	1	3	3	9	2	3	1	3	6	0	31
Clackmannanshire	Orange	0	0	1	0	1	1	0	0	0	0	0	0	3
	Catholic	0	0	0	0	0	0	0	0	0	0	0	0	0
	Other	1	0	1	0	7	0	0	0	0	1	2	0	12
	Total	1	0	2	0	8	1	0	0	0	1	2	0	15
Dumfries and	Orange	0	0	0	1	0	1	0	0	1	0	0	0	3
Galloway	Catholic	0	0	0	0	0	0	0	0	0	0	0	0	0
	Other	0	0	0	0	0	0	0	0	0	0	0	0	0
	Total	0	0	0	1	0	1	0	0	1	0	0	0	3
East	Orange	0	0	0	1	2	3	3	0	0	0	1	0	10
Dunbartonshire	Catholic	0	0	0	0	0	0	0	0	0	0	0	0	0
	Other	1	3	1	0	0	1	0	0	0	0	2	0	8
	Total	1	3	1	1	2	4	3	0	0	0	3	0	18

Appendix H

PROCESSIONS NOTIFIED TO LOCAL AUTHORITIES IN 2003

		Jan	Feb	Mar	Apr	May	June	July	Aug	Sept	Oct	Nov	Dec	Total
West Dunbartonshire	Orange	0	0	0	0	0	0	1	0	0	0	0	0	1
	Catholic	0	0	0	0	0	0	0	0	0	0	0	0	0
	Other	0	0	1	3	1	0	1	1	0	0	3	0	10
	Total	0	0	1	3	1	0	2	1	0	0	3	0	11
Dundee	Orange	0	0	1	0	0	1	0	0	0	0	1	0	3
	Catholic	0	0	0	0	0	0	0	0	0	0	0	0	0
	Other	0	0	2	2	1	3	2	2	1	0	3	1	17
	Total	0	0	3	2	1	4	2	2	1	0	4	1	20
Edinburgh	Orange	0	0	0	0	0	1	0	0	0	0	0	0	1
	Catholic	0	0	0	0	0	1	0	1	0	0	0	0	2
	Other	1	1	6	4	6	18	3	10	5	2	11	2	69
	Total	1	1	6	4	6	20	3	11	5	2	11	2	72
Eilean Siar (all treated as exempt)	Orange	0	0	0	0	0	0	0	0	0	0	0	0	0
	Catholic	0	0	0	0	0	0	0	0	0	0	0	0	0
	Other	0	0	0	0	0	0	0	0	0	0	0	0	0
	Total	0	0	0	0	0	0	0	0	0	0	0	0	0
Falkirk	Orange	0	0	2	0	3	8	4	1	1	1	0	0	20
	Catholic	0	0	0	0	0	0	0	0	0	0	0	0	0
	Other	0	0	1	1	3	6	3	4	2	0	3	0	23
	Total	0	0	3	1	6	14	7	5	3	1	3	0	43
Fife (no monthly breakdown)	Orange	0	0	0	0	0	0	0	0	0	0	0	0	13
	Catholic	0	0	0	0	0	0	0	0	0	0	0	0	1
	Other	0	0	0	0	0	0	0	0	0	0	0	0	161
	Total	0	0	0	0	0	0	0	0	0	0	0	0	175
Glasgow	Orange	0	2	5	15	36	92	69	29	12	6	15	6	287
	Catholic	0	0	1	0	5	2	1	2	0	0	0	0	11
	Other	1	4	3	6	2	5	2	3	1	3	9	1	40
	Total	1	6	9	21	43	99	72	34	13	9	24	7	338
Highland (based on Inverness figures)	Orange	0	0	0	0	0	0	0	0	0	0	0	0	0
	Catholic	0	0	0	0	0	0	0	0	0	0	0	0	0
	Other	0	0	3	1	1	1	2	1	2	2	1	0	14
	Total	0	0	3	1	1	1	2	1	2	2	1	0	14
Inverclyde	Orange	0	0	0	0	2	6	0	1	0	0	0	0	9
	Catholic	0	0	1	0	0	0	0	0	0	0	0	0	1
	Other	0	0	1	0	0	0	0	1	0	0	0	0	2
	Total	0	0	2	0	2	6	0	2	0	0	0	0	12
North Lanarkshire	Orange	0	1	0	1	23	37	63	17	3	0	6	6	157
	Catholic	0	0	1	0	0	2	0	0	0	0	0	0	3
	Other	0	0	0	0	0	0	0	0	0	0	0	0	0
	Total	0	1	1	1	23	39	63	17	3	0	6	6	160

Review of Marches and Parades in Scotland

PROCESSIONS NOTIFIED TO LOCAL AUTHORITIES IN 2003

		Jan	Feb	Mar	Apr	May	June	July	Aug	Sept	Oct	Nov	Dec	Total
South Lanarkshire	Orange	0	1	2	0	20	21	42	7	4	6	4	4	111
	Catholic	0	0	0	0	0	0	0	0	0	0	0	0	0
	Other	0	2	1	3	2	24	2	3	0	2	7	5	51
	Total	0	3	3	3	22	45	44	10	4	8	11	9	162
East Lothian	Orange	0	0	0	0	1	6	0	0	0	0	0	0	7
	Catholic	0	0	0	0	0	0	0	0	0	0	0	0	0
	Other	1	0	1	3	11	17	7	12	4	2	12	6	76
	Total	1	0	1	3	12	23	7	12	4	2	12	6	83
Midlothian	Orange	0	0	1	0	0	2	0	0	0	0	0	0	3
	Catholic	0	0	0	0	0	0	0	0	0	0	0	0	0
	Other	1	0	1	1	6	6	0	4	1	1	4	0	25
	Total	1	0	2	1	6	8	0	4	1	1	4	0	28
West Lothian	Orange	0	1	1	4	12	29	14	10	1	0	0	3	75
	Catholic	0	0	0	0	0	0	0	0	0	0	0	0	0
	Other	0	1	0	1	5	14	0	0	0	1	8	4	34
	Total	0	2	1	5	17	43	14	10	1	1	8	7	109
Moray *(no monthly breakdown)*	Orange	0	0	0	0	0	0	0	0	0	0	0	0	0
	Catholic	0	0	0	0	0	0	0	0	0	0	0	0	0
	Other	0	0	0	0	0	0	0	0	0	0	0	0	20
	Total	0	0	0	0	0	0	0	0	0	0	0	0	20
Orkney	Orange	0	0	0	0	0	0	0	0	0	0	0	0	0
	Catholic	0	0	0	0	0	0	0	0	0	0	0	0	0
	Other	0	0	0	0	0	0	0	0	0	0	0	1	1
	Total	0	0	0	0	0	0	0	0	0	0	0	1	1
Perth and Kinross	Orange	0	0	0	0	0	2	0	0	0	0	0	1	3
	Catholic	0	0	0	0	0	0	0	0	0	0	0	0	0
	Other	1	0	1	4	5	13	10	10	6	0	3	2	55
	Total	1	0	1	4	5	15	10	10	6	0	3	3	58
East Renfrewshire	Orange	0	0	0	0	2	5	1	0	0	0	1	0	9
	Catholic	0	0	0	0	0	0	0	0	0	0	0	0	0
	Other	0	0	0	1	0	1	0	0	0	2	2	0	6
	Total	0	0	0	1	2	6	1	0	0	2	3	0	15
Renfrewshire	Orange	0	0	0	1	4	13	0	4	5	0	2	2	31
	Catholic	0	0	0	1	0	0	0	0	0	0	0	0	1
	Other	0	0	0	2	0	3	3	3	4	1	9	0	25
	Total	0	0	0	4	4	16	3	7	9	1	11	2	57
Scottish Borders *(most treated as exempt) (eg common ridings) (no monthly breakdown)*	Orange	0	0	0	0	0	0	0	0	0	0	0	0	0
	Catholic	0	0	0	0	0	0	0	0	0	0	0	0	0
	Other	0	0	0	0	0	0	0	0	0	0	0	0	6
	Total	0	0	0	0	0	0	0	0	0	0	0	0	6

Appendix H

PROCESSIONS NOTIFIED TO LOCAL AUTHORITIES IN 2003

		Jan	Feb	Mar	Apr	May	June	July	Aug	Sept	Oct	Nov	Dec	Total
Shetland Islands *(all treated as exempt)*	Orange	0	0	0	0	0	0	0	0	0	0	0	0	0
	Catholic	0	0	0	0	0	0	0	0	0	0	0	0	0
	Other	0	0	0	0	0	0	0	0	0	0	0	0	0
	Total	0	0	0	0	0	0	0	0	0	0	0	0	0
Stirling	Orange	0	0	0	0	1	2	3	1	0	0	0	1	8
	Catholic	0	0	0	0	0	0	0	0	0	0	0	0	0
	Other	0	0	1	1	1	3	4	3	1	0	7	0	21
	Total	0	0	1	1	2	5	7	4	1	0	7	1	29
TOTAL	Orange	0	6	14	25	108	250	202	72	29	16	32	23	853
	Catholic	0	0	3	2	5	5	1	3	0	0	0	0	20
	Other	7	12	30	47	61	137	56	82	34	21	110	25	839
	Total	7	18	47	74	174	392	259	157	63	37	142	48	1712

PROCESSIONS NOTIFIED TO LOCAL AUTHORITIES IN 2003 BY POLICE FORCE AREA

		Jan	Feb	Mar	Apr	May	June	July	Aug	Sept	Oct	Nov	Dec	Total
Central Scotland Police Force Area	Orange	0	0	3	0	5	11	7	2	1	1	0	1	31
	Catholic	0	0	0	0	0	0	0	0	0	0	0	0	0
	Other	1	0	3	2	11	9	7	7	3	1	12	0	56
	Total	1	0	6	2	16	20	14	9	4	2	12	1	87
Dumfries and Galloway Constabulary Area	Orange	0	0	0	1	0	1	0	0	1	0	0	0	3
	Catholic	0	0	0	0	0	0	0	0	0	0	0	0	0
	Other	0	0	0	0	0	0	0	0	0	0	0	0	0
	Total	0	0	0	1	0	1	0	0	1	0	0	0	3
Fife Constabulary Area	Orange	0	0	0	0	0	0	0	0	0	0	0	0	13
	Catholic	0	0	0	0	0	0	0	0	0	0	0	0	1
	Other	0	0	0	0	0	0	0	0	0	0	0	0	161
	Total	0	0	0	0	0	0	0	0	0	0	0	0	175
Grampian Police Area	Orange	0	0	0	0	0	0	0	0	0	0	0	0	0
	Catholic	0	0	0	0	0	0	0	0	0	0	0	0	0
	Other	0	0	2	7	3	6	4	7	1	0	3	1	54
	Total	0	0	2	7	3	6	4	7	1	0	3	1	54
Lothian and Borders Police Area	Orange	0	1	2	4	13	38	14	10	1	0	0	3	86
	Catholic	0	0	0	0	0	1	0	1	0	0	0	0	2
	Other	3	2	8	9	28	55	10	26	10	6	35	12	210
	Total	3	3	10	13	41	94	24	37	11	6	35	15	298
Northern Constabulary Area	Orange	0	0	0	0	0	0	0	0	0	0	0	0	0
	Catholic	0	0	0	0	0	0	0	0	0	0	0	0	0
	Other	0	0	3	1	1	1	2	1	2	2	1	1	15
	Total	0	0	3	1	1	1	2	1	2	2	1	1	15
Strathclyde Police Area	Orange	0	5	8	20	90	196	181	60	26	15	31	18	713
	Catholic	0	0	3	1	5	4	1	2	0	0	0	0	16
	Other	2	9	9	21	12	49	18	26	9	12	45	8	250
	Total	2	14	20	42	107	249	200	88	35	27	76	26	979
Tayside Police Area	Orange	0	0	1	0	0	4	0	0	0	0	1	1	7
	Catholic	0	0	0	1	0	0	0	0	0	0	0	0	1
	Other	1	1	5	7	6	17	15	15	9	0	14	3	93
	Total	1	1	6	8	6	21	15	15	9	0	15	4	101
TOTAL	Orange	0	6	14	25	108	250	202	72	29	16	32	23	853
	Catholic	0	0	3	2	5	5	1	3	0	0	0	0	20
	Other	7	12	30	47	61	137	56	82	34	21	110	25	839
	Total	7	18	47	74	174	392	259	157	63	37	142	48	1712

Appendix H

PROCESSIONS NOTIFIED TO LOCAL AUTHORITIES IN 2004 (to Sept)

		Jan	Feb	March	Apr	May	June	July	Aug	Sept	Total
Aberdeen	Orange	0	0	0	0	0	0	0	1	0	1
	Catholic	0	0	0	0	0	0	0	0	0	0
	Other	0	0	0	3	6	0	1	3	0	13
	Total	0	0	0	3	6	0	1	4	0	14
Aberdeenshire	Orange	0	0	0	0	0	0	0	0	0	0
(partial figures)	Catholic	0	0	0	0	0	0	0	0	0	0
	Other	0	0	0	2	0	6	1	2	0	11
	Total	0	0	0	2	0	6	1	2	0	11
Angus	Orange	0	0	0	0	0	1	0	0	0	1
	Catholic	0	0	0	1	0	0	0	0	0	1
	Other	1	0	1	3	2	2	2	0	0	11
	Total	1	0	1	4	2	3	2	0	0	13
Argyll and Bute	Orange	1	0	0	0	0	0	0	0	0	1
	Catholic	0	0	0	0	0	0	0	0	0	0
	Other	3	0	0	2	7	5	6	10	5	38
	Total	4	0	0	2	7	5	6	10	5	39
East Ayrshire	Orange	0	0	2	0	2	3	9	3	2	21
	Catholic	0	0	0	0	0	0	0	0	0	0
	Other	0	0	3	1	1	4	0	0	1	10
	Total	0	0	5	1	3	7	9	3	3	31
North Ayrshire	Orange	0	0	0	0	0	0	0	0	0	63
(estimates - 2003	Catholic	0	0	0	0	0	0	0	0	0	0
figures) (no monthly	Other	0	0	0	0	0	0	0	0	0	30
breakdown)	Total	0	0	0	0	0	0	0	0	0	93
South Ayrshire	Orange	0	0	0	0	2	1	3	1	0	7
	Catholic	0	0	0	0	0	0	0	0	0	0
	Other	0	0	1	1	3	8	2	0	1	16
	Total	0	0	1	1	5	9	5	1	1	23
Clackmannanshire	Orange	0	0	0	0	0	0	0	0	0	0
	Catholic	0	0	0	0	0	0	0	0	0	0
	Other	0	0	0	1	8	1	0	0	0	10
	Total	0	0	0	1	8	1	0	0	0	10
Dumfries and	Orange	0	0	0	0	0	0	1	0	0	1
Galloway	Catholic	0	0	0	0	0	0	0	0	0	0
	Other	0	0	0	0	0	0	0	0	0	0
	Total	0	0	0	0	0	0	1	0	0	1
East	Orange	0	0	0	0	1	3	2	0	0	6
Dunbartonshire	Catholic	0	0	0	0	0	0	0	0	0	0
	Other	0	0	1	0	2	1	0	0	0	4
	Total	0	0	1	0	3	4	2	0	0	10

PROCESSIONS NOTIFIED TO LOCAL AUTHORITIES IN 2004 (to Sept)

		Jan	Feb	March	Apr	May	June	July	Aug	Sept	Total
West Dunbartonshire	Orange	0	0	0	0	0	0	1	1	0	2
	Catholic	0	0	0	0	0	0	0	0	0	0
	Other	0	0	1	5	0	1	0	0	1	8
	Total	0	0	1	5	0	1	1	1	1	10
Dundee	Orange	0	0	0	0	0	1	0	0	0	1
	Catholic	0	0	0	0	0	0	0	0	0	0
	Other	0	1	3	3	3	5	0	2	2	19
	Total	0	1	3	3	3	6	0	2	2	20
Edinburgh	Orange	0	0	0	0	0	1	0	0	0	1
	Catholic	0	0	0	0	0	1	0	0	0	1
	Other	1	0	5	2	14	19	1	11	3	56
	Total	1	0	5	2	14	21	1	11	3	58
Eilean Siar *(all treated as exempt)*	Orange	0	0	0	0	0	0	0	0	0	0
	Catholic	0	0	0	0	0	0	0	0	0	0
	Other	0	0	0	0	0	0	0	0	0	0
	Total	0	0	0	0	0	0	0	0	0	0
Falkirk	Orange	0	0	0	1	3	14	3	0	1	22
	Catholic	0	0	0	0	0	0	0	0	0	0
	Other	0	0	0	0	2	8	3	4	0	17
	Total	0	0	0	1	5	22	6	4	1	39
Fife (no monthly breakdown)	Orange	0	0	0	0	0	0	0	0	0	18
	Catholic	0	0	0	0	0	0	0	0	0	0
	Other	0	0	0	0	0	0	0	0	0	110
	Total	0	0	0	0	0	0	0	0	0	128
Glasgow	Orange	1	2	5	17	39	82	70	30	5	251
	Catholic	0	0	1	0	5	2	1	3	0	12
	Other	1	2	6	8	3	12	5	1	1	39
	Total	2	4	12	25	47	96	76	34	6	302
Highland *(estimates – 2003 figures) (based on Inverness figures)*	Orange	0	0	0	0	0	0	0	0	0	0
	Catholic	0	0	0	0	0	0	0	0	0	0
	Other	0	0	3	1	1	1	2	1	2	11
	Total	0	0	3	1	1	1	2	1	2	11
Inverclyde	Orange	0	0	0	0	2	3	3	1	1	10
	Catholic	0	0	0	0	0	1	0	0	0	1
	Other	0	0	0	0	0	0	1	0	0	1
	Total	0	0	0	0	2	4	4	1	1	12
North Lanarkshire *(estimates – 2003 Figures) (no montly breakdown)*	Orange	0	0	0	0	0	0	0	0	0	145
	Catholic	0	0	0	0	0	0	0	0	0	3
	Other	0	0	0	0	0	0	0	0	0	0
	Total	0	0	0	0	0	0	0	0	0	148

Appendix H

PROCESSIONS NOTIFIED TO LOCAL AUTHORITIES IN 2004 (to Sept)

		Jan	Feb	March	Apr	May	June	July	Aug	Sept	Total
South Lanarkshire	Orange	0	0	2	4	14	16	41	4	0	81
	Catholic	0	0	0	0	0	0	0	0	0	0
	Other	0	2	0	0	3	19	3	1	0	28
	Total	0	2	2	4	17	35	44	5	0	109
East Lothian	Orange	0	0	0	0	0	2	0	0	0	2
	Catholic	0	0	0	0	0	0	0	0	0	0
	Other	1	0	3	4	12	23	12	9	5	69
	Total	1	0	3	4	12	25	12	9	5	71
Midlothian	Orange	0	0	0	1	0	1	0	0	0	2
	Catholic	0	0	0	0	0	0	0	0	0	0
	Other	1	0	2	2	3	7	0	1	0	16
	Total	1	0	2	3	3	8	0	1	0	18
West Lothian	Orange	0	0	1	4	11	30	10	11	1	68
	Catholic	0	0	0	0	0	0	0	0	0	0
	Other	0	0	0	1	4	14	0	2	0	21
	Total	0	0	1	5	15	44	10	13	1	89
Moray *(estimates - 2003 figures) (no monthly breakdown)*	Orange	0	0	0	0	0	0	0	0	0	0
	Catholic	0	0	0	0	0	0	0	0	0	0
	Other	0	0	0	0	0	0	0	0	0	20
	Total	0	0	0	0	0	0	0	0	0	20
Orkney	Orange	0	0	0	0	0	0	0	0	0	0
	Catholic	0	0	0	0	0	0	0	0	0	0
	Other	0	0	0	0	0	0	0	0	0	0
	Total	0	0	0	0	0	0	0	0	0	0
Perth and Kinross	Orange	0	0	0	0	0	2	0	1	0	3
	Catholic	0	0	0	0	0	0	0	0	0	0
	Other	1	0	2	2	6	14	13	12	4	54
	Total	1	0	2	2	6	16	13	13	4	57
East Renfrewshire	Orange	0	0	0	1	2	6	4	0	0	13
	Catholic	0	0	0	0	0	0	0	0	0	0
	Other	0	1	0	3	0	1	0	0	0	5
	Total	0	1	0	4	2	7	4	0	0	18
Renfrewshire	Orange	0	2	0	9	0	4	10	1	0	26
	Catholic	0	0	0	0	0	0	0	0	0	0
	Other	1	4	6	2	3	1	1	1	0	19
	Total	1	6	6	11	3	5	11	2	0	45

Review of Marches and Parades in Scotland

PROCESSIONS NOTIFIED TO LOCAL AUTHORITIES IN 2004 (to Sept)

		Jan	Feb	March	Apr	May	June	July	Aug	Sept	Total
Scottish Borders *(most treated as exempt) (eg common ridings) (no monthly breakdown)*	Orange	0	0	0	0	0	0	0	0	0	0
	Catholic	0	0	0	0	0	0	0	0	0	0
	Other	0	0	0	0	0	0	0	0	0	6
	Total	0	0	0	0	0	0	0	0	0	6
Shetland Islands *(all treated as exempt)*	Orange	0	0	0	0	0	0	0	0	0	0
	Catholic	0	0	0	0	0	0	0	0	0	0
	Other	0	0	0	0	0	0	0	0	0	0
	Total	0	0	0	0	0	0	0	0	0	0
Stirling	Orange	0	0	0	0	1	2	5	0	1	9
	Catholic	0	0	0	0	0	0	0	0	0	0
	Other	0	0	1	1	1	3	2	4	1	13
	Total	0	0	1	1	2	5	7	4	2	22
TOTAL	Orange	2	4	10	37	77	172	162	54	11	755
	Catholic	0	0	1	1	5	4	1	3	0	18
	Other	10	10	38	47	84	155	55	64	26	655
	Total	12	14	49	85	166	331	218	121	37	1428

Appendix H

PROCESSIONS NOTIFIED TO LOCAL AUTHORITIES IN 2004 BY POLICE FORCE AREA (to Sept)

		Jan	Feb	March	Apr	May	June	July	Aug	Sept	Total
Central Scotland Police Force Area	Orange	0	0	0	1	4	16	8	0	2	31
	Catholic	0	0	0	0	0	0	0	0	0	0
	Other	0	0	1	2	11	12	5	8	1	40
	Total	0	0	1	3	15	28	13	8	3	71
Dumfries and Galloway Constabulary Area	Orange	0	0	0	0	0	0	1	0	0	1
	Catholic	0	0	0	0	0	0	0	0	0	0
	Other	0	0	0	0	0	0	0	0	0	0
	Total	0	0	0	0	0	0	1	0	0	1
Fife Constabulary Area	Orange	0	0	0	0	0	0	0	0	0	18
	Catholic	0	0	0	0	0	0	0	0	0	0
	Other	0	0	0	0	0	0	0	0	0	110
	Total	0	0	0	0	0	0	0	0	0	128
Grampian Police Area	Orange	0	0	0	0	0	0	0	1	0	1
	Catholic	0	0	0	0	0	0	0	0	0	0
	Other	0	0	0	5	6	6	2	5	0	44
	Total	0	0	0	5	6	6	2	6	0	45
Lothian and Borders Police Area	Orange	0	0	1	5	11	34	10	11	1	73
	Catholic	0	0	0	0	0	1	0	0	0	1
	Other	3	0	10	9	33	63	13	23	8	168
	Total	3	0	11	14	44	98	23	34	9	242
Northern Constabulary Area	Orange	0	0	0	0	0	0	0	0	0	0
	Catholic	0	0	0	0	0	0	0	0	0	0
	Other	0	0	3	1	1	1	2	1	2	11
	Total	0	0	3	1	1	1	2	1	2	11
Strathclyde Police Area	Orange	2	4	9	31	62	118	143	41	8	626
	Catholic	0	0	1	0	5	3	1	3	0	16
	Other	5	9	18	22	22	52	18	13	9	198
	Total	7	13	28	53	89	173	162	57	17	840
Tayside Police Area	Orange	0	0	0	0	0	4	0	1	0	5
	Catholic	0	0	0	1	0	0	0	0	0	1
	Other	2	1	6	8	11	21	15	14	6	84
	Total	2	1	6	9	11	25	15	15	6	90
TOTAL	Orange	2	4	10	37	77	172	162	54	11	755
	Catholic	0	0	1	1	5	4	1	3	0	18
	Other	10	10	38	47	84	155	55	64	26	655
	Total	12	14	49	85	166	331	218	121	37	1428

Appendix I

Guidance for organisers – elements of a 'How To' guide

A number of local authorities in Scotland have already produced guidance for organisers of events. I am grateful to Scottish Borders Council for their 'Organising Events in the Scottish Borders' upon which I have drawn heavily in this summary of the sorts of issues that might be covered in guidance. I am also grateful to Fife Council for their 'Events Toolkit' and to Edinburgh Council for their 'Events in Edinburgh – Planning Guide'. It would be helpful for other local authorities to produce similar guidance for organisers in their own areas. I consider that the sorts of things that guidance could usefully cover could include:

A – Legal requirements on organisers – organisers of events, including processions need to be aware of their legal requirements. They have a common law duty of care to take reasonable care not to cause foreseeable death, injury, illness or damage. Failure to take reasonable care could result in claims for damages against the organisers for injury or loss to person. Depending on the nature of the event, other legislation could apply, such as:

- The Health and Safety at Work Act 1974 and its associated Regulations which put a duty on organisers to carry out risk assessments to identify any risk and to reduce it to acceptable levels;
- The Food Safety Act 1990 which applies when food is provided or sold;
- The Occupiers Liability (Scotland) Act 1960;
- Traffic legislation – the Road Traffic Regulation Act 1984 as amended by the Road Traffic (Temporary Restrictions) Act 1991 and the Road Traffic Regulation (Special Events) Act 1994 where there is a requirement for restrictions for road users such as road closures, diversions, signs or cones when a Temporary Traffic Regulations Order may be necessary. There could be a charge associated;
- The Control of Pollution Act 1974 which makes provision about the use of loud speakers;
- Other licences, permits and certificates could be required depended on the nature of the event or procession. These could include: a public entertainment licence, a liquor licence, a street traders licence, a licence for a use of a park or open space, a lottery permit, a licence for a charitable collection or a market operators licence. There will be a fee associated with some of these licences;

- The Public Order Act 1936 which prohibits the wearing of uniforms signifying association with any proscribed organisation; and
- The Terrorism Act 2000 which prohibits the display of certain symbols associated with any proscribed organisation.

This is not an exhaustive list, but simply illustrates the wide range of issues of which organisers of events including processions need to be aware.

The guidance could helpfully cover a range of other issues including:

B – Insurance requirements – organisers of events will be subject to potential legal liabilities should an accident or loss occur. It is essential that organisers take out appropriate liability insurance to cover the event. Having carried out a risk assessment and produced an event plan will be helpful in the event of a claim to demonstrate that organisers have acted with due care and attention. Organisers will need to ensure that they record specific details of any reported incidents and report any serious incidents to the police and insurance company and, in addition, any serious accidents to Environmental Health.

C – Event planning – successful event planning requires considerable professional skill, knowledge and expertise. Guidance could help organisers identify the steps to be taken in successful event planning. Issues that need to be covered here include: a summary of the event, site plans and a health and safety policy to cover issues like:
- communication;
- crowd management;
- vehicle management;
- fire arrangements;
- event activities;
- temporary structures;
- waste and hygiene management;
- welfare arrangements;
- provision of lighting;
- insurance arrangements;
- training requirements;
- security;
- contingency arrangements;
- emergency arrangements;
- site safety inspection; and
- incident reporting.

Other issues which organisers need to address are the need to: liaise with key bodies such as the local authority, police, fire brigade, public transport, and first aid providers; ensure effective publicity and press liaison and contact with potential sponsors; oversee and control contractors, and the hiring and installation arrangements. Organisers will need to draw up their budget for the event.

D – Checklist and timeline – Providing a checklist and a timeline of what needs to be done and when would be particularly helpful to organisers.

E – Risk assessment – organisers must carry out detailed risk assessments. There already exists helpful guidance to guide organisers through the process. The Health and Safety Executive's guidance '5 steps to risk assessment' is particularly helpful in setting out the requirements. Risk assessments are not complex. However, it is important that they are carried out and recorded as that will be helpful to organisers planning and also should anything go wrong to demonstrate that organisers had taken appropriate care and attention. The 5 stages are:
- Identify the activities – for example a gala day procession involving floats;
- Identify the hazards – for example a collision with a pedestrian;
- Identify who could be harmed – for example children watching the procession;
- Control the risk – for example ensure sufficient stewards and clearly defined pedestrian areas and drivers of floats aware of any speed limits and other conditions; and
- Monitor and review the risk.

Organisers of large processions may want to employ a professional risk assessor to carry out their risk assessment.

F – Stewarding – effective stewarding is necessary for every event. The risk assessment process should identify how many stewards are necessary but it would be helpful if the guidance provided examples of what had been provided in similar events.

Stewards need to be:
- fit and capable to both physically and temperamentally to carry out their role;
- readily identifiable, in visible clothing;
- fully briefed in their duties at the event and the extent of their role;
- appropriately trained;
- in communication with the organisers and the police;

G – Essential contacts – it would be helpful to organisers for the guidance to provide a list of the key essential contacts for organising an event.

H – General code of conduct – finally the guidance could also set out the general code of conduct expected of organisers and participants of a procession.

Index

Note: References are to paragraph numbers. This index should be used in conjunction with the cross-references in the text, especially those to the Recommendations and to the Appendices.

Aberdeen, 4.57, 5.15, 6.34, 6.36
Aberdeen Trades Council, 6.36
Airdrie, 4.12, 4.13
alcohol, 8.73, 11.19, 15.37, 15.41–15.43
    recommendations concerning, 15.5, 15.43
Allan McLean Memorial Flute Band, 6.24
ambulance service, 8.60
Ancient Order of Hibernians, 4.36–4.38, 6.24, 7.4
    and bands, 4.43
Angus Council, 5.17, 6.34
annual digests, recommendations concerning, 13.5
appeals, 5.34–5.39, 6.32, 6.34
    see also case law and legal opinions
Apprentice Boys of Derry, 1.5, 4.9, 4.31–4.35, 6.24, 6.38, 8.124, 8.126, 8.127–8.128, 8.130, 8.135, 8.137, 8.141, 8.142, 14.23, 15.7, 15.26
    and bands, 15.28
    code of conduct, 15.18, 15.22
    membership, 4.34
    see also Loyalist organisations
approval, permission and, 5.19, 8.51, 14.30–14.31
    see also 'permit to process' under permits
Argyll and Bute Council, 5.16, 6.34
Armadale, 4.26, 4.47
arrests, 5.44, 16.12–16.13
arts festivals, 4.59
assemblies, 4.6, 5.13
Ayrshire, 4.12, 4.15, 4.25

band parades, 4.42, 15.1
bands, 15.27–15.30
    at Gala Days, 4.46–4.47
    at Kirkin' of the Council, 4.61
    at Melas, 4.55
    code of conduct, 15.30
    complaints concerning, 6.40
    conditions concerning, 6.26
    conduct, 15.28–15.29
    contracts with, 6.37, 15.28
    guidance concerning, in Northern Ireland, 11.19
    Loyalist, 4.44
    recommendations concerning, 15.5, 15.27–15.30, 16.20
    Republican, 4.40
    see also band parades
banners, 6.26, 10.16
bans, 1.7, 5.13, 5.16–5.17, 6.33–6.36
    in England, 5.13, 10.6
    pressure for, 8.32
    recommendations concerning, 14.19
    views on, 8.71, 8.96, 8.124, 8.150–8.152, 8.162, 8.165
Bathgate, 4.47
behaviour, see conduct
behaviour bonds, 15.19
Beltane, 4.50
Blantyre, 7.21
bonds, 15.19
Boys Brigade, 4.57

Braemar, 4.48
Bridgeton Republican Flute Band, 6.24
British National Party, 6.13
Broxburn, 4.26, 4.42
Bryan, Dominic, 4.9
Burghead, 4.60
bus operators, views on issues concerning processions, 8.84–8.86
business community, communication with, in London, 10.21–10.22
business organisations, views on issues concerning processions, 8.76–8.82

Cairde na hÉireann, 4.39–4.41, 4.43, 6.38, 7.4, 8.123, 8.126–8.128, 8.130, 8.135–8.136, 8.138, 8.142, 13.5, 14.23
Campaign for Nuclear Disarmament, see CND
case law and legal opinions, 5.6–5.10, 5.12, 5.13–5.17, 6.34
  on democratic society, 5.9, 5.12, 5.13
Catholic organisations, 1.5, 4.36–4.38, 7.4
  see also Republican organisations
Catholic processions, 1.5, 4.38, 7.4, 15.27
cavalcades
  definition, 4.4
  otherwise see processions
Celtic FC, 15.31–15.36
certifications, 5.45, 15.11
charity walks, 4.58
children, 4.46, 4.47, 6.27, 10.16
churches
  organising processions, 4.59
  recommendations concerning receiving information, 13.7
  see also places of worship
Civic Government (Scotland) Act 1982, 1.7, 5.18–5.44, 13.15
  current practice under, 6.1–6.36
  prohibition orders under, 1.7, 6.33–6.36
  see also bans
  restrictions/conditions imposed under, 1.7, 6.23–6.24, 14.20
  recommendations concerning, 14.20–14.21
  see also notification requirements

clashes, 8.136, 13.5, 15.6
clothing, 6.26
Clydeside Troops Out Movement, 6.24
CND (Campaign for Nuclear Disarmament), 4.64, 8.122, 8.140
Coatbridge, 4.15, 4.40
Coatbridge Harp Flute Band, 6.24
codes of conduct, 6.37, 8.36, 8.135, 11.17–11.20, 15.18, 15.22
  recommendations concerning, 15.14–15.18
Coldstream, 4.50
collections, 10.16, 15.11
Combat 18, 6.13
Common Ridings, 4.49–4.50, 7.5
community
  communication with, 9.19, 10.21–10.22
  in England, 10.21, 10.34–10.35
  recommendations concerning, 13.1–13.7
  effects of processions on, see effects under processions
  see also community involvement
community councils, views on issues concerning processions, 8.62–8.75
community involvement
  recommendations concerning, 13.1–13.16
  views on, 8.6–8.8, 8.23–8.27, 8.59–8.61, 8.64–8.67, 8.75, 8.78, 8.85, 8.94, 8.101–8.102, 8.115, 8.123–8.126, 8.145–8.147, 8.44–8.45, 9.18–9.19
complaints, 1.12, 6.40–6.41, 15.2, 16.14
compromise, 8.27, 14.3, 14.19, 14.23
  see also decision making
conduct
  of participants and on-lookers at processions, 15.14–15.18, 15.20–15.22, 15.40–15.43
  see also behaviour bonds and codes of conduct
consistency, 6.2, 8.32
  recommendations concerning, 12.21–12.22, 14.9
consultation networks, 3.10, 8.1–8.3
Control of Pollution Act 1974, 5.45, 6.26, 15.11
COPS CORE PACKAGE, 10.31–10.33
costs, 8.37–8.39, 9.20
  to bus operators, 8.89
  complaints concerning, 6.40

views on, 9.20–9.23
   see also under policing costs
   see also payment and policing costs
councillors
   and decisions concerning processions, 1.10, 1.11, 6.11
   processions of, 4.61
counter-demonstrations, 6.36
Criminal Justice (Scotland) Act 2003, 15.41
   see also religious aggravation charges
crowning of Summer Queens/Queens of May, 4.45
customary processions, 5.26–5.27, 6.22–6.23

Dalkeith, 4.12
danger, experiences of, 9.10
dates, 7.17, 13.5, 14.3
   peak months, 7.16–7.17
   recommendations concerning, 14.22–14.23
Deans, 4.47
debriefing, 6.42–6.44, 8.33, 14.35–14.39
   in London, 10.17, 10.19
   recommendations concerning, 12.13, 14.16, 14.33, 14.36–14.39, 15.39
decision making
   basis for, 13.8–13.9
   recommendations concerning, 14.1–14.3, 14.10–14.21, 14.24, 16.20
   views on, 8.9–8.13, 8.28–8.33, 8.45–8.52, 8.68–8.71, 8.79–8.80, 8.86–8.88, 8.95–8.96, 8.103–8.107, 8.115, 8.127–8.134, 8.148–8.155, 8.162–8.164, 8.166–8.169, 9.12–9.16
   current position, 1.9–1.13, 6.11–6.16, 6.18
   responsibility for, 13.14, 14.10
   recommendations concerning, 14.2, 14.4–14.9
   see also community input; see also procedures and decision making processes concerning processions under local authorities
democratic society, 5.9, 5.12, 5.13
demonstrations
   definition, 4.4
   otherwise see processions and protest marches
disruption, 6.40, 6.41, 7.7, 7.22, 8.15–8.16, 8.107–8.109, 8.156–8.157, 8.166, 9.9–9.10, 14.18, 15.2

   see also effects under processions
dress, 6.26, 11.19
Dumfries, 4.12
Dundee, 4.12, 4.25, 6.34, 7.21
Duns, 4.50

East Lothian, 4.25, 7.17
East Renfrewshire, 7.21
Edinburgh, 4.12, 4.53, 4.55, 4.60, 4.64, 7.17, 7.21
   views concerning, 8.82
Edinburgh Castle, 8.61
Edinburgh Council, guidance for organisers, 6.39, 15.12
emotion or personal feeling, and rights, 5.15–5.17
England [and Wales], 1.22, 5.13, 10.1–10.35
   learning from, 14.9
   legislation, 5.44
   see also Public Order Act 1986
   notification situation, 10.3
environmental hazards, 14.18
Equality Network, 8.122, 8.125, 8.129, 8.133–8.134, 8.140, 8.141, 8.142, 15.26
European Commission on Human Rights, 5.4, 5.6–5.8, 5.10, 5.13
European Convention for the Protection of Human Rights and Fundamental Freedoms, 1.6, 5.3–5.11, 5.21, 14.11
European Court of Human Rights, 5.4, 5.6, 5.9
exemptions, see under notification requirements
Eyemouth, 4.51

Faslane, 4.64
fees
   for licenses, 15.11
   recommendations concerning, 14.34
   see also costs
festivals, 4.49–4.51, 4.57, 4.59, 4.60, 4.61, 7.5
Fife Council, guidance for organisers, 6.39, 15.12
First Aid, 6.27
flags, 6.26, 11.19
Flodden, 4.50
flute bands, Republican, 4.40
Food Safety Act 1990, 5.45, 15.11
football clubs

links with, 15.31–15.36
and policing costs, 16.18
and stewarding, 15.26
freedoms, see rights
fun runs, 4.58

Gala Days, 4.46–4.47
Galashiels, 4.50
Galloway, 4.12
Gay Pride, see Pride Scotia
Girls Brigade, 4.57
Glasgow, 4.12, 4.25, 4.26, 4.30, 4.53, 4.55, 4.56, 4.61, 4.64, 8.166
Glasgow City Council, 6.45–6.47, 15.34
Glasgow Irish Freedom Action Committee, 6.24
Grand Orange Lodge of Scotland, 8.123, 8.124, 8.130, 8.135, 8.137, 8.139, 8.141, 14.23, 15.7, 15.26
and bands, 15.28, 15.30
code of conduct, 15.18
groups consulted, 3.10, 8.1–8.3
guidance for decision makers, views on, 8.32
guidance for organisers, 6.39, 8.17, 8.55
in London, 10.14–10.17
recommendations concerning, 12.22, 15.5, 15.11–15.13
Guides, 6.20, 6.22

halberds, 6.26
half marathons, 4.58
Hawick, 4.50
health issues, 8.59
Health and Safety at Work Act 1974 and associated Regulations, 5.45, 15.11
Hibernians, Ancient Order of, see Ancient Order of Hibernians
Highland Games, 4.48
Hindu community, 4.54
Historic Scotland, 8.61
Hogmanay, 4.60
human rights, see rights
Human Rights Act 1988, 5.4

impact analysis, recommendations concerning, 12.16–12.17
Inchinnan, 4.15
Independent Review of Parades and Marches [in Northern Ireland], see North Report
individuals, private, see private individuals
information
recommendations concerning, 13.4–13.7, 16.22
see also record-keeping; see also communication under community
insurance, 10.26, 15.5, 15.10
recommendations concerning, 15.19
intimidation, 6.41, 8.108–8.110, 8.166, 14.6, 14.18, 15.2
intolerance, feelings concerning, and rights, 5.15–5.17
Inverclyde, 4.38
Irish Republican organisations, see Republican organisations

James Connolly commemoration, 4.40, 4.41, 7.21
James Connolly Society, 4.40, 6.13, 7.4
Jarman, Neil, 4.9
Jedburgh, 4.50

Kelso, 4.50
Kilbarchan, 4.47
Kilmarnock, 4.12
Kilwinning, 4.47
Kirkin' of the Council, 4.61

Lanark, 4.45
Lanarkshire, 4.15, 4.25
see also North Lanarkshire and South Lanarkshire
Largs, 4.45
Lauder, 4.50
legal cases, see case law and legal opinions
legislation, 5.20, 5.45, 6.26, 15.11
concerning London, 10.20
concerning Northern Ireland, 11.2, 11.9
European, 5.5
opinions concerning, 5.6–5.10
Human Rights Act 1988, 5.4
see also Civic Government (Scotland) Act 1982,

Criminal Justice (Scotland) Act 2003 and Public Order Act 1986
Lerwick, 4.60
Lesbian, Gay, Bisexual and Transgender events, see Pride Scotia
licenses, 5.45, 15.11
Linlithgow, 4.47
Linwood, 4.15
litter, 6.27, 6.40
Liverpool, 10.1–10.2, 10.28–10.35
Livingston, 4.47
local authorities
  committees concerned with notifications of processions, 6.15
  council processions, 4.61
  debriefing, 6.42
  events teams, 6.39
  forms for notification of processions, 6.3–6.6
  and Gala Days, 4.47
  guidance for organisers, 6.39
  meetings with organisers, see meetings
  policy development, 6.45–6.47
  procedures and decision making processes concerning processions, 1.9–1.12, 6.11–6.16, 6.18
  recommendations concerning, 12.9–12.22, 13.14–13.16
  see also decision making
  'single gateway' proposal, 12.9–12.10, 12.17
  views on issues concerning processions, 8.13, 8.19–8.39, 13.14, 14.10
London, 5.13, 10.1–10.2, 10.6, 10.9–10.27
loudhailers, 6.26
Loyal Orange Order, see Orange Order
  Loyalist organisations, 1.5, 4.9–4.35, 6.13, 7.4
  and bands, 4.42, 15.30
  differences, 8.139
  history, 4.9–4.17, 4.28, 4.31–4.32
  see also Apprentice Boys of Derry, Loyalist processions, Orange Order and Royal Black Institution
Loyalist processions, 1.5, 4.22–4.27, 4.30, 4.35, 7.4, 7.17, 15.27, 16.9
  case law concerning, 5.15–5.17, 6.34
  numbers participating in, 7.21
  as proportion of notified processions, 1.14, 4.8, 7.11–7.13, 7.18–7.19
  proportion of population participating in, 7.20, 9.6–9.7
  views on, 8.166–8.168, 15.1–15.2
  see also sectarian processions, views on

marathons, 4.58
marches
  definition, 4.4
  otherwise see processions
marshalling, see stewarding
May Day marches/rallies, 4.63, 7.21
Maybole, 4.12
Mediation Northern Ireland, 11.1
meetings, 6.17, 6.20, 6.42
  recommendations concerning, 12.13, 14.25–14.29
Melas, 4.55
Melrose, 4.50
Merseyside, 10.1–10.2, 10.28–10.35
miners' galas, 4.46
monitoring, recommendations concerning, 12.19–12.20, 13.13, 13.16
monitors, 11.12
Moodiesburn, 4.25
MSPs, 8.113–8.120
music, 6.31, 11.19
  conditions concerning, 6.26
  see also bands
Musselburgh, 4.12

national days, 4.59
National Front, 6.13, 6.33, 6.36
National Health Service, see NHS
National Parks, 5.23, 5.29
National Union of Students, see NUS
NHS views on processions, 8.59
noise, 5.13, 6.40, 10.16
North Lanarkshire, 4.30, 4.38, 6.35, 7.17
North, Sir Peter, and North Report (Report of the Independent Review of Parades and Marches [in Northern Ireland]), 4.9, 11.2–11.8
Northern Ireland, 1.24, 11.1–11.31, 14.6

Ancient Order of Hibernians in, 4.36
demonstrations concerning
    in England, 5.13, 10.6
    in Scotland, 6.33
history of Loyalist organisations in, 4.9–4.10, 4.28, 4.31–4.32
learning from, 14.9
numbers and statistics on processions in, 11.30
notification period
    current practice concerning, 6.7–6.8
    in Northern Ireland, 11.18
    recommendations concerning, 12.1–12.22
    support for increasing, 1.16
    views on, 8.5, 8.20–8.22, 8.41–8.42, 8.63, 8.77, 8.84, 8.93, 8.100, 8.114, 8.122, 8.144, 9.17
    waiving, 5.24
        recommendations concerning, 12.6
        views on, 8.22
notification requirements, 5.23–5.26
    current practice concerning, 6.3–6.19
    in England and Wales, 10.3, 10.10
    exemptions from, 1.7, 4.7, 5.25–5.27, 6.20–6.25, 7.5
        recommendations concerning, 12.2, 12.7–12.8
    recommendations concerning, 12.2, 12.9–12.22, 14.24–14.34
    whether equivalent to seeking permission, 5.19, 8.51, 14.30–14.31
    see also notification period; see also 'permit to process' under permits
numbers of people counting as assemblies, 5.13
numbers of processions, see under processions
NUS Scotland, 8.122, 8.123, 8.126, 8.129, 8.131, 8.141

Occupiers Liability Scotland Act 1960, 5.45, 15.11
offences, 5.39–5.43, 15.37, 15.41, 16.12–16.13
    in England and Wales, 10.7
on-lookers
    complaints concerning, 6.40
    conduct of, 15.20–15.22, 15.31, 15.38
'opt-in' list for information, recommendations concerning, 13.7
Orange Order, 1.5, 4.10–4.27, 6.24, 6.38, 7.4

and bands, 4.42
beliefs, 4.19–4.21
history, 4.9–4.17, 4.25–4.26
membership, 4.18
in Merseyside, 10.29
processions, 4.22–4.27
see also Loyalist processions
Royal Black Institution and, 4.28
stewarding, 4.22, 10.29
structure, 4.18
see also Grand Orange Lodge of Scotland and Loyalist organisations
organisers
    codes of conduct, 6.37
    guidance for, see guidance for organisers
    identification, 8.52
    liaison with police at processions, 6.26, 15.25, 16.21–16.22
    and local authorities, 6.20
    meetings with, see meetings
    responsibilities, 6.26–6.27
        recommendations concerning, 12.18, 15.3–15.5, 15.10, 15.21–15.22
    views on issues concerning processions, 8.121–8.142
    see also notification requirements
Orkney, 4.60

Paisley, 4.12, 7.17
parades
    definition, 4.4
    otherwise see processions
Parades Commission (Northern Ireland), 1.24, 11.1, 11.8–11.29, 14.5–14.6, 14.9
    background to, 11.2–11.7
payment
    recommendations concerning, 14.34
    see also costs
Peebles, 4.50
penalties, 5.41, 5.42
period of notice, see notification period
permission, approval and, 5.19, 8.51, 14.30–14.31
    see also 'permit to process' under permits
permits, 5.45, 15.11

'permit to process', recommendations concerning, 14.30–14.34
petitions, 10.16
phone survey, see telephone survey
placards, 6.26
places of worship
   processions passing, 6.26, 8.166, 11.18, 11.20
   processions visiting, 4.56
planning processes
   in England, 10.2, 10.4, 10.11–10.13, 10.31–10.33
   recommendations concerning, 12.9–12.22, 14.24–14.29
police
   at processions, 10.5, 15.5, 15.23, 15.37–15.39, 16.9–16.13, 16.21–16.22
   and banning orders, 6.36
   debriefing, 6.43
   and decision making, recommendations concerning, 14.8
   in England and Wales, 10.3–10.6, 10.8–10.22, 10.24, 10.28–10.34
   instructions at processions, 6.26
   liaison with organisers at processions, 6.26, 15.25, 16.21–16.22
      meetings with organisers, 6.17, 6.20
      in England, 10.11–10.19, 10.29–10.30
      recommendations concerning, 14.25–14.29
   in Northern Ireland, 11.1, 11.21–11.22
      and notifications of processions, 6.15, 6.17–6.18
      recommendations concerning, 12.10–12.13, 12.19–12.20
      and stewarding, 15.23
      see also policing and policing costs
police associations, views on issues concerning processions, 8.40–8.57
policing, 10.5, 15.5, 15.23, 15.37–15.39, 16.9–16.13, 16.21–16.22
   levels of, 16.9–16.10
   views on, 8.75, 8.120, 8.142, 8.158, 8.160
policing costs, 16.1, 16.3–16.8, 16.19–16.20
   in Northern Ireland, 11.31
   responsibility for
   recommendations concerning, 16.2, 16.15–16.19
   views on, 8.18, 8.37–8.39, 8.56–8.57, 8.74–8.75, 8.82, 8.98, 8.112, 8.120, 8.141–8.142, 8.158–8.160, 8.162–8.164, 9.20–9.23, 16.2
political organisations, 4.63–4.65
   see also Republican organisations
political protest marches, see protest marches
Port Glasgow, 4.38
posters, 6.26
Prestonpans, 7.17
Pride Scotia, 4.53, 7.21, 8.122, 8.125, 8.127, 8.129, 8.132, 8.133–8.134, 8.138, 8.141
private individuals
views on issues concerning processions, 8.143–8.169
   see also telephone survey
processions, 3.1–3.2, 4.7
   arrangements for and agreements concerning, 6.16–6.18, 6.23, 6.26–6.27, 6.29–6.32
      see also notification requirements
   bans on, see bans
   categorisation, 7.1–7.4, 7.11–7.13
   combining, recommendations concerning, 15.8
   conditions for conduct of, 6.26–6.27
      see also orders in this entry
   controversial/non-controversial, 6.13
   costs, see costs
   customary, 5.26–5.27
   decision making concerning, see decision making
   definitions and terminology, 4.2–4.5, 5.28
   effects of, 9.11, 13.4
      long-term, 8.81
      views on, 8.14–8.17, 8.34–8.36, 8.53–8.55, 8.59–8.61, 8.72–8.73, 8.81, 8.89–8.90, 8.97, 8.108–8.111, 8.117–8.119, 8.135–8.150, 8.156–8.157, 8.162–8.164, 8.166–8.169
      see also disruption; see also experiences in this entry
   in England [and Wales], see England [and Wales]
   experiences of, 9.6–9.11, 9.24, 15.1–15.4
      see also disruption and intimidation
   feeder, 4.27, 4.30, 10.29, 15.2
   legislation concerning, see legislation
   local authority policy development concerning, 6.45–6.47
   in Northern Ireland, see Northern Ireland

notification requirements, see notification requirements
numbers of, 1.14, 7.9–7.13, 15.1
   recommendations concerning, 15.6–15.8
   views on, 8.15, 8.34–8.35, 8.72, 8.81, 8.89, 8.97, 8.111, 8.117, 8.140, 8.156
numbers of people participating in, 7.17, 7.20–7.21, 9.6–9.7, 15.1
occurring on same day, 7.17, 8.136, 13.5, 13.6, 15.8
orders concerning, 1.7, 5.29–5.38, 6.30–6.36
   recommendations concerning, 14.20–14.21, 14.31
   see also bans
organisers, see organisers
   outward and return, 7.7
   participants' conduct, see conduct
   peak months, 7.16–7.17
   policing costs, see policing costs
   prohibitions of, see bans
   proportion of population participating in, 7.20, 9.6–9.7
   proportions of different types (of notified processions), 1.14, 4.8, 7.11–7.13
     regional differences, 7.18–7.19
   reasons for, 4.2, 8.80, 8.157, 15.7
   regional spread, 7.14–7.15, 7.18–7.19
   restrictions imposed on, see conditions in this entry
   return, 7.7
   routes, see routes
   special events and, 10.23–10.27
   spontaneous, 8.52
   statistics on, 1.14, 4.8, 7.1–7.22
     recommendations concerning, 15.9
   see also record-keeping
   variety of, 1.5, 4.42–4.65
   violence at, 4.15, 4.25, 6.35
   whether seen as an issue, 9.12–9.13
prohibitions, see bans
protest marches, 4.62–4.65, 7.21
   proportion of population participating in, 7.20, 9.6–9.7
   otherwise see processions
protest meetings, 4.6
   in Northern Ireland, 11.23

Provincial Grand Black Chapter of Scotland, see Royal Black Institution
public assemblies, 4.6
   in England and Wales, 10.8
Public Order Act 1936, 5.45, 6.26, 15.11
Public Order Act 1986, 5.28
   application to England and Wales, 1.22, 5.44, 10.3–10.8, 14.11
   application to Scotland, 4.6, 5.20, 5.44, 8.52
public places, 4.6, 5.28
public transport, 10.16
public transport operators, views on issues concerning processions, 8.84–8.91
publicising
   of orders made under Civic Government (Scotland) Act 1982, 5.27
   of processions, 9.19, 10.21–10.22
     recommendations concerning, 13.3–13.7
   see also community, communication with and community involvement

Queens of May/Summer Queens, 4.45
Quigley, Sir George, and Quigley Review (Review of the Operation of the Parades Commission [Northern Ireland]), 5.2, 11.24–11.29
quotas, 8.35, 8.73
   recommendations concerning, 15.6

races, 4.58
Ram Lila Parade, 4.54
Rangers FC, 15.31–15.36
recommendations, 1.26–1.38
   requirements and possibilities for implementation, 1.26, 3.5
record-keeping, 6.43, 7.5–7.6, 7.21
   in London, 10.12–10.13
   recommendations concerning, 14.16, 14.29, 14.32, 14.38–14.39, 15.5, 15.9
   see also statistics under processions
religious aggravation charges, 8.97, 15.41, 16.13
religious organisations, views on issues concerning processions, 8.99–8.112
Remembrance Sunday, 4.59
Renfrewshire, 4.15, 4.25, 7.17

Republican organisations, 1.5, 4.39–4.43, 7.4
  see also Catholic organisations
Republican processions, 1.5, 4.38, 7.4, 15.27, 16.9
  proportion of population participating in, 7.20, 9.6–9.7, 15.27
responsibility
  for decision making, see under decision making
  organisers', see under organisers
  for policing costs, see under policing costs
  for stewarding, 15.23
Review of Marches and Parades in Scotland
  remit, 3.6–3.9, 4.1, 4.6
  review process, 1.1–1.5, 3.10–3.11, 8.1–8.3
Ridings, Common, see Common Ridings
rights, 5.2
  balancing, 8.28, 13.2
  restrictions on, 5.5, 5.7, 5.10–5.17, 5.21, 14.11
  see also European Convention for the Protection of Human Rights and Fundamental Freedoms
risk assessment, 8.55
  recommendations concerning, 12.14–12.18, 14.18, 14.28
road closures, 6.13, 8.84
road races, 4.58
road traffic legislation, 5.45, 15.11
roads authorities, 8.88
routes, 6.31, 6.32, 8.28, 8.31, 8.50, 8.80, 8.105, 8.140, 8.154, 11.18, 14.3
  recommendations concerning, 14.22–14.23
Royal Black Institution (Provincial Grand Black Chapter), 1.5, 4.28–4.30, 6.24, 7.17, 7.21, 8.122, 8.128, 8.137, 8.141
  stewarding, 4.30
  see also Loyalist organisations
running events, 4.58

safety, 15.12
Salvation Army, 6.20, 6.22
Scottish Ambulance Service, 8.60
Scottish Borders Council, guidance for organisers, 6.39, 15.12
Scottish CND, see CND
Scottish Coalition for Justice not War, 4.64
Scottish Football Association, 15.32
Scottish Trades Union Congress, see STUC
Scottish Youth Hostel Association, 8.132
Scouts, 4.57, 6.20, 6.22, 8.132
sectarian processions
  proportion of population participating in, 7.20, 9.6–9.7
  views on, 8.14, 8.53, 8.80, 8.96, 8.97, 8.138, 8.150, 8.152, 8.155–8.156, 8.166–8.169, 9.16
  whether considered controversial by local authorities, 6.13
sectarianism, 15.40–15.41
  complaints concerning, 6.40
  football clubs and, 15.31–15.36
Selkirk, 4.50
Sheriff judgements, 5.14–5.17, 6.34
Shetland, 4.60
Sikh community, 4.56
'single gateway' proposal, 12.9–12.10, 12.17
South Asian communities, 4.55
South Lanarkshire, 7.21
special events, in London, 10.23–10.27
sporting events, 4.58, 15.12, 15.26
  processions connected with, 4.58
Springside, 4.47
statistics
  on processions, see under processions
  on religious aggravation charges, 15.41, 16.13
stewards/stewarding, 4.22, 4.30, 6.17, 6.26, 8.55, 8.137, 15.23–15.26
  guidance concerning
    in London, 10.15
    in Northern Ireland, 11.18, 11.19
  recommendations concerning, 15.5, 15.24–15.26
  responsibility for, 15.23
  training for, 6.38, 15.26
Stewarton, 4.47
Stonehaven, 4.60
Stonehenge, 5.13, 10.6
Stoneyburn, 4.42
Stranraer, 4.12, 4.13
Strathaven, 4.47
Strathclyde Regional Council, 6.33
STUC (Scottish Trades Union Congress), 4.63, 6.38, 8.122, 8.123, 8.126, 8.129, 8.137, 8.140, 8.141, 15.26

Summer Queens/Queens of May, 4.45

telephone survey, 1.18–1.21, 3.10, 7.20, 9.1–9.26, 13.4, 14.14, 16.16
Temporary Traffic Regulations Orders, 5.45, 15.11
Terrorism Act 2000, 5.46, 6.26, 15.11
Thornliebank Flute Band, 6.24
timing, 6.26, 6.31, 7.16–7.17, 11.18
   of music, 6.26
   outward and return processions, 7.7, 15.2
TNS Social Research, 9.1
traffic legislation, 5.45, 15.11
traffic management, in London, 10.20
traffic restrictions, 6.13
transport, 10.16
transport organisations, views on issues concerning processions, 8.83–8.91
trespass, in England and Wales, 10.8

uniforms, 5.45, 6.26, 15.11

'Views Across Scotland', see telephone survey
villages, 7.22
violence, 4.15, 4.25, 6.35
voluntary sector organisations, views on issues concerning processions, 8.92–8.98

walks for charity, 4.58
warning, see publicising
weapons, 6.26, 6.31
West Lothian, 4.26
West of Scotland Bands Alliance, 4.43, 6.24, 6.35, 7.4
Whitburn, 4.42
Wigtown, 4.25
Wishaw, 4.43

youth groups, 4.57
Youth Hostel Association, 8.132